The Mind Detective is dedicated to Carl Jung.

Ex-Hollywood celebrity stylist, Shirley Yanez is a passionate social entrepreneur with a deep commitment to UK textiles and British manufacturing. After making her own fortune as a financial headhunter in the City of London, losing her self-made millions on the stock market in 2000, becoming homeless in Los Angeles in 2004, she found happiness without money through self-therapy, following a near-death experience. She has been offering free talk therapy since 2005. Shirley's common-sense life coaching began on TV in 2006 on *The Trisha Show*, Channel Five. For the last 10 years, she has worked at the highest level with corporate CEOs and business leaders and in the community with the addicted and homeless.

Shirley Yanez

THE MIND DETECTIVE

AUSTIN MACAULEY PUBLISHERS™

LONDON · CAMBRIDGE · NEW YORK · SHARJAH

A CIP catalogue record for this title is available from the British Library.

ISBN 9781528978583 (Paperback)
ISBN 9781528978606 (ePub e-book)

www.austinmacauley.com

First Published (2019)
Austin Macauley Publishers Ltd
25 Canada Square
Canary Wharf
London
E14 5LQ

"Your greatest responsibility is to love yourself and to know you are enough."

I would like to thank firstly my amazing patients, brave enough to allow me to practise my gift. The broken souls suffering in silence, unable to work theirselves out, you know who you are. Next, I would like to thank the dedicated, inspiring work of Carl Jung, a perfect example of leaving something amazing behind to mark the genius he was, helping others through his important work, the inspiration behind this book. Lastly, I want to thank my body for housing my energy, nature for reminding me I am part of something bigger and the universe for expanding since its creation, the wisdom behind the theory of life.

Introduction

I wrote this book because I believe this to be my sacred labour, to extract truth from my own experience and share it with others in hope of easing their burdens. Having a purpose today, a reason to continue living in the universe, has been essential to my own healing and survival after losing millions on the stock market and encountering a near-death experience in Hollywood, in mid-life. I did not believe in myself fully until someone revealed to me that deep inside me there was something valuable, worth listening to, worthy of my trust; that someone was Carl Jung.

On bookshelves all over the planet, in houses, bookstores, libraries, hotels there are millions of writers giving us their two pennies' worth on the vast subject of understanding the mind, from humorous self-help top tips, to serious medical mental health awareness and psychology. Everything is available from how to, what to, why you should, why you shouldn't, motivation, the power of positive thinking, self-development, personal growth, stay fit, get fit, lose weight, look great, yet our mental health is currently not thriving; we are barely surviving. How can this be? Understanding why alcoholics drink, why a person commits suicide, why someone overweight cannot lose weight, why a smoker cannot quit, why anxiety and stress cause panic attacks begins by recognising. Unless you have genuinely experienced these issues yourself and recovered, you won't have the answers.

I am not a qualified doctor, psychiatrist or self-help guru. I am a 62-year-old woman with an extraordinary tale to tell of triumph over tragedy, an unbelievable life-changing journey that transformed me beyond all recognition. Today I am celibate by choice, not religious, happy, healthy, full of life, living my purpose after working myself out of a mental health hell. I have become a mind detective, open and willing to share my own pain, problems and conclusive evidence with the rest of the world, to help save the world. It takes pain to know pain. It takes depression to understand depression. It takes courage to develop courage. It takes spirit to lift spirits. It takes compassion to have sympathy. It takes empathy to understand, and I understand because I know.

To go beyond your own personal issues and problems whatever they may be, you will need to build a solid unbreakable core foundation, which will progress you further to becoming a stronger character. It is only strength of character that helps us endure life challenges more easily. Forgiving yourself is the most important action you can take when breaking away from the self-sabotaging habit of being a victim of internal wounds, unresolved issues and past pain, which have now become part of your existing belief system. With my help, you will learn to pay close attention to your mind as an observer, a loving compassionate witness, not the victim anymore. You will start to see clearly how you think, act and behave, then discover for yourself just how debilitating your negative emotional reactions are.

As a mind detective, I am going to show you how flicking one switch in your mind can change everything in your life forever and how meditation can literally change your brain by shrinking your fear centre, which may have become enlarged after trauma through flashbacks of anxiety or panic. It is not an easy process; we all prefer a comfort zone. So before we can overcome personal misery and irrational fear, we need to go through it. Covering it up, self-medicating, living in denial or suffering in silence does not lessen the pain, it makes it worse.

Self-mastery is about being willing to find a way to transcend fears, breaking through the resistance to change, facing the weak ugly parts within, the fixed mindset, the wrong belief system we automatically follow and buy into that is simply not true or helping us evolve as mature, thinking human beings. If you want to finally discover what has hijacked your happiness and left you destined to fail, understand this truth: resistance to change brings depression and anxiety; embracing change leads to spiritual freedom with endless choices.

Once you get to hear your internal dialogue, the automatically programmed negative voice behind the illusion of your existing mindset, you can begin to push through it with hope and courage, then confidently navigate back to reconnect with your authentic truth, becoming the person you would be if you just knew how to be. As we start to grasp a new way of thinking about our life as a conscious experience, not something we just take for granted as set in stone, we begin to realise that we must take accountability for our thoughts, behaviour and life choices. As we become more confident, committed and skilled in dealing with life situations, positive or negative, we increase our access to a higher, more intelligent level of thinking, which is truly helpful in the development of the self. Each one of us must decide if we are willing and open to align with our purpose of spiritual growth, reflecting deeply on knowing our authentic motivations both hidden and on the surface. Our motivation influences our perception and our perception influences our belief system.

When I believed my life was over, I naturally began to accept myself just as I was in the moment. I detached from my unconscious ego, surrendered myself over to something more powerful than me then waited to see what would happen, embracing death as my end destination. Nothing is more powerful than knowing you are not alone. By focusing on your strengths and not sugar-coating over your wounds, you become more resilient in the face of stress, more assertive in the clutches of fear and more capable of problem-solving in the panic of the unknown. You regain your ability to think rationally. I can promise you when you recover, you'll discover how to give yourself what you need to feel nourished and healthy. You'll understand without doubt how to take care of yourself both mentally and physically, by listening only to your heart-based intuition, giving it a voice beyond your lying mind.

We only know what we know. Making any change or getting to know yourself is hard work, often impossible to contemplate tackling alone, the main reason most people fail when they attempt to work themselves out. I am very fortunate today after my own incredible life-changing experience. I know what it is like to lose everything materially, what it is like to be homeless, broke, broken, what happens when you die, how you recover and finally how you get to be your true self, without fear of being vulnerable.

Are you ready to confront your fears, your deep insecurities, your anxieties, your depression, all your unresolved pain, to begin to see through your self-deception, to dive deep head first into your past, finally being free to enjoy your future without shame, guilt or regret? If the answer to this question is yes, the time has come for you to take an active role in learning how to heal yourself. Once you identify your emotional pain and are willing and open to take the steps to resolve your internal conflict, you will begin to empower yourself, leading you to spiritual freedom. Spiritual freedom leads to your higher self, your higher intelligence, your soul, connected to the universe, the stars, the planet, driven by love, compassion, humility, empathy and gratitude, reached simply by listening to your heart.

Meditation and inner silence are how we connect to our higher intelligence. It will have a positive calming effect on the mind, creating the space by clearing out negative emotions, helping us to focus only on positive qualities, like love, humility, compassion, gratitude and forgiveness, and allowing goodness back in. This process will help reduce anxiety, depression and stress, connecting you back to a peaceful state, improving your mental flexibility and encouraging you to be mindful. It will help you move away from your lower self, your unconscious ego, your lying mind, which is always influenced by desire or energised by fear. You are going to discover that your mind is not the passive observer perceiving your reality as it is because it actually changes your reality, it is your soul you need to connect with to see your truth. For your meditation practice to be effective, you must learn to see the bigger picture beyond what you have learnt. Change will never happen until you stop blaming others. You need to change the way you think with greater acceptance. The problems you have are potentially all down to you.

Mental health, just like physical health, needs constant care if you want to enjoy a long, happy life. By making a strong commitment to expand your consciousness through your heart-based qualities—humility, compassion, gratitude, forgiveness, empathy, integrity—there is a much greater chance of gaining knowledge and wisdom during your life experience. The greatest lesson I learnt myself during my short time in the depths of despair, was the importance of walking the spiritual path to develop my own virtues, ethics and inner goodness, my solid foundation of truth, at the same time removing my fear-based ego belief system. Since what we value in life is down to our choices, our perception of what we value the most must change. There is no value in emotionally unstable, destructive behaviours. It is our responsibility to restore balance in our hearts by being open and willing to learn what our real issues are.

In our current materialistic environment, it is important to understand that money and material stuff has taken over as a priority in our desires rather than us investing in the value of our own consciousness, and there are serious consequences for this ignorance. I had it all, lost it all and spent the first half of my life covering my eyes to the reality of how much I had become disconnected from the real me. It took me reaching the bottom to seek out the truth of what was going on inside of me by following my soul without hesitation.

Trust me, you cannot afford to live in denial anymore. You need to wake up, become more self-aware and stop being pushed around psychologically and emotionally by your mind control, even if what you are faced with in your truth is painful and not what you want to see or face. Ask yourself this question right now. Has money, greed, materialism and your pursuit of your perceived idea of perfection taken over your life? If the honest answer to this question is yes, it is time to start taking an active role in healing yourself from the inside out, and identifying that your emotional pain is the reason you have become disconnected from your authentic self. By embarking on this small journey alone, you will empower yourself to take the right steps to discovering spiritual freedom. There is truly only one way to get beyond the fears we have and over the anger we feel because of them. It is about doing the right thing. By being productive in alignment with accountability, connecting with a higher consciousness, we find resolution to our life issues and problems. We tend to dislike or ignore the things we fear, often overlooking or dismissing as history any unresolved emotional conflict. When we are ruled by our fears, it means we are not dealing with our personal pain, often because of anger, blame, shame or guilt, disguising what we are feeling deep down inside, without recognising we are consciously doing it. Sadly, this lack of self-awareness coupled with a lack of consciousness results in an inability to be your authentic true self, the true nature of a spiritual being.

During this journey together through talk therapy, the healing process and reconnecting back to your higher-level heartfelt qualities, the thing that makes you a human being, once you have identified, silenced and taken back control of the unconscious ego, your dark side, we will embark on the spiritual path of developing your goodness and ethics. Without developing an inner strong core, your own natural foundation of truth, your personal integrity, you will never clear out your fear-based ego belief system, causing you to miss the meaning of your life in the present. To find yourself, you must know yourself; to know yourself, you must be honest; to be honest, you must change, and to change, you must stop lying to yourself—not an easy process when you think you are good person who is always right. So let's find out your truth, by looking at mine.

Mind You

To become an individual, an independent thinker in charge of your own choices, you must write your own story, understanding without doubt your childhood is only the first chapter of the never-ending novel of mankind.

Unlocking the mysteries of the mind means we must turn detective, collecting various clues to make a diagnosis of why we are mentally malfunctioning. All of us at some point in this life need to decide the kind of person we want to be, whether we continue to hide behind the façade, the mask created for us by others, or become independent thinkers. Opening our eyes to what we really value, how we really think and what we really need for ourselves is where we begin this process of change. To gain an accurate assessment of our authentic reality beyond our existing belief system, we must consciously make the choice to face and then clean up our emotional conflict, the internal blockages preventing our personal growth. We must be willing, vulnerable and open to explore our feelings without fear, shame, blame or guilt. By simply determining what is authentically important to you, choosing your own personal set of core values, will help you focus on these qualities, so you can align the choices you make in the future, to reflect what is right for you in the present. Once you begin the process of observing how much the external world influences your internal world and self-worth, you will be shocked and surprised how much you have allowed life and other people to hijack your happiness, leaving you a slave to your crazy mixed-up mind.

Information, your thoughts and existing beliefs are soft-wired into your brain and have been learnt consciously or subconsciously from the time you were first exposed to language; so the good news is, it can be unlearnt or changed by using different language. Your personal standards are set by your thoughts and your thoughts reflect your beliefs. Your actions are the best indicator for your behaviour. It is your job to discover the dark hidden side of yourself you may have disowned when you were a child, to uncover your inner truth, located in your core being, beyond what you have learnt, to seek knowledge about your authentic truth. The truth is what sets us free; unfortunately, most of the time, we don't want to look inside, we don't want to deal with the hurt, we don't want to see the pain because when we do, we are pushed into denial, which then creates self-delusion. As mature thinking adults, we should never be afraid of spiritual knowledge or self-knowledge, both essential learning processes to empower us to consciously engage with the soul side of self.

Through deep self-reflection, uncovering your true values, you will explore a new version of yourself, fully free of emotional and irrational fear, open and curious beyond your self-doubt. This will then lead you to a radical change in your mindset and free you to move away from your internal suffering, the main reason you are stuck. As you gain more freedom from the handcuffs of your past, you will begin to see your consciousness only lives in the present moment of now. Gaining clarity from within requires great self-awareness of your negative patterns and your attachment to them. A disciplined focus on your meditation practice, clearing out your mind and removing all connection to the old you, focusing all your energy on getting to know the authentic you, will improve your happiness levels and fulfilment. To develop a new relationship with your core spiritual mature self, you will need to face your dark shadow side, your deep hidden fears. By facing head on the denial and deceptions you have let control your decision-making process and acknowledging the time has come to awaken inside to take back control, you will begin to feel more empowered. There is always a battle going on inside us all between the dark forces and the light. The deep pressure and pain we endure because of this internal fight controlling our consciousness, often leaves us conflicted, confused and unable to be accountable for our actions. To begin to develop a relationship with your core inner spirit, the authentic person you are inside, you must face the shadows of your hidden deep fears, the denial, the deception and delusions you have allowed to control your decision-making process. Once you get to see the deceptive nature of your mind—the true nature of your reality, beyond the confusion and pain—you will finally let go of all you think you know, freeing up your mind to allow something new to manifest. Mastering the art of surrendering the old, tortured, miserable, empty you and all your unresolved fears will require increasing degrees of self-reliance and trust. A process of learning to let go in order to go beyond your limitations, developing inner strength through spiritual growth.

Before we begin, it is important to recognise we often fear and resist change. Getting to know how to overcome this resistance, is crucial to you actualising your true potential and revealing the real you. Cutting through your self-protection and many distractions will need more clarity when making your life decisions going forward. If we have little self-awareness based upon a lack of emotional intelligence, a low tolerance in handling stress, zero ability to monitor our own feelings and identify with them appropriately, we will always struggle to solve problems. To evolve into mature, responsible, independent, self-regulating adults, we need to be honest, open and curious to all the things we normally dismiss as unimportant. Managing our feelings, developing the ability to regulate them beyond the pain, stress and frustration of our personal circumstances, allows us to learn to recognise our emotions for what they are. Making the dedicated choice to begin this journey through self-enquiry and mindfulness, to define your authentic truth, your core values, ethics, behaviours and beliefs, takes conscious steps, building stable, unbreakable integrity along the way. Cultivating self-awareness and beginning to make use of the observing self is the only authentic way to building mindfulness. The observing self, your soul, is the part of you that authentically notices your thoughts, feelings and behaviours, unlike your mind, the part of you that is actively involved in engaging with them. Without understanding this, it will be very hard to tell the difference between what is in your control and what is out of your control. Practising mindfulness will help you to learn to let go of your attachment to your thoughts, feelings and behaviours, all the negative stuff that has led to your unnecessary suffering, so you can accept your reality, as reality.

We all wear many masks, a false identity, our persona, the aspect of our character we present to the world as perceived by others; the personality and social face we project as differentiated from the authentic self. We have all become experts at disguising ourselves to others, so we are protected from revealing who we really are inside for fear of being judged. The problem with this denial: in the end we become strangers to ourselves. The mask you wear, your persona, is not the real you. It is a compromise between being a unique individual, the authentic you, and what society expects you to be. We cannot just get rid of our truth without at some point being punished into a trap of anxiety and neurosis. Most people will over-identify with their persona, their social mask, to the detriment of other important areas of the psyche. It's supposed to be a small part of who we are, not the whole picture. We are not actors in our lives playing a part, giving the audience all that is great and perfect in a role we are playing. We have a dark side, an ugly side, a secret shadow side hidden deep in the unconscious, far away from the eyes of the world. We must learn to become aware of this shadow side and bring it into our consciousness. It is not an easy process but failing to do so will create chaos because unconsciously it influences our emotions, thoughts and behaviours beyond our conscious control. Most of the time, our unconscious ego wants to control the outcome of events in our favour, but once we begin to travel on a more spiritual path, we get to understand this controlling behaviour will backfire in the end, resulting in negative, obsessive, unrealistic thoughts.

Mindful meditation, the ability to quieten the mind by shifting obsessive thoughts out, releases us from the need to always be in control, helping us to become more comfortable with uncertainty. It helps us become more secure through self-knowledge, gradually developing more trust within. We become more honest, dropping the pretence, communicating more sincerely by practising forgiveness over blaming. We find the courage to start the process of reinventing ourselves with integrity, living a more transparent life, monitoring every move we make to mirror every belief we have.

During my own life crisis, I came across a mind detective who made me think. You know when someone else gets you because what they say makes complete sense to you. By listening to and learning from a master of the mind, Carl Jung, I truly got to understand myself beyond the made-up bullshit of my own self-protection. He believed in developing a wholeness inside. The individualisation process is a combination of merging the self, the shadow, the persona, the good, the bad and the ugly, all manifested by the mind in times of crisis. This is exactly what happened to me. This individualisation process allowed me to come to the realisation that there was way more to me, the real me, than the social role played out dictated by my persona. Although I believed

I was an accomplished success story on paper, in truth I was empty and lost inside.

Reaching the point where you can take off your mask, slowly peeling it back, will feel very raw and uncomfortable. You are shedding your old skin and stretching yourself beyond your comfort zone. It will open the door to your freedom if you can stay the course, slowly emerging as an individual thinker yourself. Gaining reward and benefit from any major change in your life takes patience, hard work and dedicated practice. Being happy for real is no different sadly. It is not something you are born with. Understanding this is the first step to becoming mindful of how much work you need to do on yourself.

Poor mental health, the invisible enemy, affects us all in some way. Removing the stigma and talking openly about it is vital in this difficult environment we live in today. Unless we confront and defeat our enemies, killing them with kindness, we end up at war, amidst a battle we just cannot win. The worse kind of sad is never being able to explain why. Crying is how your heart speaks out when your voice cannot explain the pain. It is hard to express what is wrong when nothing feels right. The key to understanding internal misery, the endless painful baggage we carry around day to day, is to recognise and accept that all we have learnt from birth is stored and programmed within our subconscious mind. These memories logged in the subconscious mind are often wired towards the negative bias. Think about when you were a small child how many times you were told "Don't do that", "Stop doing that", "Do it this way", "Do it that way", "Don't do it or else". Constant negative messages from neurotic, anxious, controlling parental patterns, filling you with the faults they have—and a little extra too, just for you—just spreads the misery from generation to generation. This control dilutes any unique individual talents developing naturally. Now think about being constantly told you cannot do something when your natural curious self wants to find out what is right or wrong for you, the only real way we learn to think for ourselves, problem-solve, discover our strengths and ultimately create our own footprints in the sand. If you put your fingers in the fire, you get burnt, and chances are you won't ever do it again. You learn instinctively the fire is dangerous and must never be touched. If you long to be a dancer and you are forced to be a doctor, you learn instinctively to feel disappointed every time you are frustrated or fed up with your life. By the time we can think for ourselves, we are unable to think for ourselves because we just don't know how to do it and when we do know, it is often in a negative way. We think we cannot more than we can because we have been constantly told we cannot.

Often as children when we are developing, we associate love and acceptance with pleasing our parents, doing things their way, and because they are the biggest influencers in our lives, we learn how to manage our feelings based on these influences. The problem with this fixed mindset learning: we become people pleasers in adult life and find it very hard to break away from self-sacrificing tendencies. We are not able to focus on pleasing ourselves in a self-respecting, affirming way. This subconscious programming, the negative bias we go to because we are so used to doing it, and it feels comfortable, can leave us behaving and thinking in a way that is automatic. We do it without even thinking about it, leaving us unable to perceive our own internal emotions correctly. If we are truly conscious of the things we do and say when we think about stuff, chances are we would not say and do the things we do without thinking, preventing emotional and stressful difficulties in our physical and mental wellbeing.

As we develop and stand on our own two feet, we begin to make decisions and choices, but because we have been programmed from childhood how to think, this difficult transition into maturity and action becomes fraught with peril. This causes tension, anxiety and unconscious fears we don't understand. These negative feelings can then create intense worry, stress and despair. We make choices based upon what we have been taught. We copy and model on what we see, not what we really desire for ourselves deep down inside, our own hopes and dreams. No two people will draw the same meaning from the same thing, therefore the meaning of life is unique to us all. This unique talent is our purpose. The biggest challenge we have in life is finding our unique purpose. A purposeful, meaningful, unique individual life creates a greater sense of belonging, which creates internal happiness. This then becomes our intentional life. Without a purpose, we are plagued by an empty hole in the soul, doing what is expected of us, never fulfilling our own needs. This empty hole in the soul leaves us always being driven by the opinions and wishes of others. The authentic self gets lost and buried, forced behind a mask, never allowed to shine, a false identity, a fake version of who we really are inside, easily influenced by greed, money and self-gratification.

Discovering the right path to what was already there mapped out for you in nature, healing the misery of depression from being pushed down the wrong path is like doing a giant puzzle. The key is identifying all the pieces from past experiences, putting them back together again to create a true picture of who you really are behind the mask. You may not be able to change your circumstances; however, you can change your perception of them if you are open and vigilant. Change will never just come to you. You must go out into the world and place yourself in situations that facilitate change.

As much as we don't always want to admit it, our inner core foundation and values are only established by how we build our character, especially when self-esteem and self-worth are the primary shapers of a balanced, mentally healthy individual. If we are operating in life without a strong developed core of self-acceptance and self-esteem, our personal goals and inner happiness will be directly impacted, leaving us stressed, frustrated and in crisis about our life choices and circumstances. Low self-esteem and internal chaos without a core value character in place will always make us question what is real and what is self-deception. Fear, anxiety and depression are very real to the person experiencing such negative feelings and often creep up without warning, unexplained and undeniably difficult to manage or make sense of in the moment because the underlying problem is never identified or faced openly in truth. A patient of mine recently wrote this harrowing painful expression of his internal madness on a social media site which says it all about mental health and depression today.

"No way is it anxiety when it comes on like this. Right now, I'd lay on a slab and let them dissect me to find what the bastard hell is happening at random times to me so they could just say that's what the problem is even if they have to sweep up my body parts into a furnace afterwards, at least this shit would stop."

As we gain more spiritual maturity and strength, we get to recognise when this type of accumulated inner pressure is happening. We learn how to take steps to diffuse it because if we don't find a healthy outlet, the pressure, like for my patient, can erupt into destructive, painful, uncontrollable reactions.

I am not a qualified psychiatrist or doctor. I am a mind detective, having worked myself out after a life-changing crisis. I have rebuilt my life from scratch and today work with others through talk therapy to understand further the human condition in this modern-day world. To understand your mind deeply takes revisiting the past, gathering all the unconscious evidence, fitting the pieces together like a puzzle to create a true picture of the offences you have committed against yourself, just like a clever detective would when solving a heinous crime.

To be able to think for ourselves, to manage our internal misery, the pain, the regrets, the guilt, the fear of failure, our existing beliefs, we need to start to empty the subconscious memory. We need to reframe our pain with forgiveness, humility, gratitude, integrity and compassion, developing a whole new set of core values and beliefs to live by. If you suffer anger and pain from the past, recognise that the people who caused you this pain were in fact hurting inside themselves. Projecting hurt on others was their own coping mechanism. Learning to internalise forgiveness over pain is a great healer for your soul. To change things consciously takes visiting the past and rewinding the mind, the negative subconscious memories we have stored making us miserable, to create a positive picture of who we really are and what we really think beyond what we have learnt from others.

As human beings, we have a compulsive need to feel like our life has meaning, value, not just existing, consuming, eating, drinking and ultimately dying empty shells. Without a purpose and a good sense of self-worth, we end up suffering because everything we do is driven to satisfy our external needs. A confident person without mind baggage will feel stable and balanced in their core foundation. They will be more focused and determined to establish a better connection with their state of consciousness, life choices and personal goals. I know this to be true because this is me today. If we end up valuing money and possessions over our self-worth, we create an inability to produce consistency in our patterns of thought and behaviours, greatly restricting our ability to evolve beyond self-gratification.

More than anyone, I know how hard it is to change the way we think about things. It took me reaching the bottom to realise that the person I thought I was in fact was nothing like the person I wanted to be. I was rich and successful materially for sure, but I was empty, lost and incomplete spiritually. I had become disconnected from myself, from the rest of the world, from nature and the universe. I was lost out at sea, alone, navigating the ferocious waves of my misery constantly pulling me under, constantly testing my strength of character.

The hard work of changing and evolving cannot be done by anyone else but you. Although you can learn lessons from others like me who have experienced great wisdom through hardship, we all have our own unique challenges and a personal responsibility for the choices we have made in this life. When I was growing up, my personal circumstances were not positive but my steadfast self-confidence, my core values were solid. I had a true sense of self based upon the foundations of hope and purpose. I always focused on change through experimenting, not self-improvement, sadly. I was lucky I did not model on the negative side of my childhood because it was ripped away from me very early. I was guided into higher wisdom through this experience, missing the cycles of pain, bitterness and resentment that comes from focusing on painful destructive issues. I had an innate ability to block out my truth, my circumstances and my pain to confidently create a social persona in order to get on in life. Even at a very young age, I had tremendous insight without experience, something I relied upon in times of grave personal danger.

We cannot choose our parents, or change the built-in embedded patterns they have passed on to us from their caregivers, but we can learn from their mistakes, forgive them and ourselves for how life has made us feel about who we are today. Understanding why you feel depressed, anxious and unfulfilled all the time is not easy. This has become a comfortable behaviour pattern you rely on to get through your life the best you can, often day to day. I am going to try and change this thinking for good as we go through this journey together, showing you how and why changing the negative way you think can create a positive new path to the real you, the authentic you, the person you really are behind your many masks.

There is no secret when it comes to therapy. Changing how you think to find your purpose and happiness, regardless what you have read, is all about doing the hard work without relying on quick fix solutions or emotional comfort to numb you through it. When we lose something we perceive has great value, it is true we will descend into the darkness of depression. This is what happened to me. These dark times should not be seen without worth because it is these times when we learn something new; the darkness inside suddenly gains some light. Once we understand the importance of cultivating emotional intelligence as the core of self-knowledge, we begin to regulate our feelings more accurately. We perceive our reality in honesty, helping us gain more meaning through increased spiritual growth, eventually evolving to maturity beyond the past.

Our current state of mind, our whole being is influenced by our thoughts and emotions stored safely in the subconscious, directing our conscious thoughts and feelings. How we feel and respond can be attributed to the influence of the subconscious memory. Therefore, it is critical to understand how to get a better grip on it to help create better habits and patterns going forward. This allows us to direct more desire and curiosity rather than holding us ransom, keeping us stuck with narrow-minded views like accepting and believing without doubt that nothing can ever change.

Our minds are constantly filled with everything we think, feel and imagine, all mashed up and confused in a constant state of chaos, until we finally switch off short-term through self-medicating comforts, drugs, food, sex, alcohol or some other escape route of choice. We are constantly on the go, surviving the day dealing with demons, regrets, relationships, our internal pain; and to relax, most of us turn to comfort. We all expect miracles in life without ever doing the work it takes to produce them, something I discovered myself on the journey to self-mastery, the highway to my higher self, the straight and narrow road to higher thinking, mindfulness and inner peace. Yes, it does exist! You must be sure first through deep self-honesty, the road you are travelling on today is the right road for you tomorrow and the rest of your life because the wrong road will lead you to a miserable, painful end.

You can start again regardless of your past mistakes, past failures, past upbringing, regardless of your age, gender or level of emotional intelligence. Remember your subconscious thinking can be reprogrammed and changed at any time, if you decide to do it. I had a first-class honours degree in making mistakes, bad choices and dangerous denial. I have been there, done it all and have the T-shirt to prove it. Today I have recovered and healed myself back together. Although I was lucky and started out with unbreakable confidence and self-belief, without the painful baggage of my past childhood in tow, I was not immune from the devastating effects of being an empty hole without a soul. Reaching the top when you began at the bottom is quite an achievement. Most of us remain in the middle lane of life, but there is no joy in personal success if you cannot justify the blood, sweat and tears of getting there. These days, eighteen years on after encountering a huge life-changing curve ball that knocked me off my feet, a near-death experience that almost took me down, I am an expert now in all I teach others about how to start again, healing the past to discover a future today I never imagined possible. I am living proof it is possible to master mental health, and this happens by understanding the truth about who you really are under the mask, discovering along the way that with hard work, anything is possible, including miracles. It is important to understand that where you are right now, is a direct result of how you started out, but this does not mean you have to live forever battling your unresolved issues in your past to be able to enjoy your future.

Life is a set of continual challenges. Some people manage to develop the ability to navigate these challenges successfully but the majority, sadly, are hindered by the negative bias of avoidance. Rather than facing up to these many life challenges, dealing with them head on through problem-solving, many people will descend into a passive mindset, which at the end of the day produces regrets about a life passed by. Why is it so difficult to get rid of our negative personality traits constantly hindering the process of positive change in our wellbeing? How can we understand ourselves if we don't know ourselves? Pretending to be strong if inside we are weak, is the main reason we automatically reach out for emotional comfort when we feel vulnerable. We must find ways to escape the insecurity of never feeling safe and secure or comfortable in our own skin.

Everything you have learnt and experienced in your life from birth is permanently stored in your subconscious memory. Its capacity is virtually unlimited. Its primary job is to ensure you respond exactly to the way you have programmed it. Your subconscious mind is subjective. It does not think independently. It just obeys commands from your conscious instructions. Basically, what one commands, the other obeys. It is as simple as that.

In this book, together we are going to discover why what has been planted and embedded in your memory, by the opinions and behaviours of others, does not fit a positive, healthy pattern consistent with your authentic self. We are going to look at the perceptions of your existing belief system to see how it compares with a universal core belief system, and we will work out if what you believe about yourself is real or made up in your imagination to please others. By clearing out and reprogramming your subconscious mind, focusing on new uplifting affirmations with improved self-confidence, we will begin to implement a more positive pattern of thinking, helping you to develop a happier outlook on your life.

After my life-changing experience followed by near death, I was forced to reprogram my whole mind, the only reason I was able to harness the power of positive thinking in a time of complete hopelessness and chaos. The main thing you learn with a near-death experience, your belief and faith in your ability to operate rationally suddenly returns with clarity. You are left with little choice but to feel gratitude, no matter how unhappy, hopeless and ashamed you feel about your circumstances and mistakes. It is often repressed fears and uncontrollable impulses that bring about habitual patterns of depressed thoughts and negative behaviours, often without understanding as to why it keeps happening. If you have become comfortable accepting things the way they are and can never be changed, things will remain the way they are and will never change, but what would happen if you were suddenly forced to change everything overnight like I was?

When I reached the bottom with nowhere left to go but inside myself to find answers, I was forced to unravel and clean out my own repressed fears and impulses that had led me to being so reckless with my own life. I had to take some personal responsibility for the choices, the mistakes, the carnage I created to be able to heal and face the car-crash life I believed to be invincible but was in fact nothing more than fragile and fake. It was truly difficult to start again with no one to turn to for help who would not judge me or pour their opinions over me. I needed some spiritual guidance, not from a rigid religious perspective but from wisdom and insight, a psychological bias, someone who truly understood the mind.

I was lost in LA, broke after losing all my money, devastated and depressed. Everything I had worked so hard to achieve was gone in a flash. It would take much more than a miracle to sort this mess out. For me, it was the end of the road. Or so I thought back then. I came across a book by Carl Jung in a bookstore, *Modern Man in Search of a Soul*. It popped off the shelf like I was meant to buy it. I'd never been a big reader in the past, but this title resonated with me in the moment, so I purchased it with my last few dollars before setting about trying to understand my mind and how it worked. It's not the easiest book to read, I must admit, especially for a soulless beginner, but there were some things in this reading that led me to understand more about my subconscious thinking and how to differentiate it from my conscious thinking. It made me realise I was not one-dimensional. Jung related to his patients. He realised he had the same mental health issues they did. He could see we are all fragile, fragmented and divided, and knowingly or not, we are all on a deep spiritual quest in search of our soul. This first revelation was a huge comfort for me. Reading about how I worked internally and spiritually from a master of the mind made me feel not so alone and, in turn, made me more curious to understand why I had made so many poor choices in my past. He had real empathy for suffering and was open to discussing his own weakness and flaws. I enjoyed this freedom from judgement. It made me feel better. It made me think instead of feeling bad, something I had lost sight of doing in my chaos and turmoil. I related to what he was teaching me about my internal emotional and psychological wiring. It made sense to me because I felt comfortable and connected; it helped expand my mind spiritually. I became open to learn more, so one day like today, I would become open enough to help others in the same way he helped me. The experts today say Carl Jung's theory and ideas on how we work internally are not as popular as Freud's. Jung's ideas were mystical and obscure, not easily explained, but I am convinced based upon my own personal experience—it takes one to know one—he understood perfectly how we work as human beings.

I excelled beyond belief once I discovered the idea of my undiscovered self, the authentic me behind the mask of my insecurities, alienated from my instinctual core foundation for too long. I also understand now, past childhood experiences will determine adult behaviour, so I am beginning this journey with you by simply explaining the psyche and how it works.

The psyche is a self-regulating system just like the body, processing everything in the conscious and the subconscious. It strives to maintain balance between our opposing qualities whilst at the same time develop our individuality. Most of our suffering is avoidable and can be resolved once we start to learn about the psyche, overcoming our unconscious programming producing our internal suffering. We can finally stop the constant self-defeating beliefs holding us back from developing into individual thinkers. The psyche has four main functions in developing our personality. Two are rational: our thinking and feeling. Two are irrational: our intuition and sensation. As small children when we are developing, depending on our personal circumstances, we give preference to one of these functions. This then becomes our superior function. Our consciousness is a product of both our rational and irrational processes of encountering and assessing our reality. Our perceptions, thinking objective and feeling subjective, are our rational functions. Two of these functions are related to how we take in information and two are related to how we make decisions. Some people favour thoughts to pass judgement, others follow their feelings. Thinkers will approach life with little regard for their emotions; they arrange things with logic and order. This is my own personality type and superior function. People who feel emotions embrace disorder. Sensing people will ultimately accept things as they are. Intuitive people are more interested in future possibilities. According to Jung, we have a superior function that is conscious—this is our strength—and an inferior function that remains unconscious—things we avoid. For example, like in my case, I rely on thinking to interpret information and my feeling represent my inferior function. I am now completely convinced the one switch we need to flick in our minds, to change how we think feel and act in our favour for future happiness, is to learn to think before we feel, so we can control the impulse to overreact. If we all put thinking as our primary superior function, we would not impulsively react or be influenced by illusions, other people's opinions or self-deceptions. We would consciously, in the moment, rationally think things through to the end, then respond appropriately without reacting or feeling because thinkers always decide things based on logic, and when they do so, they consider the decision to be made. The main key to becoming an individual unique thinker is all about wholeness, and this lies in the process of developing the inferior side of ourselves, the things we have buried in the unconscious like fear, regret, guilt and insecurity. To evolve and mature, be happy and achieve success beyond what we have learnt from others, liberating our authentic selves, we must strip away all our false identities our unconscious ego has created. This process will become the main trigger to eliminating all our fears.

After my own life-changing event, I realised and experienced the Jung theory for real. The point of my life was to become a whole person in my own right, reach my full potential and discover my purpose to reconnect me with my divine self within. I knew that to do this, I had to face my dark side, the parts of me I did not like or even acknowledge, my primitive side, my selfishness, my repressed instincts. The uncomfortable parts of me, my conscious mind rejected and buried in the deepest recesses of my internal self. This amazing individualisation process through my own psychological development, made me more conscious of my hidden self buried behind my unconscious ego. It finally allowed me to develop positive mental health as a mature, whole, responsible adult without any need to be accepted or validated by others. The main reason we feel permanently inadequate with others is because we have doubts about our true abilities. We lack self-confidence because we are always pretending to be something we are not to impress or please others, over satisfying our own needs deep inside.

When I hit rock bottom, I managed to face and get to know my shadow side, the dark part of my psyche, all the bits of myself I had dismissed and disowned to create my false identity, my persona. I got to understand my unconscious ego was only a tiny part of me, not my guiding light. Once I was brave enough to penetrate the core of my conflict as the authentic me, I stopped fuelling and participating in it. It was destructive and pointless and not me at all. My authentic whole self is way more refined and reliable than my unconscious ego or fake personality. Today I have become brave and capable to step outside of participating anymore in my inner conflict, with a deeper intelligence to be more aware of my essential inner dynamics. Through this journey together you will travel deeper into your own psyche to expose the degree to which you have become programmed by others, circumstances and self-deception, so you will stop experiencing your own life through a false identity. You will slowly get to know the side of yourself you are hiding from the world, the person you are without all the fake bravado, the pretence, the keeping up with the Joneses, the pressure, the stress and the endless conflict. With this greater consciousness, you will be more capable of healing the split between what is conscious and what is unconscious, to rediscover a wholeness in your psyche. You will finally become a complete human being, including all the parts of your personality you have never been conscious of before because you could not face your truth. You are going to learn to understand that you think both consciously and unconsciously, plus discover that the unlimited potential and power of the subconscious mind is available and useful, if it works to your advantage and not against you. We may want to convince ourselves in our unconscious ego state we are all conscious of our thoughts, feelings and behaviours but the reality is very different. In truth, we are mostly unconscious beings going through the motions of life on autopilot without thinking. To begin the quality process of being consciously aware of things, a mental state achieved by focusing attention and awareness on the present, not lost on autopilot, takes calmly acknowledging and accepting our thoughts, feelings and body sensations through mindfulness.

The art of mindful thinking begins with the realisation that you are in fact unhappy, unfulfilled, depressed, always anxious, trapped in a world of lies, pain and confusion, the main reason you cannot get back in control of your happiness sat nav. Mindful thinking and the practice of mediation is the only real way to clear out and silence the mind, to be able to hear the autopilot negative cruel critic inside your mind, hijacking your self-worth and self-esteem. Becoming a blank piece of paper, wiping out past destructive patterns, habits and failures will be easy for those who have already lost everything but for those who just want more from life, the process will be much tougher; for you, it's a choice. To change the way you think, you need to know how to change what you believe to be true and this is what I hope to achieve on this self-awareness journey back to a better you.

Mental health, just like your physical health, should be talked about every day without stigma because in some way everybody is mental, some more than others. No one is free from the stress and pressure of life today. You never truly know what people are going through behind closed minds, so it is important we are kind to each other and talk to each other, even strangers, showing we care. Sometimes just simply being there to listen can save lives. If this is you, I understand where you find yourself right now. I have been there myself, and in that dark moment when those black clouds came over me, it was my inner truth that intervened and saved me. Your inner truth, that voice of reason buried beneath all the burden you have let distort your rational ability to listen and understand, is not there anymore when you really need it. As the person you are putting all your faith into right now, it is important you get to know me and my own story, so you will see you are never alone. We are all unique in one way but all the same deep down, fragile, fragmented and human.

When I reached the top of the enormous mountain to self-made success, before I fell back down to the bottom, I realised I had everything materially but did not recognise myself anymore. I was alone, depressed and empty inside. I would drink too much to forget, take drugs to get a fake high, shop to buy stuff I didn't need and have sex to stop feeling lonely, then make up stories to change this truth because deep down inside I was ashamed of myself. This irrational behaviour, always escaping myself, made me feel like an imposter in my own life. How did I get to be so isolated, unable to be happy, ungrateful and not spiritually accomplished in middle age?

I did regretfully attempt suicide myself in 2000 after losing millions in the 2000 dot-com stock market crash, but thank God, I got a miracle. I woke up hung over. It didn't work. My half-hearted attempt to walk away from the mess I had created failed, the reason today I know why suicide is never the answer. I can remember feeling ashamed for contemplating such a thing after the event, but in that single moment, alone, depressed and desperate, I lost all hope and turned to suicide as the only viable way out of hell for me. For the very first time in my life, I allowed my feelings to override my rational thinking. An important thing you learn in this kind of painful situation is allowing yourself to feel incredibly uncomfortable sometimes in order to develop deeper clarity and discernment; it gives you the ability to be more transparent to yourself. Ultimately, getting to face your own weaknesses when you find yourself emotionally devastated allows you to better protect yourself in the future. You get to commit to only facing your truth, no matter how painful that truth is. In the end, you learn to cure yourself. There can be no spiritual or emotional growth without personal discomfort. It is impossible to make any internal changes if you are unwilling to learn something new about yourself and the world to improve yourself and the world, something I had to face when I hit rock bottom. Losing all your money, when money is all you value to show for a life's work, is devastating.

My failed suicide, as it turned out, was not the bottom for me. I had more falling to do until the real crash happened, not the stock market crash—that was nothing compared to this. I was looking death in the face for real. In 2005, after making the most fatal mistakes any human being could possibly make, I finally crashed out at the bottom of the mountain I'd fought so hard to climb. It was at this point I didn't have the strength to commit suicide to escape myself; I was dying for real.

The mental and physical health problems we face right now are reaching epidemic levels as our culture changes and we do not. The environment has become more competitive with medication becoming the answer over therapy because resources are limited, and human empathy has faded. Changing any problem takes knowledge, insight and a wealth of understanding. Often the truthful answer to our problems comes from a personal experience of growth and recovery, not medicating the problem away or suppressing it deeper due to pain, fear and stigma. The thing you need to know before we begin what I have learnt from my own destructive dance with self-harm and death is as follows:

There is always a tremendous meaningfulness to your life, once you can manage the unhealthy dynamics in your mind.

Together through learning how to breathe properly, meditate in silence and be more mindful, we are going to learn to become more self-aware, developing the mind and watching every thought we have. By observing the mind as an outsider, we become more aware of our feelings, not over-identifying with them but detaching from them, so we can begin to control them, making them a friend not an enemy. We increase our level of emotional intelligence to begin to experience a positive mind transformation, identifying our destructive behaviour patterns from the past. By getting to the root cause of all your mental and emotional distortions, created by your unconscious ego and reinforced by the cruel inner critic currently residing in your mind, you will begin to discover personal freedom. I can tell you for sure from my own experience of facing adversity, depression, anxiety, losing everything and near death, even though the rest of the world seems to be operating and getting on with life, most people are suffering the same way you are, living life through an illusion. I believed I was invincible, nothing could touch me or take me down but how wrong was I?

We spend most of our time with ourselves which is why it is highly important to never give up on ourselves. I am a good talk therapist because I have empathy and a willingness to share my own feelings of hopelessness with you. I also have a deep understanding of inner conflict, the power of inner weakness, through the work I have done with the homeless and addicts. I know I can teach you the principles or your inner conflicts to help you see your own psyche and true self more objectively, by breaking free of your emotional attachment to your negative destructive side. We live in an environment right now that no longer promotes or supports goals, hopes and dreams, which has left most of us dissatisfied with our lives and our circumstances, a world structured in favour of a few at the expense of the rest. The key to rising above this reality is not to give in to it believing there is nothing you can do to change it. You must instead make the effort to find the persistence to always be improving who you really are, so you can become the collective power that makes a big difference in the world.

This book is my "David"—the story of me already set in stone. It just took some chipping away and polishing for the authentic me to emerge and write it down for you. My purpose in life now is to share what I have discovered with the rest of the world. I am not a believer, I know. I faced death, lost everything and reinvented the wheel. I am living proof that life is a journey, not a destination, and for whatever reason you are malfunctioning in your own life, it will not come close to what happened to me and I survived for the better, so there's always hope for you. This book and its contents are based on my own personal journey, a brush with near death, enormous change to discover the real me, the person I was always meant to be spiritually. I have taken a leaf out of the book of my mentor Carl Jung to study the minds of those with the same internal conflicts I have suffered myself and by sharing this knowledge with you, I hope to form a deep identification with anyone who is suffering in pain. What people don't realise is that depression is not what is going on with the outside, it is all about what is going on with the inside. Thoughts are never controlled by the depressed, the depressed are controlled by the thoughts. Most people believe depression is about feeling sad, crying, wearing black, but this is not the case. Depression is about feeling numb, numb to emotions, numb to life, a constant state of emptiness, a bruise of the mind that never seems to go away.

One last note before we begin, if you have never considered doing any work on yourself through personal development, you are probably feeling quite overwhelmed and uneasy right now, believing the journey in this book will be too difficult. A sense of self-mastery is the major benefit when adopting humility. Humble people have a much better level of self-control, the dominant personality trait shared by successful people. Everyone makes mistakes, no one is perfect. We just need to learn to come to terms with these mistakes through humility, admitting them and then forgiving ourselves, understanding none of it matters in the bigger picture. Your subconscious mind will always force you to feel physically and emotionally uncomfortable when embarking on changing your embedded patterns and behaviours. You will literally feel it pulling you back to your comfort zone every time you try to do things in a different way, the main reason you have been unable to stick to changes you have tried to make in the past.

Just like my own mentor, Carl Jung, suggested all those years ago, in this book we are going to do our own psychoanalysis of the mind, body, soul and spirit, not believing we are ill but simply understanding why we have been failing to achieve fulfilment and happiness. We will learn to speak clearly with our authentic soul self and begin the journey to personal freedom away from our internal suffering. Carl Jung said, "We cannot change anything unless we accept it first."

You are a good person deep inside without the pretence. The deep built-in defences you project outwards for acceptance is why you have become confused about what goodness really means. Goodness is not about looking like you care to others. The true quality of being good is about morality, conforming to the correct standards of the right conduct, a citizen of the highest ethics and personal standards. Remember, goodness and graciousness go hand in hand. Learning to be kind, patient, aware and thoughtful towards yourself allows you to model the same behaviour for others through humility. Someone who is brave enough to live in humility is no longer proud, believing they are better than others. It does not make you a doormat constantly defending yourself but instead about knowing you will succeed with your own strength. You never have to win every argument. You never have to stand up for yourself in an angry manner. You diffuse arguments when you are humble. You learn to respond not react to unfair treatment without becoming bitter inside. We are all just small specks of rock on a bigger rock flying around a vast space, hanging on to what we know for dear life. When you really begin to think about this in an open-minded way, you truly begin to understand humility and the importance of putting things into perspective.

The Only Way Out Is Through

My new life today is so very different from the life I created for myself before my near-death experience. It was a revelation to discover the straight and narrow road I was travelling down back then, focused and determined, was in fact the wrong road for me. Today eighteen years on, I feel blessed to have hope and can promise you without any doubt that what you believe to be hopeless and impossible to change in your life is an irrational illusion created by your existing belief system. Your current thinking follows this belief system, then creates an emotional reaction in you. If you believe you are useless and a failure, you will feel like a loser and a failure, but it is not the truth, just simply incorrect evidence dictated by your beliefs. Often we become conformed to an acceptable consensus of our reality through the power of what we have learnt and experienced as children, which can feel like persecution, ridicule and control. Through these enforced intimidations, we tend to mimic the same mental rigidity, disconnecting us from our own instincts and intuitions. I have already given you the secret to changing your whole mindset in the last chapter by making one switch. This switch is all about thinking before you feel instead of feeling before you think. Ask yourself the question now:

Do you think before your feel or do you feel before you think?

If we feel before we think, we are letting our emotions be in control of our behaviours. We are acting on potentially a skewed view of the situation. If we think before we feel, we can put things into perspective, into reality ahead of time, then respond with a more rational view of the entire situation. It's common sense. Our habits in our thinking patterns, whether they are good, bad or ugly, largely determine our character and will influence the quality of our lives, due to the impact they have on our mental wellbeing. Changing your ugly bad habits into good healthier habits is what happens when you switch over from feeling first to thinking first before you react, then chances are you won't react but act. When we choose feeling instead of thinking, our brain cells never get a chance to grow. Research has proven our brain cells grow and change with our life experiences, good or bad, and keep growing as we learn new things. Our feelings and emotions often create our bad habits. These habits have a physical existence in the structure of the brain. They become our default circuit every time we are faced with temptation. Basically, we feel our emotions over thinking rationally. Changing our habits, having the courage to learn something new, so we produce more brain cells and develop our positive thinking capabilities, takes more than motivation and willpower.

I believed I was a winner, absolutely invincible, and this belief took me to the top. It made me feel like I could rule the world which fuelled my drive further until I got there. I was open to many ways of being and thinking without feeling threatened, limited or defensive. I never allowed my feelings to get in the way of my ambitions and goals. I was never a victim. This allowed me to live in the moment, never dwelling in the past, on hurt and regrets. Like I said, my superior function was always to think rather than feel. This one important skill truly helped me to climb out of chaos and poverty into the crazy capitalist world of big money and greed. The big problem for me when I finally got there, I was happy and rich materially but not spiritually mature enough to enjoy my success. I was still making fatal mistakes. The immature repeated mistake of looking outward for the answer led me to my tragic downfall; ultimately, it allowed me no flexibility for greater intelligence. I was an expert at making money and spending it, but I never realised I was part of something greater. I forgot to care about what really matters in life. I was always driven by instant gratification, was self-entitled and never kind to myself. I lost all contact and empathy for any belief in my spiritual wellbeing and was taken over by a more powerful belief in the desire for money and power. Basically, I was an empty shell.

It takes enormous courage and strength to look directly in the face of pain then try to take your own life in a split-second action, believing it is the only option you have left. If it takes courage to kill ourselves, we must also have the courage to survive and save ourselves. Not all of us have let depression, misery and discontentment drive us to suicidal thinking but many of us have wished many times we could wipe the slate clean and start again. Whatever place you find yourself in right now and for whatever reason you are reading this book, I can promise you the only way out of anything is to go through it. I know because I had to go through it to survive myself.

Back in 2000 in mid-life, after years of climbing what seemed like a never-ending mountain to a peak of personal world domination and success, never looking back, reflecting or taking a break, I found myself exhausted and empty. I had finally reached the summit, had everything materially one could ever wish for—the cars, the bank account, good looks, big houses, flash vacations, financial security and a very successful self-made business—yet I was still not happy or fulfilled. You can never judge a book by its cover, a metaphorical phrase that means you shouldn't pre-judge the worth or value of something by its outward appearance alone. Looking like you have everything to others, can often leave you a stranger to yourself.

To be able to compete in this modern-day world, we often lie to ourselves and make up stories to others to fit in and not be judged, creating what Carl Jung calls the persona, the mask we hide behind to cover our identity from the world. They say what doesn't kill you makes you stronger. I am living proof of this today, no longer hiding behind a mask, acting out a part in my perfect-on-the-surface life. Today I am basking in the warmth of a purposeful, driven life, and I never look back, I just keep moving forward. It takes a life-changing, light-bulb moment to make you realise, everything you think you are doing right is in fact all wrong and the road you have chosen to travel has led you to a disastrous end. This happened to me for real and through my story in this book I am going to tell you, at the same time hopefully help you to understand, you will never escape yourself or your mistakes. You must be brave enough to face yourself instead. When we are selective in the commitment to doing only the minimum required to change, we are selfishly responsible for the self-serving motivations only for reward. We end up never understanding the impact we have on ourselves or other people around us.

Most people spend their lives asking the ultimate question: "What is the point?" You have probably already said it today without coming up with the answer. This is what I mean by the negative bias we all turn to when we feel we have exhausted all our options and life is not working out the way we planned or hoped it would. As we begin to reflect more on the human condition, we get to understand that hardship, suffering and personal failure will at some time affect us all, its life but let me tell you now, it is only a small part of what it means to be human. We all have so much more power inside and our true potential comes from our suffering. When we reject our personal suffering because we have no desire to go backwards in time to find where the pain originated, for fear of having to face the truth then change, we end up victims of our unresolved issues. This then creates a sense of unease inside.

I was a master at escaping myself, the person I had become, so by the time I reached all my long-term goals and had made enough money to buy my freedom, I reinvented myself and my life by moving to Los Angeles, marrying a stranger and leaving behind all traces of my old life like it never existed. Most people would consider such an irrational move as complete madness. On reflection today, I agree, but at the time, it was my only way out. Money and success alone had not made me happy or provided the quality of internal peace I dreamed about as a young girl—I guess what they would call my own happily ever after. Although my life was perfect on paper, I was still not happy, but I knew instinctively if I changed my surroundings, manipulated my truth and started a life somewhere else as someone else, I might have a chance at finding happiness. There would finally be a point to all my hard work and personal sacrifice climbing to the top.

The greatest mistake people make when they rely solely on material wealth and personal possessions for happiness, believing it is money that brings joy fulfilment and wisdom—I know because I was one of these people—is they give up working on themselves spiritually. Without internal peace, joy and wisdom in place before you make it big, money does not buy or guarantee anything except freedom, and freedom is no use if you have no idea where you are going. You ultimately end up emotionally dependent on addictions like shopping, drugs and alcohol to help create an instant fix to the happiness you crave inside.

My whole life from a small child was all about reinventing myself, to be able to navigate the choppy waters towards safety, comfort and security, so this mad impulsive move to LA came very easily to me without reflection or consideration. I needed a change and that was that. In the past, I had reinvented myself many times to get on in life, always using someone else as a stepping stone, but this time around, I had the financial security to do it without having to lose any more of my self-respect, or so I thought at the time. Enduring childhood poverty and the excruciating loss of my mother, who left me when I was eight years old, ensured my future long-term goals would always include escaping and making money at any cost, to be able to survive and flourish in a life of my own. I was forced to grow up fast, missing a healthy, balanced childhood, the loving security of a content home life, with a father who worked his fingers to the bone to keep things going. I was forced to become a seasoned problem solver with no one at home to model on. I have very few memories of back then. It was all too negative; I was too consumed with my own survival, blocking out all the pain, replacing it with made-up stuff to be able to thrive and survive alone. I created and wore many masks at a very young age. My different personas became shields against the brutal lashings of real life. I became skilful at disguising my vulnerability from the opportunistic, drunken, menacing male predators lurking around the family home, ready to pounce at any opportunity. These days in my new state of complete spiritual wisdom, peace, freedom and contentment, I see this childhood trauma as a positive not a negative, because although it may not have been a fairy-tale beginning, it made me a tough, resilient, problem-solving adult.

The cycle of life, the mistakes we make, the lessons we learn, the things we change and the things we leave behind, I have recognised none of it really matters if we leave this world whole, independent and truly loving ourselves. We don't have to live with the cards we are dealt in the beginning, the luck of the draw, but we do have to resolve our issues, make peace with the past, move on from the pain and face our dark side with courage—the bits we don't consciously see or accept easily.

My whole life early on consisted of learning how to become street wise, stand on my own two feet, manipulate a person or situation to get what I needed, to be able to move forward, away from the negative mess left behind from my parents failed union. A life of snakes and ladders on the throw of a dice, always taking massive risks for big rewards, with ups and downs to compete with any roller-coaster ride anywhere on the planet. I never felt like a child. Growing up in a dysfunctional, unhappy world of pain and mistakes made me capable of riding the turbulent storms of life. There was no cotton wool comfort blanket to hide under for me.

I left school at fifteen with only one qualification in sociology. Even this was not my greatest achievement back then. I ruthlessly slept with my teacher in return for him doing the work and giving me the answers ahead of the exam— shocking, I know. You are probably judging me right now, but it was all I knew back then. If you are never given rules, boundaries or guidance from someone older and wiser who you trust, you are left alone to do whatever it takes to survive. I was the master manipulator at surviving, especially with older men, a learnt negative pattern passed down from my mother before she left me. Something I modelled on myself and used for years to come to get what I needed.

We model, we copy, we learn. We only know what we know until we know something else. A painful truth I had to brutally face later in life to be able to forgive myself, and her too, for all the mistakes I naively made as a child.

At sixteen, I foolishly got pregnant by a much older man, who stepped up to the plate and his responsibilities by offering to marry me. He showed me he loved me, but I had no feelings of love for him or the unborn child growing inside me, simply because I had never known love in the true sense. I know this sounds cold and heartless but when you learn to face your truth by going over the wreckage of your car-crash life, this happens when you reach the bottom; you suddenly realise the massive mistakes you made when you were young and naïve are not actually your fault. You compassionately learn to forgive yourself. This is where my superior function came into play through problem solving and thinking before feeling. I didn't allow myself to be driven by my emotions and feelings, I just survived the best I could under the painful circumstances I naively found myself in. I saw having an abortion as a blessing and the older man offering to pay for it as his true love for me. He knew I wanted more from my life than the council house estate jail my own mother had endured for marrying the wrong man herself at such a young age. He stood by my side, held my hand through the procedure and gracefully accepted my wishes to leave once it was all over. It was not long after the abortion I began to understand the first feelings of what being alone really meant. The drastic action of having an abortion isolated me from my family and friends, leaving me lonely and desperate, depressed and disillusioned for a while. It is true, people often selfishly judge you without understanding the whole picture.

Many people are over-compliant. They choose to live a life that is expected of them instead of building a life that fits better with their inner core and needs. They become people pleasers. I have always excelled and flourished way better alone. I was never blind to my own feelings and circumstances. I embraced my pain, my mistakes, to be able to develop a personality I could adapt to my own surroundings. I always found solitude quite stimulating and helpful. I hated the judging from others without them having the full picture.

It was not long before I moved out of the family home with my father and into a flat with a man I met at work. I was a sales assistant in a jean shop. He was the manager and much older than me. He provided the perfect haven I needed at the time to escape myself and rebuilt my confidence once again. Although I believed moving in with him would give me some independence, I soon realised it came with a price as the pressure from other people's opinions, particularly my family, forced me to marry him, making it acceptable, keeping everyone else happy. I had no real guidance or support from anyone older or wiser in my family circle. My father was probably glad to see the back of me, leaving any hopes and dreams of my financial success squashed. As the reality of married life at seventeen set in, I wanted to kill myself. Wanting to kill myself and doing it back then was just desperate thought process when feeling like a trapped animal in a suffocating cage, but a stroke of luck changed my whole destiny when the man I married robbed a bank and was sentenced to ten years in prison. Who says there isn't a God when you need one? My prayers were answered. Killing myself was put on hold as I conjured up a plan of escape with better prospects, outside the constraints of a troubled relationship with a man I didn't like, let alone love. If you really begin to look closely at this irrational behaviour, you begin to see it is often our circumstances, a lack of insight and modelling on what we see that forces us to make unhealthy choices throughout our early development. I saw my own mother walk away from a mess without ever looking back, leaving me, my younger sister and my poor broken-hearted father to pick up the pieces, so to me, this was a normal way to handle my own mistakes. We copy, we model, we learn.

I soon got a job with a recruitment firm in the local area, moved back in with my father to save money, work hard, get promoted, and eventually move up the ladder of success into a management position with prospects, something I could be proud of for once in my life. The power of intention truly works if you set yourself long-term goals, keep your head down, work hard and focus on the job in hand, never letting others influence or change the straight and narrow road you are travelling. I always had grand plans about being super successful even when I was very young, but the copying, the modelling, the negative habits of others can pull you back at any time from realising your own hopes and dreams. I already had built-in natural confidence, and once I'd made the same mistake a few times, I created a magnificent mask I could hide behind, never looking back reflecting, just rewriting the truth, reinventing my life story to fit in with my grand plan for personal success. The past became the past, a past I was not happy to brag about to others for fear of being horribly judged, so although I was able to reinvent myself and my story so far, my truth was bubbling inside me, locked away in the corridors of my mind, unresolved and festering. This is where the unconscious ego begins to win. It protects you from having to be vulnerable by allowing the lying, embellishing the truth, creating a perfect picture out of a complete mess.

I began to thrive as a human being regardless of the past baggage I had accumulated along the way. I realise now just how disconnected I was from my truth back then, but I did have the drive and work ethic of my father to be thankful for as my life began to have more meaning and structure for the very first time. I wasn't proud of my life story deep down, so to get on further, I tampered with the truth, manipulated the details and created a docu-story past for a high-flying executives future, always on a mission to succeed. After all, let's face it, marrying a bank robber at seventeen sentenced to years in prison is not the fairy-tale ending every girl dream's about, so I was forced to change it, and I never looked back. I made up some other tale to tell regarding my first marriage mistake, wiping it all out, pretending he died in a car crash. Poor bloke, this is the shadow self in action.

This was the dark side of me I found so hard to face later when accepting and forgiving myself. Once you lie because you are ashamed or embarrassed by your choices, to please others or get on in life, the lies remain with you, creating an even bigger fake persona you are forced to live with which then creates guilt.

Any truthful internal dialogue with your authentic self gets completely lost in translation. Think about how many times in the past you have lied to yourself to get what you want in the moment, later coming back to haunt you and destroy you down the line when the truth unexpectedly hits you from left field. We can never run away from ourselves forever. A big lesson I paid a massive price for when facing myself in mental crisis years later in midlife. Untangling my truth from the lies was brutal and truly painful, but it did save me in the end. Once we learn to allow the powerful feelings of our emotions to manifest in truth without over identifying with the state of being overwhelmed, we create some emotional balance and room in the mind to move forward in humility, not guilt. Today I am open to be honest with myself about my past early life. I have faced my shadow, my dark side in humility, and it was not easy but very freeing. I am not perfect but by letting it all out, I was free to be me, the whole me and nothing but me, an incredible experience of self-actualisation to maximise my potential.

It didn't take me long to climb the steep ladder to the top of the recruitment industry with my new identity and fake persona, changing firms twice along the way, relocating, ending up in charge of a team of people in the City of London, and earning enough money to buy my first flat. Life was fantastic with no regrets, no looking back and no remnants of a shaky start. I finally escaped my past, all I had to look forward to being was becoming a grand success in the male-dominated world in the City of London. Be careful what you wish for. I finally made it to the top in the recruitment firm through hard work, pure determination, a few lies and plenty of bullshit storytelling. Life was good in the confines of the bubble I had created for myself after escaping pain, poverty and the pressure of my past life. I found it quite hard to go home to see my family. They always reminded me of how guilty I felt inside. It is hard to explain why but maybe you will understand if you have ever changed who you are to get what you want. Sudden death is always a reason you are forced to go back and face your family. In the space of a six-month period, I lost my brother and my father both to heart attacks. It was my first experience of deep loss and great pain. It hurt so bad it almost took me down. It was at this point I should have reflected on my lifestyle, stopped rushing around for a while, taken some time out to mourn the loss. They say when a parent dies, it sets you free. It did make me more determined to fly higher, selling my soul to the highest bidder but free I was not. I knew I couldn't go backwards to a small provincial life in a small town where it had all begun. I instinctively knew it had to be London all the way for me.

As busy frantic human beings, we easily become alienated from our deep inner needs and feelings, something I experienced myself for over half my life. Today I understand to begin any inner work, we need solitude, something necessary for us all to become free from the constraints imposed by others. After both funerals, I returned to my life in London as a hotshot businesswoman even more focused on making money, until my whole life was completely consumed with working hard, escaping my truth and my inner needs. I was so driven I had no real idea about solitude outside my compulsive need and greed to succeed. Making millions was the goal at any cost and working as a woman in a man's world, the cost—trust me—was high, very high and often compromised my morality; it tested my core values to the limit, forcing me to forget about developing my internal spiritual needs.

As more and more people in the current consumer driven world cut themselves off from time in solitude, it is unlikely any of us will become unique thinkers, separate individuals from the pack. We will live being chained to what is expected of us instead of living the life we truly deserve. Although my start in life was grim, money scarce and boundaries non-existent, my father was a Victorian-minded man with good morals, modelled on his mother with her own strict morals, so I did have some values of my own deep down. I often felt very compromised working in a male-dominated environment, many times pushing my own morals to one side to close a deal, always feeling guilty, but alcohol is a great medicine for blocking out the truth. You soon learn how to use it to medicate and forget by turning a blind eye. Although I did shamelessly participate getting my male clients sex with prostitutes to close deals, participated in providing tawdry tactics to do business—the city works this way—I never slept with any of them myself. The key to my success was getting them to make the mistakes, then through guilting I got them to do the deal with me. It works like this. When you are a strong woman in a man's world, they become weak and easily influenced when high or drunk. The business always went to the broker who gave them the best time and I was the best back then, the ultimate party animal with scruples but never addicted. I was blessed. I knew how to win friends and influence people naturally. I had been doing it for real for years, so it didn't take me long to build solid relationships with a network of important clients who respected me as a woman in business.

In my mid-thirties, my biological clock began to tick so loud, I had no choice but to listen. Once again through the opinions of others, I was tempted away from my long-term goal of business success and drifted once again into the arms of stranger I met on a blind date after getting blind drunk. They say the definition of insanity is to repeat the same mistakes and expect a different result, so all I can do is put this period down to that, temporary insanity. For a short time, I completely lost my mind, imagining myself living a simple quiet life outside a world of money, greed and success. On reflection, the truth was I was not insane, just lonely, tired and burnt out. Working so hard in the city, entertaining my clients in late night strip clubs, consuming too much cocaine with zero focus on my mental and physical health, I found myself empty inside, guilty and sick of acting like a ruthless male.

I married the stranger quite quickly after moving in, gave up my ambition for world dominance and moved away to live in Jersey of all places, to build a new life and think about having babies, my own happily-ever-after moment in housewife heaven. It is here you can see how embedded negative patterns from the past can resurface at any time, even when you believe you have evolved and changed into someone new. You automatically get dragged along and pushed back into the life template before you realise it is happening. This is how powerful the subconscious memory can be. Although I already made the mistake once, copying my mother and marrying the wrong man to escape misery, I continued to make the same mistake all over again.

The wedding was white expensive and not me at all, but I put on the big frock, a big smile, drank too much champagne, worked the room, playing the part until falling into bed, legless and married to a stranger, once again complete cringe-worthy insanity when I was forced to reflect on my choices, when facing my dark side. If I am honest, and these days I am, deep down inside I knew I was making a huge mistake marrying someone I knew very little about, giving up my freedom for an easier life, losing my drive and ambition in exchange for becoming another half of someone else. Many people believe by marrying their other half, they will finally become whole. Sadly, this is an illusion often ending up compromised and unfulfilled. The half of you that you think you are missing has nothing to do with anyone else. It is to do with you finding the whole of you, the good, the bad, the ugly and the lonely.

The new husband wanted children quickly. I thought I wanted them too in my new role as a stay-at-home wife and domestic goddess, but I soon discovered getting pregnant would not be as straight forward as we planned on the honeymoon. It turned out having an abortion at sixteen had given me pelvic inflammatory disease and chlamydia. I was infertile and my only option for having children was expensive rounds of IVF treatment, with no guarantee of a baby at the end. When God closes one door, they say he opens another. In truth, I was ready to find any excuse to escape this new life I found myself trapped in with a man I had nothing in common with except when drunk. It turned out destiny forced me to change direction once again and re-think my plan for world domination. I had no desire to go through the unnatural painful process of getting pregnant through IVF. Although my new husband loved me, he wanted kids more, so we got divorced and I moved back to the City of London to start again, this time around in the cut-throat world of financial headhunting.

The thoughtless mistakes we make in the past have a nasty way of turning up later in life, changing our destiny. A reckless, promiscuous past proved fatal when trying to conceive a child, so once again I wiped the whole thing out, didn't face the mess, instead bulldozing my way back to work without regret or reflection. Every time we bury the pain deeper, hide the misery further, ignore the problem longer, it gets pushed down deep into the subconscious, stored like ghosts in a cupboard, always waiting to jump out when we least expect it. By now, the ghosts in my subconscious closet were so crammed in and agitated, banging the door down, desperate to burst out and be released like a pressure cooker, it made me want to escape myself even more. I had taken little responsibility for my deep internal feelings, my soul self, my guilty conscience, never understanding my emotional boundaries or limits. I had become negligent and careless of my core values and morals, never being realistic or genuinely sincere about my authentic needs inside. I became the ultimate capitalist bull-shitter without ever truly understanding the self-harm and damage I was subjecting myself to behind the painted smile. In truth, the shameless pursuit of greed in the nineties took me over. I was driven by money and power, nothing else. I slowly began to drink more to forget, take drugs to escape having to face myself and my mistakes, and even though the pressure and pain was building inside, this self-medicating kept me travelling down the straight and narrow road towards world domination, a world I believed would provide the life I longed for in the end.

You might be reading this cringing for me right now, as I bare my soul to you all. You may be judging me, feeling uncomfortable but remember Carl Jung believed to be whole and free from our past mistakes, we find the key through self-honesty to becoming a unique individual, recognising none of us are perfect. It is in understanding this freedom that creates a new healthy space for self-reflection, without the guilt, the regrets, just facing all the bits we dislike about ourselves. Regardless of how or why, it allows forgiveness, then healing, so stick with me without judging because you will have to face some of your own ghosts very soon if you want to evolve and mature. Living life in the fast lane is brutal for anyone. It takes its toll regardless of how successful you become. It leads you to believe you are invincible, when in fact inside you are fragile and fragmented, going along with things to simply survive life.

I was headhunted twice and eventually set up my own firm with a mere five-thousand-pound investment from a friend, to finally make millions, secure my future, buy my freedom then find the happiness I believed I deserved right from the start. I will repeat the mantra here once again. Stay focused on the straight and narrow. Don't stop to reflect until you reach the goal and lo and behold the things you truly desire with the power of intention in the end will manifest what you think you want to make you happy. The problem is getting what you want is very different to getting what you need.

Although I did have massive success from nothing but hard work and drive, I lost the real me along the way, the price you pay for chasing power and money over ethics, values and morality. Finally, after all my focus and drive on the straight and narrow road, I reached my long-term goal of becoming rich powerful and successful, with my own flourishing firm. Sadly, when I arrived there, I was not happy or fulfilled. I was rich financially, that was not in question, but I was not rich spiritually, and this was a real shock to my system. I had convinced myself I was a happy fun person with everything anyone could ever wish for, the flash properties, the designer life, the perfect paradise everyone dreams of in this thing called life. The ghosts in my closet were slowly banging the door down, as I played catch-up with my successful life, realising in truth I was drinking too much, using drugs like cocaine to keep it all suppressed, covering up my internal misery, hiding my inner truth from the rest of the world.

Climbing the mountain had consumed me, compromised me and caused me to forget about the important things in life internally, my authentic self, my spiritual needs. I was alone and empty, even surrounded by all those hangers on I called my friends back then. My family was proud and although I had not been there for them with my time, my money in my mind made up for that. I was able to buy them stuff in return for being accepted by them. The only thing you can do when money defines who you are.

The wayward girl from the council estate finally made good, appeared established and accomplished, never allowing the world to see the truth behind the glitter and the glory. It was all about showing off shallow empty lies, pretending to be happy, believing my own bullshit over being brave enough to change. The truth is, you only change when you realise you need to change. Unlimited financial security is amazing on one hand. You can buy your freedom and anything you fancy but money can never buy real happiness, unless you understand happiness before the money comes. A truth you should all take note of the next time you find yourself imagining money is all you need to make you happy.

I was miserable. No matter how much money I spent on trying to feel good, I always felt bad and empty inside. I couldn't work out why my life was not full of joy, full of fabulous people inviting me to fabulous places, just like you see in the movies, the media and the glossy adverts. Trudging to my office in the city every day was a real struggle, but the drugs and the drink helped. I had a gold Coutts card. This helped too but with every trinket I bought, nothing inside changed. I was still lonely going through the motions of a pointless materialistic sad life. I was living a false reality, mirrored by self-delusion, never telling myself the real story, promoting my own lies, unable to make informed decision through ignorance. I had become so conditioned into believing in the façade, my mental mind programming, my negative patterns and self-deception, I was totally desensitised to hearing my inner instincts and heartfelt intuitions, my truthful satnav. You are probably thinking right now how can this possibly be? All that money, all that privilege, all those designer handbags but you only know what you know. Trust me, without being completely centred and spiritually grounded before you make it big, no designer handbag or VIP privilege will make you feel happy or fulfilled, regardless of what you think.

Once again, the insanity of pattern behaviour comes back with a vengeance in this tale of the unexpected. Even though it makes you rich, accomplished, secure and respected, money and success does not make you immune from your past patterns and mistakes if you have not worked on yourself spiritually before getting there. Out of the blue, I was asked by my best friend, who had moved to LA a few years earlier and was about to marry a stranger herself to escape a chaotic drunken past in London, to be maid of honour at her upcoming wedding. I didn't hesitate to accept; having reached my journey to the top, there was nowhere left to go except backwards to revisit an old friend, potentially making a fatal mistake herself, marrying a stranger on a whim. Too much hard work and no play makes for a dull existence. Working so hard had left me short of real friends. My clients had become my friends, but they were all married or addicted, so this escape to LA came just in the nick of time.

At this wedding, after too much wine, some very long lines of some very good cocaine, an amazing speech from me, the best man, my friend's new husband's brother, asked me in a slow dance to join him on a late-night ride on the back of his Harley Davidson to visit the bright lights of Las Vegas. I have had many moments of temporary insanity in my life as you now know but this one goes down as the most stupid of all, not once stopping to think about the consequences of such madness in the moment. I realised when I arrived in LA, my best friend was too far gone to be saved from herself. She too had created a docu-story life to die for and was drinking herself into oblivion without ever facing the carnage life she left behind in the UK. So, when in Rome and all that, I decided without much rational thought to take the brother up on his exciting offer, throwing caution to the wind and sped off to Vegas on the back of the Harley, leaving my friend back in LA making what turned out to be the biggest mistake of her life. I woke up three days later in a big fancy suite at the Bellagio Hotel somewhere on the strip, surrounded by rolled-up hundred-dollar bills, a marriage certificate from the drive-in Little White Chapel, where a look-alike Elvis performs a cheesy ceremony in a white Stetson with a mammoth hangover. God when I think about this right now, it makes me cringe with embarrassment. To think I had all that money, all that success. It just shows you how empty my life was back then to make such a poor judgement call in the moment.

Once again, I had married a stranger on a whim, when totally high and clearly not thinking straight. My old pattern behaviour returned with a vengeance, leaving me with no other choice but to embrace the mess, drink more and thank my lucky stars he was at least good-looking. Not going to the negative bias but finding a positive spin on my ridiculous insanity, I eventually decided moving to LA—the ultimate escape from my reality—was maybe not such a bad idea after all. It is a place where dreams come true. The new husband, Mexican and poor, was good looking; I had enough money to reinvent him and myself to start a new life in the sun in Hollywood, somewhere nice on the beach where no one knew me. Looking back, this was the point I should have realised I was completely out of control. I was too consumed by creating the fairy-tale ending that had eluded me for so long to worry about being out of control. I wanted the dream. I wanted to be happy. I wanted to live in the moment. I wanted the life I believed money would buy me. It was time to enjoy the fruits of my success, find a point or purpose to my life and finally grow up.

I had no idea back then I was having what they call a mid-life crisis.

Las Vegas is a very toxic, unhealthy, unethical place for people who love to gamble, drink and do drugs, so the mini honeymoon with the new husband prevented me from questioning myself further. I was at home. I had made my bed and I would literally lie in it. It's funny, people imagine somewhere like Las Vegas to be the ultimate rich man's paradise, but to be honest, once you peer behind the veneer, the biggest persona of them all, it is nothing more than a sleazier version of Butlin's, without the sea and the candy floss. Like us all, Vegas has a dark side, a shadow side, so ominous, so oppressive, it crushes your spirit. A shallow man-made humongous concrete casino, a mirage I was happy to leave behind, once the drunken crazy honeymoon was over.

I remained in LA for a couple of weeks getting to know my new husband, his cultures, drinking too much red wine with my friend, delighted by my crazy impulsive move to the US. Suddenly, life for us both was beginning to look up. Once I acclimatised myself to the idea of moving to LA full time, I returned to

London, sold my properties, gave up my business and ploughed all my money into the stock market. Once a gambler, always a gambler and that was that, the end of the road, the end of an era. When you begin to look at this thoughtless stupid behaviour, you begin to see the patterns emerging again, always escaping, always running, always taking no personal responsibility for the mess created. Again, it is the price you pay for having money without a purpose. You might still be finding yourself judging me right now, looking at my car-crash life and believing I was truly stupid this time or you might be thinking how much fun it all sounds but whatever you are feeling, what you see is never really the whole truth. It is just an illusion.

It is at this point in this tawdry tale you should begin to think about your own life choices now. Have you made mistakes based upon what you believed was right for you in the moment? Have you been pushed down the wrong road by circumstance, the opinions of others or because you believed it was the only route available to you? What if everything we have been programmed to believe in, the life template created to keep us away from thinking for ourselves, outside of the box mentality is not real? Compared to what we should be as whole thinking human beings, we are only half-awake, living within our limits, rarely going beyond what we have been programmed to believe. A fulfilling life comes not from avoiding our suffering and mistakes but by confronting and overcoming them. I thought this new life in LA would be the beginning of my happily-ever-after fairy-tale. I truly believed changing my environment would change my life. We all make mistakes.

In January 2000, internet and telecom stocks were booming. I was invincible as I moved into a massive house on the prestigious Strand in Manhattan Beach CA, to live the dream and embrace my happily-ever-after ending at last. Leaving London was not so hard after all. The weather was cold, I needed a change. What could possibly go wrong? Three months after moving to LA and embarking on my new life, the stock market crashed, the dot-com bubble burst, and I was left hopelessly watching my portfolio dwindle away to almost nothing overnight until I had lost the lot, my virtual millions gone, ending up owing my bank money. It is hard to believe such a cruel blow could be delivered so quickly. When you take your finger off the button even for a moment when driving your destiny based upon your feelings without thinking, it is inevitable you will crash and burn in a world of greed and fantasy. This was Hollywood after all. The virtual money market casino they call the stock market had made me rich and was now ruthlessly taking it all back, without mercy, just like the roulette table in a Vegas casino. I have never really thought about the stock market being a money market casino. I just followed the instructions of my broker, watched the financial news now and again, checking my positions making sure they were moving up, not down. It never occurred to me the price of my stocks could ever drop so low. The internet had massive growth potential according to the experts. The dot-com business was booming, I was greedy, the perfect combination for any Gordon Gekko wannabe storyline. What I needed to understand, I know now in hindsight, is how these small businesses inflate their share price by insider trading—*Blue Horseshoe loves Anacott Steel*—to look bigger than they are. When one person panics and sells in fear, the rest follow like sheep. I had no understanding of how the markets worked to be honest. Someone on a night out gave me a tip, I purchased a load of shares and before I knew it, my financial portfolio was bulging at the seams. I guess like everyone else back then, I became addicted to making easy money, based on little more than a future idea, the companies I was heavily investing in would one day be valuable and I would rich beyond my wildest dreams. Even when the share prices were dropping in the crash, my overly optimistic broker was advising me to buy more. He believed it was a blip. Buy low, sell high. He convinced me things would improve because it always did. Everything would be fine if I could hold my nerve long enough to weather the storm. I stupidly took his advice and the rest is history. The dot-com bubble burst dramatically. Billions wiped off the markets overnight. I was left owing the bank money, a truly disastrous start to my new fabulous life in LA.

It had taken me all those years of hard slog, climbing out of the gutter, working day and night, never standing still until I made it and within just one week, my whole fortune was wiped out, just like that. I wish I could tell you now, for me, this was reaching the bottom, ending up with suicide as my only option but losing the money was nothing compared to what was around the corner. I remember thinking back then my story was like one of those Hollywood blockbuster movies, where the story line is so unbelievable and unlikely, you leave the cinema wanting your money back. Sadly, this was no movie. This was payback for being reckless, greedy and naïve with my investment strategy.

I can imagine if you have stayed with me and got to this place in my tawdry tale, you may not be thinking about your own misery anymore. Sometimes escaping into someone else's mistakes and misfortunes, even if only for a short while, can help buy you the time you need to accept and face your own mistakes and misfortunes. You can see now you are never alone. There is always someone else much worse off than you, with an even more miserable tale to tell. Life is tough. No one is perfect. We all make stupid mistakes, but we can all grow and learn from these stupid mistakes in the end, if we can survive, change and evolve beyond them. Hope is an amazing thing to have when all else fails. Once I had accepted the money was gone and not coming back anytime soon, divorcing the new husband followed. Good looks without money and different culture to contend with was impossible to face, so the short, loveless marriage ended, not just for me but for my best friend too. At least we had each other, and living in Hollywood how hard could it be to start again and reinvent the wheel, even old, poor and not thin?

I had always relished a challenge in the past. Although losing the money was painful, it was my own greedy fault, the big lesson you learn if you rely on gambling to provide you with a secure future. I did take it all quite well at first and in some ways, I was a little relieved to be honest. Deep down inside, I knew I was living a lie, drinking too much and not taking care of myself. There was little I could do without the security of money. The sale of the big house I was buying on the beach had not yet gone through, thank god. Surviving by selling my possessions was all I had left to rely on.

It was a rollercoaster ride from then on for five long years with its ups and downs, highs and lows. So much happened during this time, we ended up writing a book called *Looking for Harvey Weinstein*, the only man in Hollywood who can help you make it big, if you can find him that is. We managed to survive quite well financially. I did have material possessions from my out-of-control spending habits before I moved to LA, pre-loved affordable luxury for anyone prepared to buy secondhand. I had designer bags galore, luggage, art, diamonds and jewellery. You get quite a shock and a rude awakening, the things you have paid a fortune for at Tiffany and Chanel have little resale value when you are starving down and out in Beverly Hills. You cannot eat a Rolex watch, and after five long years of struggling, possessions all gone in 2005, bleeding with no medical insurance to see a doctor for diagnosis, I collapsed with heart failure. For a brief few seconds, my life was over until resuscitated by paramedics and admitted into an expensive hospital I couldn't pay for.

When you are trying hard just to survive, with no money, in an expensive place, no direction and little thought for anything except where the next meal is coming from, the state of your health is not a priority, especially in the US where you need health insurance to stay alive. It turned out after being admitted to intensive care, my blood count had dropped to three point seven. I had pretty much bled to death. It was curtains for me until I had immediate blood transfusions and an emergency hysterectomy to remove what they suspected was an eight-pound tumour in my uterus. It was at this point I suddenly realised I was finally at the bottom and if you want to know what fear feels like, this is it. I was so scared, any fight left inside was gone. I had no medical insurance to pay for the operation. Three transfusions had already sent the hospital administrator into a phoning frenzy, demanding my credit card details to pay the anticipated fifty thousand dollars to save my life. At the same time this unbearable madness was happening, I had a kind priest on the side of my deathbed reading me the last rites, the only free service offered in the US when you are about to die without the money to pay.

I tried hard to pray to God for a miracle for real this time. Although it was difficult having never in my life believed or even thought about if there was a God out there, somewhere waiting to sort out my mess if I said sorry, but nothing came back. I was alone and this was it, 'The End' for me. I had nowhere to turn and no one to blame but myself.

I understand now what it feels like to have nothing, even the prospect of my life. This empty, scary feeling is like being numb. You are helpless, hopeless and truly humbled. You have no choice when death knocks on your door for real but to gracefully accept it.

All alone in that small private hospital room, in that tiny bed, next to all those noisy machines, with nothing but regrets, I suddenly panicked as my reality played catch-up with my mind. I knew I was dying alone without the chance to put things right. Accepting death for me came with huge feelings of remorse and guilt. I remember closing my eyes, floating in and out of a state of semi-consciousness, feeling quite calm and ready to go where you go when you die. It had to be better than being in an expensive hospital bed with no way of paying, feeling like a complete loser, without a miracle in sight. I began to talk to myself like I was talking to a stranger in my head. I handed myself over, gave up, gave in and waited to see what would happen. I guess this was my final attempt at truly praying in desperation, I might get a miracle at the final hour, suddenly waking up from the nightmare I found myself in.

I must have fallen to sleep eventually or slipped into unconsciousness. Although I could feel my body still lying in the bed, my actual body appeared at the end of the bed, looking right back at me. For a split second, I somehow knew I was dead. The feeling was surreal, calm and almost pleasant to be honest, like I had escaped my old self finally. Any panic, pain, fear, guilt or emotional fracturing seemed to be left behind along with the empty vessel of my fragile body in the hospital bed. I could see my blood all over the floor, over the white bed sheets, over my still, lifeless, empty shell of a body, cold and pale like a corpse in the morgue waiting to be zipped up in a plastic bag. As I write about this today, I can still remember the feeling of peace I had in that second like it was yesterday. I have never felt such a feeling before. All I can tell you is I knew my spirit; my energy left my physical body that night to go back into the universe, free and finally at peace. My whole world had collapsed before my very eyes, all my hopes and dreams gone, all the chaos and pain gone. There was nothing left for me. I was finally over and done, or so I thought, but it ain't over until the fat lady sings and she was silent.

This amazing out-of-body experience was interrupted by what felt like an electric shock, a tingling sensation in my arms and legs, like pins and needles. Within seconds, I was awake again back inside my body with a transfusion needle pumping fresh blood into my veins, with a kind nurse gently reassuring me it was all going to be alright. She sensitively explained the blood transfusion given during the evening when critically ill had been rejected by my body but I was now stable, and things would get better once I'd had a hysterectomy the following day. The doctor on duty that evening informed me that the suspected tumour was in fact an eight-pound fibroid. I would be OK if I could come up with the money for life-saving surgery and if not, tablets to suppress the bleeding would be prescribed until I could get a flight back safely to the UK.

I was completely penniless with not even enough money to pay for the pills to suppress the bleeding. Asking my friends and family for help was so difficult. I was ashamed and afraid they would judge me for being so stupid to lose everything, including almost my life. It is impossible to explain over the phone to people you love that you are penniless, dying and desperately in need of their help after years of lying and exaggerating. They probably would not have believed me anyway. I had to deal with this mess on my own.

My sister-in-law and best friend was now my new nurse. The hospital gave her strict instructions on what I needed to do if I was to make it back to the UK in one piece. I had one painting left from my precious art collection, my favourite, most treasured, limited-edition Mick Jagger print, given as a gift by a grateful client back in the city. Selling this provided enough money to pay for the pills and healthy food I needed to keep me alive short term, so thank you, Mick Jagger.

Two weeks after being released from the hospital, still unwell and unfit to travel back home, I was cruelly evicted with my sister-in-law from our house. It was brutal. We had nowhere to live and found ourselves in a homeless shelter in Compton, one of the most dangerous places in LA. Can you imagine living a millionaire lifestyle one moment to dying in a homeless shelter the next? Now that is a Hollywood movie someone like Harvey Weinstein should produce one day. Just like the hospital situation, when you have no insurance, you are given the minimum in terms of support. The same goes when you are homeless. There is no safety net option available. You must get creative and just find somewhere safe to eat and sleep. I was alive and I was grateful, regardless of my misfortunes and mistakes that had taken me to such an unimaginable place. The place you go when you reach rock bottom. Trust me, there is nothing worse a human being can face in life than losing everything.

The first night in the shelter was more horrific than the first night in the hospital bed. It was not for women like us. It was for poor drug addicts, drunks and dangerous gang members with guns and disturbed personalities. The tragic forgotten faces of extreme poverty, left to rot in the dark side of downtown LA. We found this place through the doctor in the small free medical centre that provided the pills to suppress my bleeding. A free clinic for immigrants and those too poor to pay for health care. There is a whole underground network of independent passionate people doing their best to provide free services for all the people outside of the system, something today I will always be eternally grateful for and never forget for as long as I live.

The shelter was a noisy scary place with no one in charge. With few speaking English, it was hard to communicate the fear or problems we had but eventually I dropped off exhausted, until I woke up with someone beside me, breathing close into my face. I could smell a combination of strong stale tobacco and pungent sweat as I slowly opened my eyes to find a stranger intensely staring back at me without mercy. A dangerous, dark, tattooed, tortured face with cold eyes and a distant stare, chilling me to the bone, sending shivers down my spine, forcing himself on top of me. He held a small knife in his hand close to my face; I knew he was going to rape me even without him saying a word. He was high. He was desperate and not someone I wanted to mess with in that moment. I was not afraid to be honest. I knew if he saw my fear it would fuel his aggression, so I kept my composure by looking direct into his eyes, through to his soul. I told him to do what he had to do. I was going to die anyway. His English was broken but he understood me somehow and in what seemed like seconds, he produced a better pillow, an extra blanket and was guarding me like a princess in a castle. When two desperate souls collide beneath the human crust, formed to protect and preserve life, both from different worlds, both the same with nothing to lose, fear turns to empathy and miracles do happen. I was no different to him really.

45

We were both at rock bottom with nowhere to go, so letting him see into my soul and me into his created sympathy. When you have a genuine understanding for life, recognising we are all fragile and complicated regardless of where we come from or how we end up, in the end, all we have is each other.

When we have a clean energetic balance with ourselves, we become in line with our spiritual selves. We connect and listen through our hearts not our minds. We regain our emotional balance. In that dark almost impossible moment to imagine with the stranger by my bed, I woke up from a long coma, entering into a new phase of complete empathy, compassion, humility, gratitude and forgiveness. I finally felt something real for the first time in my life.

For the next few weeks, things began to look up, as the men around us began to talk openly about their own tragic stories, some so horrific it made our plight look like baby food. It is amazing how empowering it is to learn there are people much worse off than you. Even when you find yourself at the bottom, there is always hope. This life-changing experience inspired me to use my time to life coach the men and encourage them to do something positive with their lives, regardless of their desperate circumstances.

It was not long before my ex business partner sent two Virgin airline tickets back to UK. Finally, we were going home, on our way back to safety. This brief period of escape from my own problems gave me my purpose and changed my life forever. It gave me an opportunity to do something that made a difference to others less fortunate than me, my very first taste of truly feeling happy inside, understanding what a genuine miracle life is at the end of the day. All my money had bought me stuff, experiences, travel, freedom but it never gave me peace, humility, grace or gratitude. These qualities only came from finding my purpose back then when I reached the bottom.

Within two weeks of getting home, the NHS saved my life by removing the giant fibroid. A real gift in the bigger scheme of things and something we should not take for granted because without the NHS, only hard cash will save your life in the US. Once I recovered, I signed on the dole back in Leicester, my hometown where it all began, to start again from scratch with only one purpose: to learn from my mistakes and be grateful for my life. I had survived not the life I planned, imagined or created but a life I deserved.

After about a year recovering, meditating, in splendid isolation with my Carl Jung book and working on myself, I made the choice to give up everything that had taken me down—my addictions. Once I gave up drinking, smoking, drugs, sex, shopping, meat, caffeine and lying, I was stripped back pretty much to a blank piece of paper, ready to start a new life in the Leicestershire countryside with no material wealth or aspirations. When you are given a second chance at this thing called life, you wake up and smell the coffee. There is no room for excuses. You just get on with things in gratitude. My story was so massive for most people to comprehend or even imagine, but I did not hide away from talking about it because it was my truth, my mistakes and my misfortune. I hoped by talking about things openly it would help others look at their own lives and make the changes necessary before it was too late. I started talking more with damaged homeless people and the addicted, forgotten and left by society, soon realising just how many people in the world have mental health issues and depression. I knew myself in my heart what it felt like to want to die. I had experienced feelings of hopelessness and unbearable anxiety, trying to sort things out alone, so this work gave me my true purpose. I had empathy for those suffering because I had suffered myself, something very powerful when you have the courage to be open and truthful about who you really are, without the fear of being judged.

During the mayhem of losing everything materially before my near-death experience, I was overcome myself with an unbearable, unexpected flash flood of emotions. I now know this to be what they call depression. It was in this dark moment I contemplated suicide myself. I had no one I could call on for help. I had let everyone down. I was ashamed and desperate, unable to see the wood for the trees. Losing all my money, when you are only defined by what you have materially you suddenly realise, ignorance is defined by that which is only identified in the material world. Who was I without the money, without a purpose, without the façade, without the bullshit? I was nothing, so killing myself in that moment seemed like the only available option left for me. Maybe if I had killed myself successfully back then on that lonely night in LA—I did take the tablets and drink the tequila—I would never have found my true sense of self to tell you all this tale.

Not long after the failed suicide attempt, I got a call from my family back in the UK informing me my mother had died. I remember feeling anxious and depressed, unable to confess I had lost all my money, attempted suicide and did not have the airfare to return for her funeral to say goodbye. Although I desperately needed my family at that moment, it was her funeral and not the time for me to get the attention I needed. Later that evening when I felt truly desperate, I had a light-bulb moment. Although I was broke, broken, ashamed and alone, my mother dying would set me free and give me the momentum I needed to fight back. I have made so many mistakes in my life but today I have forgiven myself and, through self-mastery, I have learnt I am never alone. Inside of me, there is always my rational voice of reason.

These days my time is spent making money again; we all need to eat but I am more focused today on making millions again, this time to use the money to give something back, making free talk therapy available to anyone who needs it. I want to save the world one by one, sharing with you all I have learnt about why your life, regardless of what you think in this moment, matters in the big scheme of things. Thank you for sticking with me and listening to my story, which like all life stories, feels so much better out than in. This sets you free.

It is true for all of us, regardless how depressed, miserable, unhappy unfulfilled we are, the only way out of anything is through it. My own story is the perfect example of how even the most confident, successful people who appear on the surface to have it all, can be a crumbling mess inside, just waiting to be discovered as an imposter. This massive life-changing experience for me evoked a powerful sense of purpose and discovering this purpose has provided the true joy and happiness that was missing in my life, even with all the money in the world. This journey of self-discovery and personal growth allowed me to widen my range of experiences, coming face to face with a brave part of myself I had no idea even existed. I faced enormous fear. I found courage. I overcame depression and guilt. This allowed me freedom. The road I travel now, every day without doubt, the straight and narrow road to higher thinking and spiritual development, is an amazing journey. You never get there but you are always working towards a bigger better goal.

If we don't monitor our actions, we end up paralysed with no self-esteem, so we must always be true to ourselves and be productive, going beyond our perceived mental limitations. If we are going to begin to recognise and establish the qualities that define who we are, we need to first understand what these qualities are and why we need this zone of safety to overcome our fears. For you to begin to heal your own mental and emotional pain, you must learn how to establish a real safety inside by recognising what it is that makes you feel unsafe in the first place.

Once you become more competent in understanding how to be more self-regulating of your emotions, your inner safety becomes more enhanced and trust can be established. A strong spiritual foundation is built on moral character development. Nurturing trust inside ourselves is built on consistent ethical conduct and what we fear the most is hidden in the unconscious. Until you are willing and open to face up to these hidden fears inside, you are likely to continue projecting your fear onto others. I chased money and power which closed the pathway to my heart but after my near-death experience, I found the courage and confidence to do the work necessary to re-open it. The lesson from my story is to never let your emotions control you. You can never stop them, but you can have strategies in place to reduce the impact they have, once you learn the triggers that make them happen. Learn to be the master of what you do and not what you feel. Life is ten percent what happens to you and ninety percent how you react to it. Always remember your feelings begin or are triggered by a real or imagined situation, and your body will automatically respond without your awareness. Mindfulness will help you enhance this awareness, then help reduce your physical response, reducing the frequency to avoid emotional situations altogether. By being mindful of overreacting to my own feeling during my mid-life crisis, I created awareness and distance as an observer, rather than participating, allowing a more mature and wise ability to always think rationally.

I Have Complete Confidence in Myself

I have the confidence to walk into a room of complete strangers and immediately start a conversation, so when I talk to you about the meaning of this word confidence, I am talking about certainty, a knowing when you don't need validation or permission to be you. So to begin this chapter or any new chapter in our lives, we must determine if confidence is already encoded in our genes or not. Recent research has suggested it possibly is. Our personality is biologically driven. It is both nurture and nature that affects the biology of the brain to create our temperament. True confidence is not about whether we can do a task, it is more about whether we assess ourselves as capable of doing the task. I am of the opinion from my own personal experience, confidence is not genetic, the luck of the gene pool, a predetermined gift from our parents but something that is determined by our environment and the positive attention we receive when developing as small children. We model, we copy, we learn, three important things I will keep repeating throughout this book to help you understand why the things we do automatically often go against what we really think and feel inside. We are all creatures of habit. The process of identifying our own destructive habits, copied patterns and being willing to change and heal them is all down to confidently developing spiritual maturity beyond our existing belief system.

Small children are just like sponges, soaking up every feeling, message, instruction and visual stimulation. If you tell a child enough times they cannot think for themselves, controlling how they think and what they feel, eventually the child will be unable to problem solve, ending up with little emotional intelligence in adulthood. On the other hand, if you tell a child they are amazing, beautiful, can fly to the moon, the child will develop an innate intelligent personality believing they can do anything, even fly to the moon. If a child is left to problem solve, make mistakes, make up their own minds in a safe, secure, loving environment, they will develop useful skills and emotional intelligence to then be able to nurture their own unique talents.

What is planted in our subconscious mind, as we have established from the beginning of this book, will remain in the memory forever. It will reflect how we feel about ourselves in everything we do as we travel through life on our own journey into maturity. Normally when we begin to self-analyse, we start by looking at the superficial reasons why we are failing to be happy. Once we begin to delve deeper into the bigger picture, the whole story beyond what we perceive, we begin to understand ourselves much better. We understand ourselves better by recognising the difference between who we are and our behaviours; this allows us to stop beating ourselves up, focusing on who we are and not what we do.

Self-confidence in my opinion is the most important ingredient missing in people today, which has created a society of underachievers with a sheep-like mentality, following an ego-driven life template from birth through to death. We are copying, modelling and learning from generation to generation with little concept or thought of an individual unique direction. I know this sounds harsh, but it is true when you study why you keep doing the things you do, over and over without thought, then complain and remain stuck in the cycle of life and traditions passed on by our parents from their parents. Once you are conscious and you see these patterns emerging, recognising you are being led and not walking on your own path, you begin to question your motives, and this is progress.

As we expand our consciousness awareness through self-enquiry, we begin to discover what is important to us, what our priorities are in our own life, what is motivating us. We learn to have resistance against being influenced by other people's opinions, gaining more knowledge about ourselves and our own opinions, without feeling worthless or stupid. Learning to stand up for yourself and go against the pack begins in early childhood. This is what happened to me. I had the built-in confidence required to handle difficult situations and circumstances, to become a leader not a follower. I was able to confidently heal myself inside by recognising and identifying destructive patterns in those around me. I may not have had the best start on paper and as you know I made some massive mistakes, but I never suffered with a lack of confidence. This is because subconsciously I was told from the beginning I was a winner and I believed it.

As a life coach right now, I could give you five ways to build your confidence. I could tell you to act the part, dress the part, be self-assured, think positive, be more assertive, but this would all be easier said than done for you; for me, I know how to do it instinctively and I always have. I believe the reason for this is all down to my own start in life as a miracle baby.

When I was born, my parents, who had few skills themselves and four other children, there was a ten-year gap in an unhappy relationship before I was conceived. I was a miracle baby that gave them hope again in a dead union. My birth gave them something fresh and exciting to bring them closer together again in the moment. For the first eighteen months of my life, I was over adored, shown off like a prize turkey and told repeatedly how beautiful and special I was by my parents, my siblings and all the people who lived in our street. This was way back in the fifties. We were poor and the community all pulled together, so I was looked after by many different people—thankfully for me, all optimistic, happy and loving. I was given constant attention, positive affirmations and compliments that were all planted deep in my psyche and subconscious right from the start. These positive, almost euphoric subliminal messages in my subconscious mind helped me to develop a strong unbreakable self-belief and confidence, so much so I could talk heads off at eighteen months before I could even walk. I instinctively knew right from the start I wanted to be somebody rich, powerful and successful. As you know, my life did not always have a happy positive follow on, but I believe this gift at such an early age was the main reason I managed to survive and escape all the emotional turmoil thrown at me during my development into adulthood. I believe if with that confidence had come a happy, stable upbringing with centred, happy, developed parents, my own life journey would have been very different.

Today in my more spiritually balanced mature life, I see this early stage in my own life as a miracle, considering the chaos and trauma I see in others, completely ruining their adult lives. I was one of the lucky ones on reflection.

My younger sister was born when I was eighteen months old and by this time, my parents had remembered they were not so happy before I came along, so the joyful euphoria of my birth had worn off, and she began her life very different to mine. She was not the centre of attention, not shown off like a prize turkey and not told repeatedly how special she was. Don't get me wrong, she was loved and wanted but the intense attention I got was missing for her start. The difference in nurturing confidence is very plain to see in us both today as adults. I am too confident, and she has no confidence at all which has left her struggling with fear, and the trauma of our mother leaving made her retreat even more into herself. At eight years old, I became her mother when ours walked out and my childhood after this was non-existent, explaining maybe why I had the ability and confidence to escape and find a new life as a new person somewhere else, away from such huge responsibility, so young.

I have no idea why other people lack confidence because for me it comes so naturally but I am almost certain it is down to past trauma, buried deep down under all the burden of baggage we carry around, passed down from others like the plague. I can tell you now, positive thinking, practice of patience and talking to others are all useful ways to improve your confidence but real confidence comes from feelings of wellbeing and acceptance. Getting over shyness and feeling inferior with a lack of self-confidence, those deep painful feelings of worthlessness, only happens when you start eliminating social fears, becoming a leader, so people begin to respect you for having the courage to stand up every time you fall down.

Talk therapy is all about having the confidence to face yourself without feelings of guilt, embarrassment, judging and is an important part of the treatment for anxiety, bipolar disorder and depression. A good listener and therapist can help you to cope with feelings and symptoms, changing your pattern behaviour, constantly contributing to and distorting your thinking before every move you make. During talk therapy, we can focus on how our negative existing beliefs and thought patterns change our moods, which can be very effective when dealing with depression, changing a negative mindset back to a positive one. Like I have said, I am not a doctor. I am not trained and qualified in the general sense, but I am a survivor having dealt with my own depression, suicidal thoughts and negative actions, making me, in my opinion, a qualified person for you to relate to right now. The more disconnected we are from our spiritual consciousness and heart-based emotions, the more pain, unease and lack of confidence we have, preventing us from understanding why we feel the way we do. I am your only hope if all else has failed or you cannot bring yourself to talk to a professional. Maybe you cannot afford to see someone. Maybe your medication is not working but whatever the reason, I take my work seriously and I know I am good at it. This is what they call confidence.

I have worked in talk therapy sessions with the homeless and addicted. The people society have forgotten about, truly damaged, those who have given up on life as we know it, so I have practical experience in listening, based on my own spiritual journey of recovery. Sometimes a dose of the truth and a bit of common sense can completely change a negative mindset very quickly, but with addiction and deep depression, the path may not be so easy to clear. Often those suffering have become comfortable with their destructive patterns. Maybe this is you? Can you imagine your life without drinking alcohol? Can you imagine your life without eating chocolate? Can you imagine your life without other people? Can you imagine your life without your unhappiness? Can you imagine a life where you feel happy all the time? We spend most of our time imagining things rather than planning an action to make things happen. This means we get the feeling we are happy, but it is always short-lived because it's based on what could be and not what is.

The world has changed so dramatically today. This competitive environment we live in right now puts so much pressure on us to be perfect, be accepted and fit in, regardless of our own needs and desires, insecurities and internal pain. It is ruthless and relentless out there. We may have money worries that build up and get out of control, seem impossible to manage, or maybe we have been hurt by divorce, been rejected or find ourselves relying on food, drugs or alcohol to cope. Whatever the reasons are you cannot cope anymore, you cannot see the point, believing you'd be better off dead or stuck with what you've got, learning how to change your pessimistic beliefs into optimistic thinking surely is worth a try if you want to change things for good. Making slight changes in your life, like resolving a demanding situation with an action, talking about your problems, getting more sleep to relieve anxiety or taking a walk outside, can often improve your mood dramatically. If your low moods persist too long, they will eventually become deep depression and often become impossible to change, even with talk therapy. Never getting any enjoyment out of your life, constantly feeling tired with low energy, comfort eating, feeling hopeless, unable to concentrate on everyday things are triggers to let you know you are in trouble. Making any change in your life will take inner confidence and it must be done by you and you alone. No one else can help you get there. Once you understand why you are failing, it will help you regain power, and power is confidence.

Expanding our consciousness, increasing our clean energy with a higher frequency, our highest level of intelligent energy beyond our mental knowledge, allows us to see things as they really are, not what we want them to be. Basically, by expanding our thinking beyond our consciousness, decreasing our self-deception, lies and illusions, our wishful thinking, we can begin to face then resolve our mental blockages. We can move away from our limited thinking capabilities, expand from our narrow-minded perceptions and stop being stuck with what we believe is all we deserve.

A disconnection from the authentic self happens when we deny or refuse to acknowledge and accept our emotions, our pain and our fear because we repress them into becoming ghosts crammed in the closet of the mind. To be able to repress these negative emotions successfully, we subconsciously need defence mechanisms in place to help keep us in denial about our memories and impulses that are consciously unacceptable. The things we dislike about ourselves. When we deny intense and uncomfortable negative emotions rather than facing them and dealing with them in the moment, we either project blame on other people or we get lost and distracted in our comfort zone. The comfort zone is that place where we covet our addictions and our imagination. The place where we turn off our awareness to anything we feel is painful or unwanted.

I can tell you with complete confidence that repressing your painful and unwanted emotions will keep you stuck, unable to develop or mature emotionally, spiritually or psychologically. It is this that is causing your anxiety, stress and frustration, leaving you forever struggling in the darkness of your denial. Any negative feeling, memory or emotion that is repressed for too long will always become exaggerated and eventually manifest into something more significant. An underlying sadness never addressed becomes deep depression. An underlying fear becomes permanent anxiety. I can also promise you when we repress our negative painful emotions, refusing to acknowledge and face them, we lose a bit of who we really are deep down under the mask. This is exactly what happened to me. I became a stranger in my own life.

Today, I don't care about what others think of me anymore. We all have our own crosses to bear and a big dose of self-reflection, developing positive self-talk got me back from the brink of despair when all else failed, including my steadfast self-confidence.

Life changes like our moods, which go up and down like a yoyo depending on our circumstances. They can affect every move we make, so we need to find the middle ground, that space in between the mood swings. This is called being centred. Most of us perceive the external structure of our reality based on information conveyed by our caretakers through our main senses. Very few of us have the confidence or incentive to expand our senses to reach a higher level of thinking beyond this mind control. Thinking in a one-dimensional way contracts our consciousness, limiting our ability to expand our main senses like our intuition. This then shuts down the pathway to the heart, closing us off from our real feelings. We end up with unconsciously uncontrollable mood swings without ever understanding why. So how do we begin self-therapy to be able to lift low moods when they hit us, bringing us back to a more centred positive internal place, before the flash flood of negative emotions takes over and we are lost out at sea in choppy waters?

Training your mind to go beyond your one-dimensional thinking expands your consciousness, your clean energy, connecting you back to your heart and your intuition. The place you find your true feeling centre and your core built-in values, like gratitude, empathy, integrity and compassion. I encourage you to begin to get in touch with your negative emotions, not repress them or block them out through denial or projection. Start to have the confidence to bring them fully into your conscious awareness as much as you can. The stored-up ghosts trapped in the closet of your mind, the repressed unresolved problems that have now become your pain, will only be acknowledged when you are prepared to experience your reality. Your problems are buried in your pain.

Breathing and mediation help us to focus on one thing at a time in silence. When our heads are filled with chaos and we are in pain, like any other practice, it will take time, focus and enormous patience to master, but it is how we begin to expand our consciousness and connect back to our heartfelt feelings. When you start to think about your subconscious mind being filled with everything you know from birth, you will begin to see how all your thoughts come and go. The main reason most people fail when they try and meditate. The continued rushing of automatic, mostly negative thoughts take over the one conscious thing we are trying to do—stop thinking. The reason it is important to slow down and silence the mind in order to listen more clearly. Once you begin to acknowledge and listen closely to your automatic negative internal dialogue as an observer, detached from the emotional attachment to your perceived feelings, you begin to see just how chaotic your mind has become.

I began to learn how to slow down my own mind, clear out the chaos and automatic rushing thoughts by doing the following daily breathing exercise and trust me it does work, even without confidence and hope in play. Learning to breathe properly allows us to focus the mind and bring us back to the moment every time we find ourselves drifting back to the chaos of the past or our negative internal dialogue. As we keep breathing deeper, this practice gets easier with time. Awareness of your breath, pulling in and pushing out, helps to nurture mindfulness and develop a deeper insight, which eventually leads to enlightenment and an awakening, calming the mind, so you can relax without anxiety or pain. It finally gives you the space and freedom to find the relief from having to listen to that cruel critic in your mind.

Nurturing compassion, the main ingredient needed to develop a loving kindness towards ourselves and others, is an important core value required when expanding consciousness; it comes naturally when you learn to meditate. You begin to question your existing beliefs, learning to be less afraid of the consequences of having to change them. Through nurturing some basic core beliefs in meditation, you are going to become an observer outside your mind, sitting on the fence, looking in at what the hell you are dealing with inside your head. You are going to take a long hard look, without being emotionally connected, at your negative automatically generated chaotic self-abuse, potentially something you are not even aware of. Think now. Have you ever stopped in the stillness and asked yourself how you are feeling in the moment, outside of the misery of your mind?

The first step to building self-confidence comes from being aware of the inner negative dialogue you are having with yourself everyday automatically, without ever questioning why you are doing it or taking back control. It is this inner self critic making you feel worthless, hijacking your self-esteem, keeping you a slave, uncomfortable and insecure in your own skin. How stupid is this when you put it into perspective. Trust me if you just allow your emotions to be, let them manifest and proceed, then learn from them, you can begin to repair your relationship with yourself beyond the invisible cruel voice in your mind. Your meditation allows you to oversee your thoughts as the conscious you and not the unconscious automatic dialogue planted by others, the past, memories, unresolved issues, constantly tying you to your pain. Once you have the confidence to reconnect with your authentic self, the real you, beyond your imagination and pain, you can begin the process of maturing psychologically, developing spiritually and increasing your emotional intelligence. So let's begin, shall we?

I want you to lie on your bed after you have closed the curtains and try to shut out any noise around you. I want you to relax and focus on the breath you take in and the breath you take out, feeling your chest lift like you have an invisible piece of string pulling you towards the ceiling and back down again, as you breathe out. Once you have this focus in place, take in a deep breath to the count of eight, hold for the count of six and then breathe out for the count of eight. Keep repeating this exercise until your body and muscles feel rejuvenated with oxygen, which will automatically give you a feeling of wellbeing, helping you to feel less anxious in the moment. You should try and have a routine where you do this every day when you wake up and every night before you go to sleep. I can promise you, especially if you have trouble sleeping, this simple daily action is way more effective and healthier than having a big glass of wine or taking a pill to help you relax. I know it sounds difficult to imagine something so simple as learning to breathe correctly would change the way you feel but, trust me, most anxiety is caused by an inability to breathe properly in panic, which creates internal stress and further panic.

Getting a good night's sleep is never easy when your mind is running like the wind, your worries are overwhelming, your diet is bad, and you have been unable to do any exercise because you cannot be bothered. I found going out for a long walk in the countryside, just focusing on the sound of the birds, the wind through the trees and the colours around me, all helped lift my mood. Find that private place yourself in the park and make it a mission to walk there every day, even if your mind wants to remain inside. Push it out. Regular exercise like walking can help you to feel more in control and able to cope better, giving you a change of perspective, which will change your mood in the moment. Again, it sounds simple, but it works. Once you take the plunge and create these new simple patterns of behaviour with regular practice and patience, you will replace your old habits with new healthier ones.

I suggest you take me with you on these walks, you know my voice now. You can trust me because I have been open and honest with you about my own problems and downfall. Imagine me as someone you can talk to in your mind, to offload everything on. It will stop you automatically participating in your own negative thinking and help you clear the air. If you can stop feeling like your life is not worth living and self-harming is your only solution, eventually with time and confidence, you can begin to tackle the root cause of why you are depressed and begin intense work on yourself to encourage more positive, clean energy.

Every negative word you use to describe yourself or your situation through your inner dialogue, the automatic internal unconscious chatter with yourself will instruct your subconscious how you are feeling. This will then play out in how you behave. You may not even be aware you have an internal chatter with yourself right now, but we will discover more about this as we go through this journey. It will be a real revelation when you begin to breakdown how you communicate with yourself and how this affects how you feel about yourself. There are many simple practical things you can do to begin the process of self-therapy, like the breathing, the walking, the confidence building, but none of it will work without personal desire. It is only you who can change things if you truly want to. I can encourage you, even instruct you on how to begin the process of self-reflection, but the hard work must be done by you and you alone. I have no miracles right now. They come later with the hard work.

I wanted to write this book because right now there are many people with mental health problems and there is very little free help available when it comes to talking to someone, which in my experience and opinion, is the best medicine for modern-day suffering. I am sure in some cases of mental health issues, medication is essential. I also recognise medication is an easy quick way to mask the problem and suppress the root cause deeper inside. Talking it out in my mind makes way more sense than suppressing it. Remember all those ghosts I had trapped festering in the closet of my subconscious mind? You don't want to end up like me when they burst out one day when it all goes wrong.

When we look at mental health in this book, I am not just talking about those who have clinical depression, suicidal thoughts and other severe conditions of the mind; I am talking about negative thinking, unhealthy lifestyles, personal misery and all the underlying problems that manifest from how we see ourselves. You may think you are operating in a perfectly normal healthy way with no mental health issues, but you would be wrong. Living your life without a point or a purpose will inevitably cause you internal misery at some point, especially if you have unresolved issues from your past living in your unconscious. There are many people who have resigned themselves to the idea they cannot change anything because everything is already mapped out for them through the choices they have already made, especially in midlife, but this is not the truth. I want you to learn and understand that we never stand still as human beings. We should always be evolving. We can never be truly happy or satisfied with our lot unless we change, develop and mature into adults, not be stuck with our existing beliefs and false perspectives about who we are, handed to us in childhood from others.

Understanding why we do the things we do automatically without thinking, without ever really challenging our minds, comes from listening to how we communicate with ourselves through our internal dialogue. Like I already said, learning to listen as an observer, not participating emotionally, is the key to changing how you feel about yourself. To learn to talk positively to yourself in this dialogue, you must find the desire inside to change and by this I mean you must truly want to be honest with yourself and then want to sort yourself out more than anything else. For example: if you genuinely want to lose weight, you must find the desire within to be thin overeating a dozen cream cakes every time you automatically want emotional comfort without thinking. You must start listening consciously to your body instead of unconsciously going straight to your bad habits and patterns. The fix, the comfort, the high you get from eating the cream cake is what you believe to be satisfying, when it is not. You are not hungry for food, just desperate to feel better in the moment. The reason the cream cake is as addictive as drugs or alcohol is because of the high fat and sugar content creating a trigger chemical reaction in the brain, inducing feelings of perceived pleasure and satisfaction. It is a very powerful feeling and it can make people feel better in the moment, but we all know deep down inside the desire for this kind of uncontrollable eating is not healthy or the secret to real happiness. All this does is fill a void momentarily, eventually making us fatter, unhealthier and even more miserable—the vicious cycle. Then there is the other extreme where the desire to be thin can be so powerful, a person can starve themselves, ending up with an eating disorder or even death. Anything you do unconsciously that is excessive or based on emotional control is never going to work when it comes to feeling happy or discovering your power within.

As we go through this journey together, climbing towards higher thinking, getting closer to revealing the authentic self, I will explain and repeat many things because processing information is about having the insight to change embedded beliefs, patterns and habits. If you have never even considered working on yourself or your mind, you are going to find it tough to keep focused. You will feel uneasy and uncomfortable, so the meditation and breathing techniques are crucial to start the process off. Changing your negative habits and patterns, especially those connected to food and other addictions, will require extra focus. Often we have no idea or understanding why we cannot get on top of them and, trust me, they do affect our emotions and our moods. It is important also to understand that cravings and hunger are not the same thing. Most people get cravings now and again, but if after you are full, you still crave more food, this could be a sign something else is going on in your mind. If your cravings happen too often and you have absolutely no control of them, this is a simple indicator you have lost control. It is not a need for nutrients for your body, it is your addiction calling for dopamine in the reward system of your brain every time you feel miserable about yourself. Asking a food addict to cut down on portion size is like asking an alcoholic to go for a week without a drink, impossible, so we must understand how powerful your cravings can be. Admitting you have a problem is the start of facing the problem, be it food, drugs, drink, sex, depression or anxiety, because until you face it, you deny it and denying it can lead to more dangerous problems further down the line.

The word addiction is derived from Latin to mean enslaved or bound to, and anyone who has tried to break addiction or helped someone do it understands why it bears this name because it truly does keep you imprisoned and enslaved. We must be willing to expand beyond our existing beliefs to find inner confidence without fear, making a stronger connection with the rational side of who we are and not be mentally closed off, rigid and inflexible, wallowing in self-pity. It is important to understand any addiction hijacks the brain and changes its structure. Alcohol and drug addiction are the worst of them all and the most powerful because we can excuse it as having socially acceptable fun.

There are many things we are facing right now in the world and in our own lives that are challenging and painful. Often it is hard to feel or find happiness without comfort and addiction, but we must get to a point where we grow beyond this by understanding it. The further away you get by pretending or hiding behind a mask or a glass of wine, acting out different identities, eating and escaping in the comfort zone, the harder it will become to maintain your truth. To go beyond these different identities, be it mother, father, daughter, clown, career role, extrovert, peeling off the mask to reveal the real you, is a process that can feel raw and uncomfortable. You are being stretched outside your comfort zone. However, once the mask is fully peeled back, you will have a new sense of freedom, a new level of clarity about your self-direction, leaving you free and excited to begin a new chapter in your life. Remember, we all have a choice in the perceptions we have about what we see and how we feel. The truth is if you are feeling pain, you are at least feeling something, and feeling something in a deep way is the only sure way to get to know the real you. There are no shortcuts to true happiness. All the pain and discomfort you feel for a short while when peeling off your mask, stretching you beyond your comfort zone and limitations, will slowly disappear. When we have limitations and are ruled by defence mechanisms, we are unable to free our minds and be real about who we really are inside.

To achieve inner clarity and peace we must never allow other people's expectations to dictate who we are or what we feel. Once we can learn to create the silence and space in our meditation, to communicate compassionately with the authentic self, we can begin to start the process of releasing our suffering.

Nurturing compassion through our meditation practice is the main ingredient to developing our unique potential, the higher thinking we need to stop us feeling like we are not good enough, an unrealistic feeling of inadequacy created by the mind. An inferiority complex, the painful feeling you are not good enough, not as attractive as, not as intelligent as everyone else happens because of an unconscious emotional reaction delivered somewhere in your childhood. This often plays out in ways of you overcompensating for these negative feelings through the imagination later in life. This is described by Freud as an avoidant personality disorder and stems from early shyness and inferior feeling towards maturity, identified in individuals who subordinate their own needs. Basically, taking no personal responsibility for their lives, handing it over to the control of others. This then results in clingy behaviour, always eager to please, strong fears of abandonment and is one of the most common personality disorders today, resulting in a total lack of confidence with a fear of being isolated. When we begin to understand more about self-knowledge, we begin to see we have developed our negative unconscious ego as our primary identity through repetitive conditioning when young. Basically, this becomes recognised as self, who we believe we are. It is not possible to just think yourself into a higher level of consciousness. You must develop deeper heartfelt feelings and emotions to override the control your unconscious ego has over you. Practising daily meditation is the only way to achieve this skill and it must be done religiously to take you forward and evolve your ability to remain focused on you, the real you.

When we are around age three, we begin to develop our own sense of identity and personality, learning to make our own decisions; if we are painfully shy and introverted instead of maturing and developing, we will allow our parents to remain in control of how we think. By the time we reach adolescence, this control and not thinking for ourselves can leave us feeling totally insecure and reliant on others for what we need. This then creates an irrational fear of being abandoned, resulting in untrue beliefs delivered by the unconscious ego, the times we feel unloved. If we cannot think for ourselves, have never experienced problem solving, constantly feeling insecure and afraid of abandonment, we will grow up feeling inferior, then create a complex. Often something will happen in adolescence, a traumatic event like the death of someone close or a parental divorce. The anxiety connected to this kind of bad experience then becomes so overwhelming, the intense fear of being inferior develops into a made-up protection strategy, a fake persona, to fit in outside the parental control. The fake confidence, becoming someone else because the inferior child inside cannot cope anymore, cannot stand the control anymore and cannot problem solve, turns into an over-confident young adult without skills and little experience of managing their feelings in the real world. Here you can start to see what happens to us unconsciously as children will damage the natural development of the maturing process into adolescence, leaving us feeling inferior and not good enough as adults, which stops us fitting in socially and being accepted by others. Without learning to take personal responsibility for our life, it will descend into a spiral of pain and suffering with all the excuses in the world why we continue choosing negative unhealthy thoughts and behaviours over being in control of our choices.

As we go through this journey together, regardless of what anxiety, stress, depression, suicidal thoughts or irrational fear you suffer from, separating yourself from your subconscious thoughts and diluting your unconscious ego through being mindful, will help you start to grow and understand yourself more. I want to help get you thinking again by challenging the reasons you do the things you do without thinking, and maybe give you some food for thought why you are unhappy, unfulfilled, miserable, and forever asking the question, "What's the point?" Your life is short and goes by in the blink of an eye, so wasting any more of it, wallowing in misery, harbouring regrets from the past without understanding why, is not an option anymore if you truly want to find happiness. We are going to learn to develop a new strategy towards liking yourself more and stop you being controlled by your negative thinking. This long but enlightening process of learning, self-observation, gaining increased self-awareness through dedicated meditation practice, reaching a higher level of consciousness, connecting to the soul self beyond the unconscious ego, takes you listening only to your heart. It takes a great deal of courage to admit you have a problem, an issue, an addiction, a fake existence and even more courage to admit the choices you have made have left you in misery and mental turmoil but, to be honest, there is not a person on the planet who is perfect, even with social media and photoshopping at our finger tips.

The greatest gift in life is being able to laugh not only at yourself but with yourself. After all, it is only you who really matters. The opinions of others belong to them and will only contaminate your thinking, if you allow them to, so don't do it anymore. It is hard when you have allowed your self-esteem, self-worth and self-confidence to reach an all-time low because you just don't feel good enough to speak out and contribute when the rest of the world seems against you. Do you really want this to be your calling card forever, the way you portray yourself in your mind? I am a great believer in the wonderful teachings of amazing people in history like Oscar Wilde who once said, "There is only one thing worse in the world than being talked about and that is not being talked about." So very true in my opinion and something worth thinking about the next time you feel insecure or picked on by others. Let us remember, it is not only you who is feeling vulnerable and worthless, most of us have the defence mechanism, projecting on others what is wrong with us, our dark side, so try and give yourself a break.

Let's with confidence begin to look at why you have given up on yourself, constantly feeling uncomfortable, on the back foot, forever feeling like a complete failure, lost, lonely, unhappy, unable to change your deep-rooted fears and anxieties, keeping you trapped, tortured and lost out at sea, drowning in your own misery. I would imagine if you are currently consumed and bogged down by feelings of depression and anxiety, you are in a passive behaviour state, avoiding any expression of opinions or feelings, unable to meet your own needs. People with passive behaviour patterns when it comes to learning positive self-talk will always struggle because they will tend to go backwards to the past for comfort rather than remaining in the present with courage.

Self-talk, your subconscious internal dialogue with yourself, like any other therapy must begin by understanding where the root cause of the problem began, the reason good therapists take us back to childhood in sessions to discover and uncover where our painful feelings began. We must rewind for a healthy mind, understanding all repressed feelings and emotions are waiting dormant in the unconscious, ready to attack when we least expect it because although we believe we have consciously dismissed them, the subconscious is not so kind, always ready to remind.

In our early years, each of us forms a composite picture of ourselves and our experiences from others. What we were told back in childhood has today become the foundation for the mental programming we live by but what if you have been told how you think about yourself is all wrong? Now think about your life and this incorrect information planted in your mind, creating the person you are today, like a computer program incorrectly wired with bad conditioning, malfunctioning and breaking down. This programmed negative conditioning by others is the main reason you are unable to change your existing beliefs and negative patterns, leaving you constantly at the mercy of your destructive thinking, emotional reactions and unpredictable impulsive behaviours. The good news is with learning to positively self-talk, just like your computer you can reprogram yourself, replacing the unhealthy parts with happy, positive new parts, putting you back in control and in tune with yourself in your own mind. If everything you tell yourself is a directive in your subconscious mind—if only I was thinner, brighter, younger, prettier—your conscious behaviour will reflect the same feelings back to you and others around you. You are what you think. If you put negative bad energy out into the world, accept this is maybe why you are failing to connect with others positively. We attract ourselves and no one is ever attracted to someone down in the dumps and down on themselves. So shifting negative energy out is the main key to creating self-esteem and self-confidence. Every time we have been told we cannot do something, this is a directive to our subconscious mind, and because of negative conditioning by others, we repeat the same negative conditioning to ourselves and end up full of self-doubt, forever feeling like the underdog. In this state of negativity, we have learnt to automatically go straight to the worst-case scenario first and best-case scenario last when it comes to making decisions and choices about the future. We believe we will fail before we have even tried to win.

We are not born with our beliefs, they are created and handed to us by other people, just like they give us their faults and unhealthy habits, which repeat like a chain reaction in how we see the world and ourselves. It is important to remember, anything you have been taught by someone else is not your truth or what you really believe, this is something truly important to recognise when working yourself out of your own misery. If you have been in a controlling relationship with your parents as a child, growing up your programming and conditioning is likely to destroy any natural self-confidence you have and create secrets and lies inside instead.

This negative lying creates your negative beliefs and your negative beliefs then create negative attitudes, creating negative feelings, which then create depression and anxiety. We cannot be authentic because we have no idea who we are or what we think for real, our thinking has been done for us. This is how the subconscious mind works and if you truly want to change your programmed mindset because you have recognised the person you really are, is nothing like the person you portray, then it is possible to do so with hard work and positive self-talk therapy. Once you have the confidence and desire to work yourself out from the inside out, you will be on your way. The voice inside your head is the way you override past negative beliefs and conditioning, by replacing it with conscious new thinking and beliefs, the opinions and values you really believe in rather than the passive acceptance of things taught by others. Can you honestly say right now you always practise what you preach?

Personal choice and positive thinking beyond your irrational fear, anxiety and depression is the most empowering feeling you will ever have. It is this change in you that will set you free, even if you have failed in the past, and there is no race going on here. You must just keep trying. Every time you say to yourself you cannot lose weight, you could never do that, or you are just not good enough, these negative doubts become self-professing and manifest into exactly what you say. You must learn to type and translate into your subconscious memory only positive and empowering thoughts, your thoughts. I can lose weight, I can do that, I am good enough, and eventually this new programming will respond into your conscious thinking. Remember your existing beliefs create your negative thoughts, create your negative emotions and your emotional reactions dictate your behaviour. This I will keep repeating as we go because if what you think is all wrong, then how it makes you feel is all wrong and simply explain why you behave the way you do, automatically.

Being aware of your inner chatter—the voice that daily gives you an unconscious running monologue, be it happy and positive or negative and self-destructive—is known as self-talk and combines your conscious thoughts with your subconscious beliefs. It is an effective way for your brain to work out your experiences and how you feel about things. Human nature, as I have said before and will repeat again, is always prone to negative self-talk. Even though we understand the sweeping negative assertions we make to be untrue, we do it anyway. The truth is that the negative bias can be changed. We just need to be more conscious of when we are doing it—the hard bit. How you begin to orchestrate and conduct your inner monologue with yourself, can have a massive effect on the success you create in your life. I told myself right from the get-go I would be rich and successful, even coming from a bleak start, and sure enough eventually I got there. The use of positive self-talk in my own internal monologues growing up created further self-confidence, freeing my brain to perform at its best, not being bogged down by feelings of self-doubt and failure. Of course, I was young and immature, made some massive mistakes and failed in many ways, but I had the drive and confidence to bounce back without any fear of what others thought about me. My subconscious was trained by only me, through constant steadfast repeating the idea in my mind that I would escape poverty and become someone rich and successful one day and sure enough it happened. I was lucky because I was not programmed or influenced by my caregivers constantly telling me how to think. I grew up knowing how to think for myself.

By changing how we address the self, the first person or the third, we flip a switch in the cerebral cortex according to the psychologist Ethan Kross. The centre of any thought from another in the amygdala, the seat of fear moving closer or further from our sense of self. Gaining this psychological distance allows us to have self-control, helping us to think and perform more competently. Every time we complete a task, we gain positive perspective, releasing us from negativity, allowing us to focus more deeply then begin to plan with action, not through fear but from feelings of personal achievement. We can pat ourselves on the back which gives us confidence, creating positive self-talk, and the negative bias we are tied to suddenly loses power. We can take back control of how we think about ourselves once again.

The inner voice always begins positively in childhood, then remains with us throughout life, like a companion, often getting clogged, confused, distorted and buried deep inside until it can no longer be heard or reached consciously. It can turn on us and become the cruel critic, forever battering us with negative self-doubt, destroying the positive, beautiful, naïve, childlike curiosity we once had. We end up contaminated and destroyed as we become negative, consumed people pleasers, unable to think for ourselves. Think about it deeply right now just how many times you go to the negative first, believing you will fail when you try and do something new. Think about how many times you please others over pleasing yourself for fear of being told off or rejected.

Self-talk in childhood before it gets contaminated, I believe to be the soul, the inner divine you and because it is the common sense stable consistent thought of reason and goodness, when misused or pushed to its limit by the unconscious ego or through the control of others, will create psychosis. This becomes a long-term failure to operate or create any personal success and spiritual development beyond one-dimensional negative thinking, the reason we let the cruel voice take over making our choices.

Everything you say to yourself from now on matters. If your inner dialogue with your self inhibits you, limits you or prevents you from pursuing the life you want and deserve, robbing you of your emotional wellbeing, the time has come to face it that this is the reason you are always depressed with anxiety, have no confidence, and are always ruled by your fears. It is time to stop punishing yourself through negative self-talk monologues why you are a failure and begin the reward process of shaping new and positive belief patterns, no longer focusing on what you are doing wrong but instead on what you do well. This small switch alone in your mindset will begin to create the inner self-confidence you need to take you to more action-driven daily tasks, like the meditating, the walking and keeping a journal of how you are feeling moment to moment. Start to forget about what everyone else is thinking. They are not thinking about you as much as you think. They are too busy pretending they have their own act together. Start working on being the better you, the real you and leave everyone else to get on with their own lives.

During my own journey with negative self-talk, I learnt to talk back to myself to take away its power. I imagined my inner voice to be a separate entity like the cruel critic I did not agree with or even like. It didn't know me—the real me. It was made up, mixed up in my mind, ready to take me down. I gave this critic a name 'Mood Hoover', and every time it told me I was an idiot for losing my money or a failure for wanting to end my life, I simply replied I had no interest in what it had to say anymore because it was lying. The more I took back control of my real thoughts, the weak inner critic, my own worst enemy, began to lose power and it was not long before my positivity returned. I was kind to myself again and my inner confidence returned with a vengeance. I am not saying it will be easy to defeat the inner enemy you live with; it is all you know right now. We are all different with various levels of personal persecution to deal with, but I hope you can now begin to see a light at the end of the dark tunnel you have been lost in for too long. There is always hope even when all hope seems lost. None of us want to fail because that would be tragic for humanity and the wellbeing of our planet.

My purpose with you is to try and make a shift in your thinking. Opinions are good and we all have them but if your opinion of yourself is damaging to the outcome of your happiness and wellbeing, then this is not good and probably happening because you only know how to listen to your negative self. You don't believe in the real you. Have you ever asked yourself who that negative voice belongs to inside your head? The one that keeps telling you you're a failure. Remember this voice is not you because why would you tell yourself you are a loser and a failure even if you have made a mess of your life. Failure does not make you useless, it makes you human and just like everyone else in truth. None of us have the perfect life, and perfection does not come with money possessions, status, marriage, kids, it comes from understanding yourself completely, the real you buried beneath the layers of what you have been programmed to believe will make you happy. Think about as a child how you were given all your information before you could think or decide for yourself what is right or wrong for you. It is a real eye-opener when you ask yourself if what you believe is what you really believe or what you have been programmed to believe by others.

Learning to fill your mind with what you need to exist in a happy harmonious environment with your thoughts, your truth, your actions and your words all making complete sense, to present a true picture of who you are and what you believe for real, is your only goal going forward from now on. It all begins by understanding mindful thinking, the state of being conscious and aware of what you are thinking, focused only on the present, the moment from a positive loving perspective, always with a good sense of humour. This is progress.

Mindful thinking involves acceptance, meaning simply we must always pay attention to our thoughts and feelings without judging them, without believing there is a right or wrong way to think at any given moment, always with realistic expectations. When we practise mindful thinking, all our thoughts tune into what we are sensing in the present, rather than reliving the past or imagining the future, creating a mental state achieved by focusing awareness on the present moment. Everyone has difficult thoughts, feelings and memories. It is all part of life. Trying to just wipe away the negativity and belief in these irrational thoughts and feelings is useless. We must let them in, own them, deal with them through forgiveness and compassion then no longer identify with them.

When I began to work with mindful thinking myself, to acknowledge my inner voice, I would breathe, meditate and focus on removing each thought that came into my mind one by one. I did this by imagining in the back of my mind there was a giant tennis racket; every time a thought came into my head, I would bat it back out until my breathing became the only focus, I had. It was such an effective way to help me see just how much rubbish was entering my mind with absolutely no purpose in the moment.

Cleaning out your mind is the most important job you have as a human being if happiness and personal growth is what you desire and unless you do it, you will be left consumed with all the wrong information, passed on from others with nothing to do with what you think anymore. We are old enough now to think for ourselves as mature adults with our own minds.

Mindful thinking allows us to understand we have become comfortable with discomfort. An almost radical acceptance as a society that what we have become is normal and OK, primarily because those around us follow the same patterns of over-eating, drinking too much, being medicated, obese, addicted and so on. If everybody on the planet became a non-smoker because smoking is bad for us and can kill us, it would be very hard to be the only smoker, wouldn't it? We model, we copy, we learn, we follow the pack like sheep, and we all fall off the cliff into choppy waters, lost out at sea, suffering in silence, until we die full of unease. If everyone was fed the correct information about how to create a happy, healthy and purposeful life, there would be empty hospital beds across the land and very little need to be obsessed with dieting or boozing, constantly escaping our reality to become someone else because we like the look of them better.

As a society we have become oblivious to our own behaviour through denial, running away from taking personal responsibility, jumping in and out of binge purge patterns whenever possible. I understand life today is tough, where money, looks and aspiration drive everything we think and do, where social media is more important than a real connection, and self-image is distorted because to be attractive, we must copy someone we think looks perfect. Our idea of perfection is skewed based only on the external with little regard for what we have to offer internally.

We are all a work in progress and this work is never finished. The more we understand the less we know, until we realise we know nothing in the bigger picture because it is all just an illusion to keep us running around in circles. Understanding how you work, how much your subconscious memory affects what you think, which dictates how you feel about yourself, will help you get back in control of your behaviours and ultimately set you free.

In AA recovery, the first step back is to admit we are powerless over alcohol and living a normal healthy life has become unmanageable. Alcoholics lose control when they drink, addicts do the same when they use drugs and food addicts do the same with eating. When we can no longer control what is happening, we are out of control and always remember the worst lies are the ones we tell ourselves.

With practice in the next chapter, your ability to translate your good intentions into mindful actions, through practising positive conversation with yourself, will start to become second nature. By learning to shift and relocate your mindset, you will become better equipped to redirect all your attention away from a negative stress response to your problems and will push you towards a more realistic interpretation of what is really happening in your head, not what you are imagining. It is true to say by changing your relationship with your thoughts, feelings and behaviours, learning to accept them for what they are, rather than how you would like them to be, you literally begin to change your brain and decode networks important in managing your stress, depression and anxiety. Over time with mindful thinking and a clear understanding that what you think you know is not always real, you will begin to develop a greater capacity for self-observation, and growing optimism will lead to better control of addictive behaviours, improving self-control.

It took me reaching the bottom as you know to let go of the past and cross over into maturity, taking personal responsibility for my life's mistakes to be able to achieve my full potential. If throughout this life, we have been able to get through it without taking any personal responsibility for it, we must face we have not grown up yet or learnt anything new. We remain immature children stuck in misery, blaming everyone else for our own mistakes.

Today, I am a self-actualiser. I have been able to achieve everything I believed I can achieve. I have a real sense of purpose and I experience moments of profound happiness with great compassion and empathy for all. I accept fully who I am. I can laugh at myself and my mistakes with an ongoing appreciation for the goodness in my life. I am a survivor, proud of all I have achieved. I can exist alone and do not need other people to validate who I am. I have learnt through self-mastery how to achieve happiness, fulfilment and personal pleasure beyond my dreams. Through this book, I want to help you become problem-centred rather than self-centred, to appreciate fresh thinking rather than stereotypical thinking, the stuff you have learnt, and most of all, I want to teach you to transcend the environment, not copy it. I have had a profound spiritual experience with near death, not a religious one. This has created a need for detachment and privacy within me, something I love and gives me a great sense of peace. I think this is what they call wisdom. Getting you to this place will not be easy but it is possible if you are able to put your confidence and trust in my teachings, derived from a personal journey of growth, overcoming monumental mistakes and a shaky start in my own life. Gaining an accurate assessment of what you are good at might be tricky to begin with because building confidence does not come from being told how good you are, how clever you are. It is built through experiencing achievement, not through hollow praise. Always remember, a confident person accepts a new experience and understands mistakes happen, and if they do happen, the person will handle it without falling to bits. This is what having a confident attitude is all about. Learning to not take something going wrong too seriously, always with a good sense of humour, curiosity and fun. Treating each experience as a building block towards a better more grounded you, is the process of enjoying just how far you can go.

When you look at very young children who are learning something new, you can see such curiosity and wonder, as they approach every situation without fear. They have no understanding of failure yet. They just go for it. You need to rewind and go backwards to being like that curious small child again, understanding, experiencing something new is a chance to learn, shedding your inhibitions and limited beliefs along the way. You have become unconsciously incompetent. Going back to your childhood remembering how you would just go for things without fear will take you back to a time when it would never occur to you learning something new could be so hard. I want to get you back to this place where you can be happily unaware of the fact it doesn't matter how hard things are; if you persevere, you will eventually get there. Your greatest weakness is, if you are completely honest with yourself, you simply give up too soon. It's easier.

Unhappy, unconfident people spend their whole lives unconsciously living in the past, dwelling on the things that went wrong, the opportunities they missed, the unresolved issues they harbour, forever resentful, believing things will never work out the way they planned or hoped they would. Confident happy people on the other hand, people like me, live only in the present, in the moment. They see the past as wisdom, they have learnt from their mistakes, battled the storm within and come out the other end much more centred because of the experience. When your perception of a goal matches your perception of your ability to achieve the goal, you get confidence. How you see yourself, your self-image, plays a massive part in building your self-confidence. If you can see and believe in the person you long to be, beyond the irrational picture you have painted, you will have a more realistic approach to building your confidence. Who you see yourself as, is often a fantasy self, a persona, the role your personality plays out for the rest of the world to see. If the gap between the persona-self and who you really are inside is too big, you will never live up to the expectations of others. Uncovering your authentic self is now our goal together, so you no longer need to live up to the expectations of others. We are going to get your beliefs and expectations of who you really are more closely aligned, so who you believe you are is much closer to who you want to be, matching your abilities with your expectations. Setting yourself up with unrealistic expectations and standards will produce failure before you even start. The only way we are going to build you up and get you operating more confidently is by you doing something new, experiencing the fresh feeling of achievement firsthand.

We all know that being confident gives you edge in life, the catalyst for you to gain more confidence in your life, giving you an edge on others is to recognise, your actions influence your results. I can tell you from my own experience, confident people always grow up with a realistic appraisal of their abilities; they just know instinctively where they stand. This knowing allows them to build a life strategy to strengthen themselves, creating a positive perception they can influence an outcome, reducing anxiety when under pressure. Confident people will always develop themselves further by making a note subconsciously, celebrating successes, to create positive expectations in future experiences. They tell themselves they did it once, so they can do it again. Once we believe in ourselves and our abilities turning our experiences into actions, we can then risk curiosity and delight because we will be revealing the human spirit.

Mindful Thinking Can Change Your Brain

Recent studies have shown that an eight-week mindful meditation course can lead to structural brain changes, including increased grey matter density in the hippocampus, the region in our brain that regulates our emotions, known to be important for our memory, learning, self-awareness and compassion. The aim for mindful meditation is to boast your happiness levels, moving you away from a fixed mindset into a growth mindset, so you can focus on the smaller things that really matter, moving away from the bigger things that consume your thoughts, especially when they all come flooding at once. Understanding more about yourself through being mindful means the more you become in tune with understanding your subconscious mind, the closer you become to successfully acting to stop being pulled in by your self-limiting beliefs.

As we learn to observe our thoughts, our actions, our behaviours and ourselves externally, through our meditation, we begin to become more aware of how often we operate without intention. We get to see how much of what we think is automatic. In the early stages of understanding this lack of intention, it will be hard to learn to remain still and quiet in your mind. Over time with patience and dedication, you will learn to observe every single thought as it enters the space in your silent mind.

To be able to allow a deeper comprehension of your true self to disarm the programmed functions of your mind and accept them without judgement, you will need to become more focused and disciplined towards a higher level of consciousness. Higher consciousness is the consciousness of a higher self.

So how do we bring mindful thinking into our everyday lives as a habit, part of what we do without thinking and not a chore, i.e. something we dismiss as pointless hard work? I can only tell you how I did it and why it helped boost my mind, changing the way I thought about things, helping me to become more positive and focused in the present, away from the past without regrets. Think right now about how over-busy your mind is at any one time and how hard it is to focus on something with your full attention. Think about the last time you had a good mind clear-out to make more room for fresh creative positive thinking. You spring clean your home, so why would you not spring clean your mind occasionally too. When you focus only on yourself in meditation, you'll begin to lose sight of everything else around you and this feeling, once you get used to it, is peaceful and calming, creating the right atmosphere to remove stressful anxiety or panic. It stops you getting taken over by your excessive thinking and irrational fear. When you only focus negatively on yourself in life, your everyday challenges and movements, you become consumed with what you think you want to make you happy and not what you need to grow and mature.

I discovered, even with millions in the bank, it was not money, stuff or things that made me feel happy. It was only when I had nothing materially and only myself to give to others, I began to know true happiness for real. Doing something good to help someone else helped me take the focus off my own problems, making me feel good about myself, which produced an overwhelming warm fussy feeling of achievement inside. I suddenly felt like I had a purpose. There was a point to my life. Giving my time to be helpful or useful to others created a kind of new reasoning behind my own life, the life that had eluded me in the past. I volunteered my services in a local charity shop when I was on the dole, recovering from my near-death experience and lifesaving operation. I couldn't get a paid job; this made me depressed, sitting at home feeling useless and uninspired, so this was a miracle for me. By getting outside and doing good helped me get out of a negative mindset and it was this small positive action of being kind to others that helped me find my inner strength again. I had skills they needed and getting out of the house was life-changing. Interacting again with people was truly the key to fuelling my continued strength and recovery. Trying something new, at the same time helping others, can inspire you to begin the search for your true purpose in life, the thing I believe to be the key to happiness, without the constant searching outward for false comfort or fixes. If you can get completely absorbed in something you love, detox your negative thinking, keeping it real, staying positive on what is important to you, there is a good chance you will get in touch with your spiritual self. This is the rational voice inside of reason beyond the lying cruel critic in your mind and it is how you reach a higher level of thinking.

I am not remotely religious as you already know by now, so when I talk about your spiritual self, I am talking about your higher self, the real you, your soul consciousness and the part of you that holds the key to your positive future. Your physical self is your body. The most finely tuned complex container that works without you having to do anything, other than keep it healthy with the right fuel, just like you do every day with your car. If you abuse it and do not take care of it, it breaks down and cannot get you from A to B. Understanding your mind, body and soul is the same principle. If you abuse them, eventually, they too will break down and you will become unable to interface purposefully with your environment and fellow human beings. You are potentially at this stage right now if your depression and misery has taken hold of your thinking, crippling any desire to make the necessary moves to restore the functions of your mind, body and soul. Basically, chances are you have probably given up on yourself. Now I want you to really think about that. Why would you consciously give up on yourself?

The best way to reconnect with your authentic self is through mindfulness, to start to notice your feelings at any given time in what I call a place of splendid isolation, your meditation. You will create the time you need to enjoy being free from your internal chaos, through breathing properly, meditating in nature, forgiving yourself with compassion, the perfect ingredients for creating a better you. Surely being the best version of you there possibly is beyond the perceived pain you have become used to living with, without question, must be better than giving up on yourself?

We are having a highly personal connection on this journey together through my own experiences. This is called a text to self-connection. What you are reading, and learning, is hopefully reminding you of your own experiences and feelings. Finding yourself outside of this personal connection means you can create a new life timeline by writing down daily after breathing and meditation new goals you hope to reach. Setting yourself goals will give you challenges, exercising your mind and changing your thinking, helping you focus more in what you truly believe in and not what you are used to accepting as your truth. Consciousness work, being aware of everything we are doing is very taxing, but it must be done until old habits and patterns are erased, and we have learnt to no longer indulge in mindless activities by escaping. The stuff you do without thinking. For example, escaping into a TV show, especially when you are in turmoil to mindlessly ignore what is really happening, is not going to help. Take a walk outside in nature instead, a much better way to calm your mind and reconnect with yourself, not escape in your imagination.

Beginning to distinguish your own thoughts from those of others and relying on yourself more, means you can create a clean slate, the ultimate chance to organise the world you want to live in, rather than a world you are forced to live in by your circumstances. We need to start learning to trust ourselves again, getting rid of our negative thinking bit by bit, experiencing new ways to think beyond what we believe is set in stone. Remember, beliefs create thoughts, thoughts create emotions and it is our emotions that dictate our behaviours.

Keeping a mood journal was an amazing exercise for me when my mind got locked inside a prison cell, with my depression holding the keys. By writing down my thoughts, it helped me notice what triggers upset me and what changed my moods. It helped me look at the times I felt overwhelmed with anxiety and the times I reached for comfort or fixes to feel better. Getting my madness and confusion out on paper away from me, separating it from me, was quite empowering and enlightening because I didn't recognise myself when I revisited later, outside of the misery. My journal of a mad woman gave me real insight into my negative patterns, and I began to see what was happening to me and when. This encouraged me to keep working and slowly get back on top of myself. I noticed going through my mood journal every day for a week, at almost the same time every day, I would burst into tears for no reason. It would just happen, so I began to become conscious of the crying episodes ahead of time and shifted the pattern by going outside for a walk instead. Noticing this embedded pattern and recognising it for what it was, made me very aware I was no longer in control or had any reason for feeling this way. The slight change by just pushing myself out for a walk changed my whole focus. The more I could see where I was going wrong, getting stuck or repeating things for no reason, the more I was able to take back control of my irrational thought process.

I was alone in chaos for weeks after losing all my money, riddled with fear, anxiety and stress. My emotions left me feeling hopeless, confused and sacred. It was not easy to face myself for being such a stupid, greedy idiot and being lonely in my misery did not help me either. My journal became my constant companion and friend in the end, as I watched the old me on paper being erased, overtaken by the emerging new me. This was a truly cleansing and helpful process to go through, especially when it came to tackle the negative inner critic constantly putting me down in my subconscious mind. This process helped me survive and flourish in the most demanding and difficult five years in Hollywood, which led up to my near-death experience. Documenting and juggling my emotions became my way of coping and recovering. Once we begin to observe the way we communicate with ourselves through our internal dialogue, we begin to reveal our underlying thought process and existing beliefs operating in our minds. All the things we do automatically without thinking. This was a particularly enlightening time for me. I had always been so busy and focused moving forward, driven towards success, I had absolutely no idea of the voice inside my head. Once we can observe our actions, how we talk, behave and respond, we can observe and direct our thoughts and feelings to make sure they are the same. The idea of this is to become aware in the moment, to observe our outward actions, at the same time observing our inner thoughts. This is not easy and takes practice, but through your meditation and mindfulness, you begin to understand self-awareness creating more internal peace, our objective on this journey back to the real you.

I know this is a lot to take in and hopefully you are still with me. You know deep down inside being that stranger who wants to keep failing is not the authentic you. As you begin to work on being mindful and you think consciously about one thing at a time in the moment, you will get to see the barrage of overwhelming information you deal with every day and how it affects your thoughts and perspective of how you see yourself. Think about a time when you have intended to do one thing, then found yourself unconsciously doing three different things unconnected to the one thing you intended to do, before the overload of information entered your mental space. Your conscious mind can only focus on doing one thing at a time, and unless you are mindful to focus in the moment on that one thing, your subconscious patterns, habits, fears, anxiety and memories will take you over before you can say Jack Robinson. If you are consciously focusing hard on feeling hopeless, your subconscious overload of emotional barrage will enter into your mental space, the self-doubt, the self-loathing, the million negative programmed thoughts, it is easy to see how suicide happens. This overload of negative thoughts already buried in the subconscious, hitting all in one go, prevents the one conscious focus—to stay calm—from happening. It is so powerful, any positive focus gets lost in the moment.

I found once I was able to manage the dynamics in my subconscious mind through not focusing on the past but only on the present, I began to grow beyond my memories to become a better person inside without the self-doubt and the negative self-punishing stopped. If you can fill your subconscious mind with joyful, positive, truthful, confident and solid messages, whilst being mindful and grateful for them every day, eventually, you will become what you think and your mood will lift. Of course, being joyful, positive, truthful and confident is not possible when you have no idea what it feels like. I understand this but somewhere in that massive memory bank, you will somehow pull out a time when you felt happy. You just need to persevere and go through the pain with gratitude, remembering that happy time to give you momentum. Getting to this place for somebody who is severely depressed, living with hopelessness, will not be easy, even with the idea of one happy positive thought but anyone can literally reprogram their memory, once they have the tools and the desire in place.

The main reason most of us fail in life is because we listen to others for answers to life dilemmas and not to ourselves. Every decision we make determines the road we travel down. We cannot make any authentic decisions until we get to know our authentic selves because we will always be travelling down the wrong path towards the wrong hopes and dreams, potentially the reason you are depressed. We are all guilty of blending in with the crowd, going along being influenced by others, even when we know deep down we are not being authentic. This is because it is easier or we are not confident enough to say, "No thanks, that's not for me." If you spend your life blending in, never being real, you end up doing things that go against your core values and beliefs to please others, until you don't recognise yourself anymore. You end up feeling empty, numb and depressed. Then you get anxious, miserable and unable to see the wood for the trees. This is not progress. Once you start to be mindful with confidence, standing out from the crowd, being unique and authentic, following the straight and narrow road, your own unique path, you will begin to shine out as different from the rest. Being different from the rest is what you believe to be the reason you feel scared, depressed and unhappy but if you change the way you look at things, why would you want to be like everyone else?

The reality is you probably have no real understanding of who you are inside. You have been hiding for way too long under your personality persona, never questioning why you feel so bad all the time. The realisation you don't really know who you are is the first step to listening to your inner soul, instead of creating mental images you cannot live up to, for fear of being found out, the biggest mistake we all make in this thing called life. Once we become experts at living up to these imagined images of ourselves, we totally forget and give up on who we really are inside. Deep down, our subconscious already knows we are being fake, pretending we are something we are not to impress others. This becomes our unconscious ego in play. The big problem with creating a false image of yourself occurs when you present yourself outwardly as a confident clown, when you are really a shy introverted insecure mess on the inside. If you are exposed publicly and outdone by someone else, your self-worth becomes shattered. You begin to feel insecure and your whole belief of self becomes unstable and compromised. Basically, you malfunction, get even more depressed and give up trying.

Our unconscious ego always wants to be right and will often argue black is white when we know black is black. This is because it is protecting the false image we have created for the outside world to see when inside we know we are lying to ourselves. Honesty is the best policy when it comes to being authentic. Telling the truth without shame and forgiving yourself, shedding your social personality, your persona, confidently revealing who you really are, is the key to bearing your soul. So, what is your soul? Have you ever explored the idea it exists? Do you believe you are soulless? Do you ever imagine there could be more to you than meets the eye? Have you ever considered the possibility you are more than a miserable useless mess?

We know what our tangible body is. We know if we don't take care of it, it will break down and become useless, unable to house any healthy, happy, clean energy. This clean energy is the important natural signal we project outward to others in our everyday lives. Our clean energy is the positive, healthy, happy and optimistic self, and it encourages permission for your soul to shine out into the world, attracting the same back from others. If you are happy, optimistic, full of the joys of spring, you will cause tremendous stress to someone who is down in the dumps with life. They will potentially hate you for being happy. It is true and works the other way around as well; if you are miserable, unhappy, negative, pessimistic, preaching doom and gloom on the world, you are likely to find yourself alone without any friends. It is important to understand your soul is your energy. The vital thing that shines out from your being and it can be so powerful sometimes, it can literally attract anything you desire, without you realising it is happening.

The soul is not tangible but the immortal, incorporeal essence of a human being, which drives and guides us towards growth, change and wholeness, so it is important to recognise it exists, needs to be valued and protected by you. Your soul or your psyche are the mental abilities of a living being, reason, character, feeling, memory, perception, thinking, and depending on a philosophical system, can be mortal or immortal. Plato considered the psyche to be the essence of a person. He considered this essence to be incorporeal. The external occupant of our being and just in case you don't know what the word incorporeal means, the definition is 'not composed of matter, with no material existence'. I have come to my own conclusion outside of the philosophical and religious debate about the soul or the psyche. I believe it is the open curious internal dialogue, the voice inside, the one we start out with as young children, when discovering how to do things instinctively through private talk.

If this open, curious self-talk is subjected to the harsh nature of life trauma, such as abuse or neglect, control or insecurity, it can become shattered and buried deep inside, unable to be heard positively in an open way. The voice becomes the negative cruel critic instead. We talk to ourselves in silence unconsciously all the time, often distorted by the wishes of our unconscious ego self to be heard correctly. This inner talk at the beginning of life helps instruct our development and our thinking automatically. We are our language and through this speech we discover our own identity, concepts and meanings. We create our own world by problem solving and developing a social personality. Think about this inner voice at the start of life as a dynamic that shifts between words and thoughts, something that keeps moving because it is learning. Once we begin to use social talk, the stuff we learn from others, this dynamic takes on the role of what we learn from others and it loses its authority. In short, the authentic thoughts and inner voice we are born with, to help us be unique and individual, all changes when we are influenced and moulded by our environment and those who have control over what we do and think. It all gets contaminated.

At the core of each unique individual, there is a powerful creative energy. It is this energy that cuts through to find expression in the individual psyche, and Jung identified this energy as a rising from the collective unconscious, which contains the whole spiritual heritage of mankind's evolution. Obviously, this is a complicated subject matter but if you think about it in simple terms, it does make sense we would be born with a built-in set of self-regulating instincts and intuitions, and as we make mistakes, we would naturally learn to do what is right for us.

I am at this place right now and can tell you in all honesty my mind is free from everything. I am focused and curious for all that enters my mind instinctively through my feelings, senses and inner dialogue with my divine higher self. I have had things come to me naturally—inspiration, ideas, messages, things I would never have believed possible like miracles, the unexplained. I never doubt this anymore. I just have faith now, following only what feels right and it is never wrong.

When children are working alone on a problem-solving project, they must be allowed to talk to themselves to focus attention, be able to develop self-motivation and self-praise because this is how we learn to feel good about ourselves internally and how we develop self-esteem. When problem solving as children, we are constantly told how to do things; we never learn to do things our way. We end up never feeling self-motivated with little self-praise or self-worth developing inside. Basically, we develop self-doubt over developing confidence.

Cognitive development stems from independent exploration in which the child can construct knowledge of their own. They learn instinctively how to make the right choices, how to make mistakes, how to feel about their choices and then decide what is right or wrong for them instinctively. This is exactly what happened to me as a child. The environment in which a child grows up will without doubt have an influence on how and what they think, as they develop and mature into adults through attention, sensation, perception, and memory. We copy, we model, we learn, we become. The way in which an adult transmits information to a child is critical. The type of language used becomes a powerful tool for intellectual adaptation. The more a child engages in private speech, it acts as a tool to develop and facilitate cognitive process such as overcoming obstacles, thinking and conscious awareness. If this inner self-talk in a child is developing in a controlling or abusive environment and is subjected to mental or physical abuse, it can become a voice of negative destruction, creating depression, anxiety and unbearable unconscious pain later in life. This becomes a mental health problem when someone may not always be able to distinguish their own thoughts and feelings from reality because their natural learning curiosity and healthy development has been shattered. Even if we have not been abused or controlled as children, the way others communicate with us can influence our internal dialogue which can become distorted, often unnoticed. We learn to lie and make up stuff or change who we are to please others for our safety, gaining their approval. How many times have you done something you know to be wrong because that little voice inside has let you know, yet you have been unable to stop yourself doing it anyway? How many times have you lied to not hurt the feelings of someone you care about?

I understand there many psychological explanations for this self-talk and how we develop from children into adulthood, but I have my own theory about this voice. Like I said, I am convinced it is what we call our soul, our internal spirit guide.

Through the work I have done with talk therapy and damaged people, it is very clear to me to see why so many use alcohol and drugs to help block out the inner voice of self-destruction when painful memories become unbearable. The truth is because we are not taught to naturally listen to our own instincts and intuitions, we are not allowed to think for ourselves, we end up unable to self-regulate our behaviour in adulthood because we simply don't know how to do it. I guess this is where confidence came in and saved me. Although I had many traumatic experiences growing up, having enormous amounts of confidence and self-belief made me fearless, which allowed me to make mistakes then self-regulate, without the mistakes defining who I was. I had no one in charge of me, shouting at me, controlling me, telling me how to think or what to do to please them. I was a natural self-regulator. I learnt the hard way but at least it was my way. Of course, there is no right or wrong way to bring up children I hear you all saying. All we can do is our best. My point is, understanding what we are subjected to early on as learning empty vessels will ultimately dictate how we operate and handle life later down the road.

As we develop a stronger, more resilient character, devoting ourselves to the practice of listening to our authentic self, the good angel on our shoulder expressing love and unity in all we do, we begin to gain more strength, repelling all the negative, dirty, emotional energy away from our consciousness. To be able to change how we think to feel happier, more fulfilled and satisfied, we must understand that not everything we have been taught is necessarily the right way for us to develop as unique individuals. The very best recipe for self-reflection is to take a long, hard, honest look at your own character, then decide if what you are putting out in the world matches your authentic values or are you just being dragged along doing and thinking what others expect from you.

It was only when I was forced to face the car-crash life, my unauthentic fake persona created, I realised it was not me I wanted to kill but the person I had become in order to survive and fit in to a perceived environment. The aim of my unconscious ego was not for me to see things clearly and objectively but to be somebody. All my focus on the conscious attention of outward self-satisfaction became an obstacle to uncovering my true purpose and unique gift—the point and meaning to my life. I had completely ignored me, my soul self, my authentic self-talk, my instincts, my inner clarity, my super knowledgeable self, and continued through my life like a bull in a china shop, listening only to my ego to get what I thought I wanted. I tried to do the template life thing through peer pressure, listening to my biological clock, copying the rest to fit in but as you know, my drive and desire to be rich materially put an end to all that and for this today I am quietly grateful. Reaching the bottom surviving the crash was a real miracle for me, the best thing that ever happened. It made me finally grow up, face my old self to be able to uncover the real me, the person I am now proud of from the inside out. In this life, you can either be a host for your soul or a hostage to your unconscious ego. I was forced through horrific personal circumstances to make this choice which at the end of the day was the biggest miracle you could ever imagine. It changed me forever. I wanted to shed my old skin like a lizard and be free of it once and for all, to start again from scratch as a blank sheet of paper; that's exactly what happened after my unexpected near-death experience. I was so happy and grateful to be alive. I let all the other stuff go and began my journey to mindful thinking, just as you are about to do right now if you have the desire and the courage to take the plunge and jump in. You are lucky. You have not been forced to the bottom to recognise; if you do not change now, chances are you never will. Do you want to die never knowing who you truly are inside?

Whenever we are trapped in unhealthy thinking patterns, the negative bias, it becomes so tempting to hang onto these thoughts, giving them more power and strength than they deserve. This usually happens because we have become comfortable with feeling anxious and stressed. It is important to allow yourself to have negative thoughts now and again. It is normal but we must never let unhealthy thoughts run riot or get out of control, creating an invisible barrier to our daily reality. Sometimes your stress level created by your uncontrollable chaotic mind will lead to a numbness, like an out-of-body experience. You begin to feel disconnected from yourself, from your reality. This is when you are automatically going through your life without thinking or feeling anything real. Think about how many hours in the day go by before you realise your reality again. All the time spent zoning out instead of being present in your awareness. This happens because you are not being mindful of how you are feeling. You have become disconnected from your truth, if you look at how negative unconscious thoughts play out in self-judgement. When you over-eat something like a whole packet of biscuits, your false image of yourself feels bloated and fat; you know after the event how you feel but during the compulsive overeating, you are in fact zoning out. This negative feeling towards yourself of feeling fat comes via feelings of guilt and will go round and round in your subconscious mind, constantly reminding you how fat you are. This will then lead to more eating to soothe and comfort your failure to resist—another vicious cycle.

Your body, when you are healthy, happy and full, becomes satisfied. It lets you know you have eaten enough. Your mind is never satisfied if you are miserable. Subconsciously, it will always instruct you towards emotional comfort to make you feel better. It's not about feeling hungry. It's about fake pleasure. Mindful thinking allows us to avoid extreme levels of high and low moods, preventing us from suppressing or allowing them to rule our lives. It keeps us balanced in the present, the moment, the centre, always observing that our actions mirror our thoughts.

It is estimated by experts that seventy-five percent of us over-eat to satisfy our emotions. Certain foods will trigger cravings likened to self-medicating. As humans, we are only motivated by our feelings and sensations, so it is vital to be mindful how you feel if you want to stay on top of your negative habits. Negatively harmful destructive thoughts become very powerful when we engage and get entangled with them, mixing them with our emotional energy. Learning to take time out every single day to notice your thinking patterns and your negative feelings, especially those you go back to again and again, will help map out what triggers them and how you feel when this happens. You will begin to listen to the positive voice inside your mind again with more clarity, not blocking it out anymore, and with more work on yourself, you will begin to see this voice as your guide and not your enemy, something quite powerful and empowering when you get the hang of it. Have you ever thought about what this voice inside you head is or who it is? Think about it now. How many years have you been communicating with yourself and someone inside of you without ever questioning who it is? You may even begin to see now why you drink sometimes because you just don't want to listen to what it is telling you anymore, preferring to drown out the truth, escaping and pushing it further in the closet of your subconscious mind. You tell yourself you hate yourself. You are a failure. You are fat. No one likes you. You are stupid. You feel insecure. You turn to drinking. Your subconscious knows this negative self-talk always wants to be drowned out. It all just happens without any conscious participation from you. When this automatically happens, you then feel stressed, unloved, unhappy, and without keeping all these thoughts and feeling in check, they become mental torture inflicted back on the self. Once the escape, the comfort is over, there is still no resolution to the unresolved issues of the negative destructive thinking. Do you really want to be this person who always runs away from your uncontrollable chaotic mind?

Right from the beginning of your life, when your parents held you in their arms and fed you, your brain has been trained to associate food with comfort. It is hard wired in your subconscious. Remember the sweets the doctor gave you as a child to comfort or reward you? Your brain as a child was not developed enough to use the right words to deal with complex feelings, so using food to self-regulate your emotions is something we learn to do very early on to find comfort. When a desire or craving comes from something other than feelings of hunger, eating will never satisfy it. If you are eating but don't physically need the food, you are numbing yourself rather than dealing with your feelings. This is what causes stress, weakening your immune system. If you feel bad about eating a cream cake, this excess guilt may lead you to eat a box of cream cakes, destroying any pleasure you hoped to gain from eating the one cake in the first place, affecting your mood in a negative unstable way. This is a perfect way to use your journal. Writing down how you feel in the moment, seeing your emotions on paper in black and white, helps you to understand what is going on inside. It helps you to see the times when you are more likely to eat something other than when you are hungry. Always remember your strongest cravings hit you when you are at your weakest emotionally. You will turn to food subconsciously or unconsciously for comfort when faced with a stressful situation, a difficult situation or just when you are bored. Your emotions can become so tied to your eating habits, you automatically reach for comfort, a treat, when you feel stressed angry or unhappy, without even thinking about it. The food serves as a distraction whenever emotions drive you to overindulge. The result sadly is always the same, a temporary fix and not a solution. The emotions will always return. Your emotions are what trigger you to over-eat. You then beat yourself up, feeling like a failure. You fall off the weight loss wagon feeling so bad, you begin to over-eat again through the additional burden of guilt—the unhealthy vicious cycle. Instead of participating in this constant conflict the next time you fall off the weight loss wagon, forgive yourself and try again the next day. It is important to remember physical pain comes on gradually. Emotional hunger comes on instantly. It hits you and feels very overwhelming, leading you to mindless eating. Always be mindful whether you are eating in response to physical hunger or because you crave comfort. By just being mindful of this small area, how your emotions affect your eating behaviour, you get to understand how important it is to remain in the present on top of yourself, instead of zoning out automatically how you are really feeling. You are always a work in progress, remember.

As you begin to learn to breathe deeply, you will become more aware and present with the presence of the self. This focus through your guided breathing switches off your body sensation and your nervous system, allowing you to fully relax. Once your deep breathing meditation process is complete, you will find peace and calm, and this state of no worries, no thinking, no self-abuse, it is what they call serenity.

Being the master of your own selfish world is just not enough in truth, the main reason many people feel empty and lost. I can only talk to you about the soul, the psyche, the spirit from my own experience and perspective. The reality is just like science, no one knows for sure where we come from, how we evolved, or if we are the only living beings in the universe. It is all down to theory in the end. All I know for sure myself, we must face, feel and see what is hidden to overcome it, get beyond it, then transcend into a new compassionate way of healing, evolving, developing, maturing, growing upwards, reclaiming the authentic person we deserve to be. I have isolated myself for quite a few years to continue my own spiritual development after the process of taking full responsibility for my chaotic mind mess. I have fully accepted the death of my unconscious ego, my fake persona and today live an authentic—as much as I can—life, without regrets. I know how much damage the unconscious ego does to your soul. It destroys any heartfelt intention to do good, be good, feel good, it just keeps you believing that escaping your mind and your madness is the key to getting you through your life. What is broken inside can be mended, once you let go of the past, relinquish your unconscious ego, connect back with your heartfelt intuitions and begin to start thinking more, over letting your feelings lead the way in your choices and decisions.

I imagine my subconscious mind today like I imagine my soul. It knows everything, hears everything, understands everything, and I am responsible for setting it in the right direction, giving it what it needs to make me happy and successful, without doubt or fear. I am now fully engaged with what I believe to be my soul, my inner voice. The one voice I hear that fills me with love, protects me, makes me feel safe and guides me beyond what I see as reality. It has taken me a long time to hear this authentic voice in the silence of my mind, but it is there now, and it is this I believe to be a universal wish we all have inside to be loved, cared for and protected by something all-loving and all-powerful. I will repeat here again, I am not religious but like Freud, I believe the idea of God to be a regressive return to our childhood, the powerful all-loving protecting parent father figure and religion to be the universal neurosis of mankind. I am not sure what it is in terms of an explanation or what it looks like. It is just always there when I listen, when I am open. It is me, the real me, the honest loving whole me. I never have moods anymore. I never wake up feeling anything but ready, focused, engaged, curious and open to explore my purpose, my goals, my hopes and dreams, just like being a small child again with mature eyes of wisdom. Through the religious practice of an almost silent prayer—and by religious, I mean without fail, believing in the power of love for myself, cultivating my soul perspective in a spiritual direction—I connect to a powerful light and energy source. This energy source helps me to be more receptive to others and the universe. This powerful personal knowledge has stopped me hiding behind a false fantasy. It has healed my emotional wounds, creating a real stability in my assessment of what is important to me. Any inner healing is more likely to occur when we can use all the means at our disposal, therapy, talk therapy, spiritual connection, the psyche, the soul, the self, all that makes us whole. All we need to do is consciously have the courage to engage them all in a dialogue. The power that unites us all beyond the divisions of our perspectives and learnt beliefs is a knowing. Despite the fact we are all different, we all share something in common, a desire to mend our broken hearts and to live a life full of intention.

I am of the absolute understanding now; the soul is not something that comes from outside of us. It is a collective energy within us all and unites us all together if we are all working on the same page for the good of the planet, the universe and the whole of mankind. I found this peace, this powerful energy in the silence of my mind and connected back to it despite my own suffering. My near-death experience made me more open to listen beyond my unconscious ego voice. I handed myself over, waited for inspiration, and eventually, it came. As I began in meditation to confront the ultimate mystery of understanding myself, I realised I was way more than just a persona, a mask, a personality type, the person I knew myself to be. I became more curious entering into a dialogue, with my deeper sense of self, and this whole experience has been life-changing in terms of how I feel inside, how I think about myself, the world, the planet and my life to date. I am genuinely happy, fulfilled, driven, passionate and purposeful. I never waste time or energy questioning or doubting myself anymore. I just do what feels right and it works for me.

This personal journey for me becoming whole would not have been possible without learning to love myself before I began. Digging up the roots of all your negative thinking, the ugly side of yourself you don't recognise or wish to face, will require a true sense of self-love without judging or self-blaming. You know inside when you are being the unkind you, the selfish you, the unauthentic you. It makes you feel bad and uncomfortable. You cringe, then either face the pain or deny it with comfort through defence mechanisms like guilt or shame. These feelings of guilt and shame get trapped inside with the knowing, fermenting over time into dirty energy that is never released and never dealt with, which then manifests later into all kinds of negative fears, emotions and thoughts. Remember we are what we think. Through nurturing integrity, a universal core belief, you have nothing to fear thus you have nothing to hide. You do the right thing, so you have no feelings of guilt and this is common sense in my opinion. Building solid core values to replace your existing belief system, starting with integrity, the foundation to build an honest character, is the most important asset for your authentic self to begin to emerge. It represents your truth, your strength and your authenticity. The answer to all your life problems lies within you, not outside of you. The true version of who you really are comes from looking inside your heart with forgiveness and compassion until you can recognise this pain you feel does not belong to you. Recycling your old negative belief system, your emotional pain, the wounds, the scars, the false perspectives, the unconscious ego demands, that cruel inner critic, is what our whole journey together is all about. Hopefully, in the end, recycling your mind rubbish will help bring you closer to yourself, the real you behind your mask. You will finally find out what has caused you to want to be so destructive with your life and why you hate yourself for being the way you are. With time, dedication and practice, you will eventually begin to understand the person you hate and constantly want to destroy is not the real you but the person you have become. The real you is happy and productive, can do anything it wants to, can fly like a bird, sing like a songbird, swim the ocean, so open your eyes and see you must believe in yourself to manifest the power within. Behind the mask, the created persona holding you back, lives a miracle, the secret, the thing you are all looking for, so start looking today.

Life is about choices. If you have made all the wrong choices based on all the wrong information, passed on from others, it is potentially not your fault you have made all the wrong ones. Stop beating yourself up and give yourself a break from your unconscious ego. Let it go. Lighten up. There is way more to your life than misery and suffering. When you have more choices, you have more hope. More hope produces more positive reasons to wake up and do more things, rather than being stuck, waiting for someone else to sort it all out for you. None of us are the same, we all have unique DNA, unique fingerprints and we all have a different perspective on reality, yet we all follow each other when it comes to the meaning of life, looking outward for the answers to our problems. Poor mental health, and sadly this is what the sheep mentality is, clouds our awareness to inner power, leaving us crippled, consumed and preoccupied with our pain, disinterested in the idea we can work ourselves out. We have forgotten how to love ourselves because we no longer know ourselves. We are lost out at sea, unable to feel anything, numb and disconnected, not open to explore, forgive and move on to calmer, happier shores, beyond the violent choppy waters of our internal storms.

Learning to move on from your mistakes and false beliefs, once you have taken personal responsibility for them, you can begin the process of healing the pain, the shame and the anger, leaving you free to have a positive dialogue with your higher self. It is not as hard as you think to connect and talk with your higher self. The key is to always be open to loving yourself, then all the answers to all the questions you have will come to you naturally without constantly trying. Once you begin to understand what you are thinking and doing, all the stuff causing you to have your negative destructive bad habits, you will begin to see the fear and false beliefs you have been harbouring can no longer hurt you. They are just illusions created by your mind. People able to learn self-love know what they think, what they feel and what they want. They are more mindful of who they are and how they act.

The big downside for me, when I took personal responsibility for my own mistakes, I punished myself hard at the beginning before I realised it was this self-punishment in the end that made me become a stronger person. I had no idea how strong and steadfast I was when pushed against the indestructible wall of defeat. It quite shocked me and motivated me more to work harder on developing my strength of character. We must accept when learning to love ourselves, none of us are perfect, so practising the art of forgiveness is the only way to lead us to a better understanding of our chaotic minds. The biggest problem today with life in my opinion, people put more effort into building relationships with others than building a solid relationship with their selves. If you really think about it now, you have probably felt more love from others than you have ever felt from yourself, understanding this is a big eye-opener. Love is not a feeling because feelings change; it is a constant unconditional acceptance of self first.

I am on the journey every day to understanding more about myself. It is never a destination to be reached but a work in progress. If I never get there, I am not worried anymore. The travelling and wisdom gained along the way is amazing and so much better than standing still in ignorance. My advice is simple, learn to respect yourself and treat yourself like the other people you say you love in your life. If you cannot do this for yourself, the love you feel for others will never be the real deal. Understanding every day can never be perfect is the key to understanding balance. Love for others is the same. One day, we can feel love and be happy because the other person has done something right, the next day when they do something wrong, we can feel hate. Our feelings will always create turmoil until we have worked on ourselves and we know without doubt who we are and what we expect from ourselves. We have to have standards and boundaries that satisfy our own needs, never being tempted to cross the line to please others.

It will take great courage and true clarity to be able to see your true self emerge, once you knock down the wall erected to protect your persona, your unconscious ego; it has been with you for a long time. Self-loathing, hating yourself, is the worst pain any human being can feel, so why would you treat yourself this way when you would never treat someone you say you love this way? If you are willing to face this, you will gradually stop abandoning yourself. Any process of self-discovery will not happen overnight. Like I have said before, feelings change and your emotions are tricky to control but practice makes perfect. Are you ready to change?

Mastering mental health through awareness, this is what we are doing right now in this book; identifying triggers, learning how to deal with these triggers to change situations that cause the triggers in the first place, is the key to successfully preventing your repeated patterns. Mental health triggers are external things that happen to us, bringing stress, anxiety, irrational fears and negative self-talk. If you find yourself getting trapped in a mindset of negative thinking, it can feel like you are trapped in a prison cell, held captive by the constant inability to escape your bad thoughts. Being aware in the present, facing any situation that triggers mental health problems like stress, anxiety or fear, preparing for them in advance, can help you create better coping skills going forward. Always be prepared like they say in the Boy Scouts. This will include situations like being alone too much, being yelled at, bullied, judged, criticised, in family tension, so start to become aware of these triggers happening and be ready for how they will make you feel the moment they happen. To become free of our negativity, we must be aware of our thoughts by paying attention to what is going on in our minds at any time. Begin to visualise yourself as a curious observer, outside of your own mind madness, watching the same sad movie over and over with the same mistakes until you get sick of watching then recognise, if the character in the storyline did things in a different way, the outcome would be much happier. Once you can step outside of yourself and fully observe your negative thinking and behaviour patterns, you will soon realise you are somewhere in the past, consumed with guilt or fantasising about a future that isn't real. The problem with these two patterns of thinking, you are completely missing the magic of the present, the moment, the point. This positive move to observing yourself and changing your habits is all connected to your conscious thinking. What you must become aware of is your subconscious thinking. This is where the real problems you have live. It is never going to work in your favour, if you keep saying to yourself, I am a winner, I am going to rule the world, but deep down inside you struggle with feelings of failure and insecurity. Your subconscious mind will soon begin to remind you of past events where you have failed and any idea of being a winner immediately gets squashed. It is always better to see real change in your subconscious thinking by asking questions, not giving commands. This switch really helps when the negative voice inside your head throws negative accusations at you, like you will never be successful, or you are useless. As the observer, you must begin to fight back and challenge this by asking yourself questions, like why won't I ever be successful? Why am I a loser? Standing up for yourself through self-enquiry can truly help educate and train your brain to begin problem solving, shifting you away from fear, creating a positive spin on things with an open mind. If the negative subconscious seeds of doubt are constantly bombarded with questions, every time they surface, to pull you down or drag you under, eventually, you will overpower your existing beliefs and replace them with confidence.

Mindful thinking is the key to healthy eating. If your mind is full of rubbish, chances are you will eat rubbish, and with no self-control or self-respect, taking back control will be tough. You are already addicted. Like any other way to get your mind and body to communicate, we must slow down and understand how we work internally by listening to the signals we receive in our brain. I always go back to looking at eating when it comes to mindfulness. It is a very simple way to show how much we do to ourselves without thinking. Being mindful about how you eat and the way you eat is an amazing practice to help you begin to be more mindful of emotional triggers. I try and be mindful to always remember that my stomach is the size of the palm of my hand and if I am eating more than fits into this space, I am eating more than my body needs, which will eventually make me fat. It's common sense. I no longer use food for comfort or fixes; I have worked on my emotions and food now for me is about fuel and not always pleasure. There is a balance though. I sometime have the odd treat without the guilt, enjoying it without beating myself up. A simple way to help your body catch up with your brain when it comes to healthy eating is to try and be mindful to slowly chew every mouthful at least 25 times, putting your knife and fork down in-between. You will learn to get real pleasure from what you are eating and not the false comfort you crave when you mindlessly cram it all in. Rather than just eating mindlessly when you get emotional signals like loneliness, boredom or stress, listen out for your tummy grumbling instead, the body signal to the brain to let you know you are hungry for food, not comfort or fake pleasure. If you are living your life busy doing what you do, your body will let you know when your energy is low, and you need to eat something, so stop listening to your mind and be mindful to listen to your body instead. By understanding your emotional triggers, understanding your body sensations, you will begin to see you are not an empty void but a human being with a complex internal digestive system that constantly needs your care and attention, if you want to work properly. We will never get on top of our thinking until we get our bodies healthy and operating properly. Unless the right signals travel to the brain, we will be listening to and receiving all that is bad for us. The main reason we feel unhappy, unhealthy, depressed, constantly at the doctor, demanding a magic pill to make us feel better. Our ability to do, to think, to feel are all functions of our mind, the things we do consciously and unconsciously. As we learn to become more conscious of our actions through mindfulness, we begin to wake up and notice what we do automatically without thinking. If you are unable to find the incentive to practise mindfulness for better wellbeing and your negative thinking has made you physically unwell, scientists have discovered that mindfulness techniques can hugely improve physical health in many ways, including reducing stress, heart disease, blood pressure, chronic pain and insomnia. A healthy mind will always result in a healthy body. An unhealthy body is the road to early death.

In my work with the homeless and addicted, I use mindful meditation techniques, an important treatment for many problems including depression, drug, alcohol abuse, anxiety and OCD. It helps people face their problems, accept them, take personal responsibility for them, rather than blaming others through avoidance and the more work I do with the mind, the more I understand why people are stuck. If we think about the idea of self-regulation, for most this is a difficult concept. We are driven by our emotions, our social needs and ultimately our perceived pleasures, over our physical and mental health needs. Sticking to a plan of positive action to get back in control of our bad habits, to be healthy, takes more than just believing we will succeed; it's about acting with lower expectations, so if we fail, we are not too disappointed to try again.

Mass poverty has created a mass malaise when it comes to health and wellbeing today. Big brands have hijacked our happiness, gone head to head in a price battle and the consumer has been tricked into believing that what they are eating and drinking is good for them and will make them happy. The reality is for these brands to compete, they have compromised and then lied to the customer through marketing the ultimate dream—eat this burger and you will be happy, when in fact it is more likely you will be slowly poisoned. Did you know to remove an oil stain from a concrete floor, you can use Coca Cola? If you are having a coke now and again, this is not such an issue but if you are drinking two litres a day, imagine the state of your poor insides. It's no wonder you don't feel good anymore or function properly. In these kinds of situations when we are mindlessly driven by our habits, patterns and social pressure, mindfulness works because it is a state that is characterised by introspection, openness and reflection. An acceptance of oneself which means mindfulness is correlated with positive effect, life satisfaction and overall wellbeing.

Everyone is feeling some level of pain right now, no matter who we think we are or where we are going. We need to return to inner balance through being mindful, through breathing practice in meditation, to release mental anxiety before we all lose control and the planet dies. The older you get, the more inflexible you become, yet in the current environment, things seem to be changing, as young people become stuck in a rut, repeating habits learnt through mindless activities. When we are in a rut, we have in fact mindlessly outsourced our brain control and we are operating only on autopilot. The key to changing bad habits is to understand your brain is lazy; when it can, it will put your thoughts, emotions and behaviours into circuits below the surface, so they become automated habits then allow your brain to work on autopilot. Always remember to be mindful. Habits are hard to break; never beat yourself up when you relapse. We are what we repeatedly do, so imagine yourself as positive, not as an act but as a habit.

Fear Uncontrollable or Unavoidable?

Fear is closely related to, but should be distinguished from, emotional anxiety, which occurs because of threats perceived to be uncontrollable or unavoidable when we are faced with danger for real. In this book when I am taking about fear, I am talking about emotional fear, a chain reaction in the brain that begins from a stressful stimulus and ends in a chemical release, causing heart raising palpitations, erratic breathing and other symptoms known as the fight or flight response.

Everyone without exception experiences and handles fear in different ways. Each one of us has individual personalities. We are generally not afraid of the source of our fears but the sensation of fear itself, the irrational feelings that cause anxiety and stress. Avoiding unhealthy habits and behaviours that make us feel bad about ourselves, overindulging with food, shopping, drinking, unhealthy relationships, restricts the opportunity to be the authentic self, resulting in fear, anxiety and depression.

Almost every mental illness stems from a fear-based experience or problem from somewhere in the past. Our brains are very clever at searching for patterns. As human beings, we instinctively draw conclusions from our experiences. Feelings expressed through our emotions affect our thought patterns and our long-term habits, and many of us today in this current chaotic environment somehow manage to survive by blocking them out of awareness over facing and dealing with them head on.

Over time from childhood, our emotions and experiences gradually become our core set of beliefs and values. A set of accumulated ridged beliefs gained from our caretakers, our environment and our early learning. We copy, we model, we learn, we repeat. Our minds are constantly trying to make sense of our internal world, forming opinions and judgements about every situation or experience we face. Our core beliefs and values shape our perceptions. The way we chose to react to all of this dictates the course of our life experiences. Everything we do starts with one single thought. This thought then attracts other thoughts until we have a mind full of thoughts. This becomes our pattern thinking and then forms a habit. Think about lying in bed in the dark. You hear a noise. You automatically think it is an intruder. Your mind fills with other thoughts in panic—he has a gun, he's going to kill me, he's going to rob me, he's going to tie me up—all based on irrational fear in your imagination. It is good we are alert thinking about potential danger, this is natural but when irrational excessive overthinking floods the mind, it will drain your energy, preventing you from concentrating enough to accomplish a rational action in the moment. Having these racing thoughts becomes disturbing and frightening, creating a real sense of being out of control but you are not out of control, you are simply anxious and stressed. Racing thoughts, fast repetitive thought patterns and excessive overthinking are all common parts of anxiety and mental health problems, often a replay of something from the past or worries about something bad that might occur in the future.

Now think about your childhood, your parents telling you to stop doing something because it makes them angry. You think they don't love you. You think you have upset them. You fear they will punish you. This kind of pattern of excessive irrational thinking forms the habit of anticipated fear every time you get shouted at, which then gets applied to many different situations as a default setting throughout our lives. Our minds will usually worry about things it is convinced are true when often they are not at all. The mind likes to predict the worst possible scenario happening because we are set on the negative bias default based on our past experiences. Once again returning to the present, the moment, through your breathing and meditation, will start to help you to accept and then let go of what you cannot change, the past and the future, helping you concentrate on the now, for now. If through mindfulness we can exercise more choices, remain more centred over our unconscious irrational thinking through an internal selection of rational conscious non-fear-based thoughts, we manage better to get our thoughts back under control in the moment.

Fear is an unpleasant emotion caused by threat, danger, pain or harm. An emotional response induced by a perceived threat, which causes a change in organic function as well as in behaviour. It can lead us to hide, run away or freeze in our shoes. It can also come from confrontation or discovering something shocking like we have a fatal illness. Some people can get so overwhelmed by fear and avoid situations that might make them frightened or anxious. It is very hard to break this cycle. Once in fear, it is impossible to remain rational or objective. Unfortunately, whilst most of us control the fears we experience, not everyone is so lucky or successful. An inability to control fear can lead to paranoia and other serious mental health issues, resulting in mental misery and uncontrollable anxiety for the person suffering. I know this to be true. I have worked with and helped many people create ways to feel less fearful in the moment, so they can cope with life situations better, things which in the past have stopped then living a full life. The invisible enemy, the thing we know we feel for real but cannot rationally explain, like the anxiety created by fear, is a crime against our freedom. It keeps us stuck as a prisoner of the mind, unable to escape or rationalise why we are afraid. I think two of the most common fears I have come across in my work are the fear of failure and the fear of being judged by others. This I believe is because we live in such a brutal environment right now, where keeping up appearances has taken over from living a full abundant life. Our emotional response to fear is very personal. Some people thrive in fearful situations, others have a negative reaction and avoid them like the plague. Other fears such as fear of death, fear of flying, fear of success are all emotional anxieties, and these kinds of emotional fears transform into negative beliefs, leaving us avoiding situations, resulting in other unhealthy behaviours like OCD, Obsessive Compulsive Disorder.

I recently worked with a very successful person in his sixties. On the surface, he appeared strong, balanced, operating quite well through his daily life at the top of his profession, managing to hide his many deep-rooted insecurities and internal issues from his past. I knew he lacked confidence inside due to a childhood traumatic experience, which lasted for years and created the need in him to use fake confidence, his persona, to survive and hide behind in his successful working life. He often used alcohol in social situations to appear more confident and feel better about himself—they don't call it spirit for nothing—but take the drink away and I would find him paralysed by negative thoughts and fears, believing always something bad was going to happen. It was a real feeling, a real belief so powerful he would follow daily rituals to ensure his day run smoothly, without something bad happening along the way. He was always checking, always meticulously following the same routine and patterns without fail. This ritual of his pattern behaviour, a form of OCD thinking, believing if he followed his routines to the book, he would be safe, nothing would go wrong became his natural habit and something he based his every move on. He was a manic, depressive, often overwhelmed by fear, but he never allowed his feelings to overwhelm his rational thoughts, He never contemplated suicide; instead, he used alcohol to block it all out and help him get through his day. It took years for me to make him see the things he feared were not real, simply a reaction to repressed feelings in his unconscious mind, connected to a past event, a bad memory. I did this by making him confront his irrational fears one by one. The real things he needed to be afraid of like alcohol damage and other physical problems connected to his unhealthy lifestyle, he didn't even acknowledge. In his unconscious ego and fake persona state, he convinced himself he was invincible. You get to see here how an existing belief, based on a repressed experience from the past, can play out later in life without understanding why, in false fears, negative feelings, thoughts and behaviours. You can also see how the persona outside of the anxiety and fear, usually through alcohol and fake confidence, allowed him to hold down a demanding, successful job and somewhat normal family life.

As we did more work on these anxiety and irrational fear problems, we uncovered more of his self-loathing. His weak negative thinking came from being abused as a child by a stranger and no one believing him, including his own mother. This dark, damaging, uncomfortable experience in early childhood created internal fear and insecurities of never feeling good enough to be believed or loved. This deep-rooted painful experience through his unconscious ego and persona character learnt how to tell lies to please others, to be accepted, loved by his mother and compete with his sibling, who was always perceived as more loved by his parents in his eyes. I helped him face these negative OCD daily rituals by making him confront them, the very thing he was afraid of, until eventually he managed to let them go. Today he is more confident, drinking less, not always using food for comfort and likes himself for the first time in his life.

It was not easy. It took a lot of painful exposure for him, collecting the evidence through talking it out, going over the crime. In the end, it set him free. He finally realised it was not his fault but the fault of his abuser and his mother. Once he managed to forgive himself first for self-harming, then his mother—she had since passed away—he started to feel better about himself inside and the anxiety slowly lifted.

When everything we do is a lie because the person we have created to fit in and be accepted is not authentic but a shield to cover the battered damaged self, the child buried beneath the fake persona, blaming themselves in fear, we begin to understand how it is possible to experience anxiety and unconscious irrational fear, later in life. It happens when the inside is totally out of control, deep down afraid to speak out for fear of not being heard, becoming a people pleaser, going through daily rituals to prevent something terrible happening. All of this was triggered by his repressed unconscious beliefs, memories and negative associations from the past trauma of the rape event. In this kind of situation, it is not difficult to understand why the person suffering would turn to alcohol to suppress the problem further inside. A ticking time bomb always on the verge of exploding.

Anxiety tells lies. It tells you you're in danger when you are safe. By understanding this simple idea, we learn to see through it to gain freedom from it. Alcohol is s short-term way of medicating our emotional fears away. It helps us to ignore our problems in denial but if we don't deal with things compassionately, eventually they become magnified, causing further internal chaos. After we worked on my patient's fear and OCD habits, changing his beliefs through forgiveness and compassion, I began to tackle his drinking habits by getting him to become more self-aware of his feelings, outside the fear and anxiety. I encouraged him to ask himself as an observer of his habit, to look at the real reasons he wanted to drink to decide if it was triggered by over-excitement, influenced by others or if he used it to shut out his pain. The more he questioned his habit, the easier it became to control his drinking behaviour. The more he self-monitored, the more he realised he was now drinking because he was surrounded and influenced by other drinkers. He didn't need it anymore to self-medicate and it was a true revelation to recognise how many people he was surrounded by were addicted to alcohol. His fear was not a reality in his present life but a possibility in the future that may or may not happen. The drinking was a result felt in the base of his memories of the situation he faced in the past. His drinking was his coping mechanism. He managed to finally understand his irrational fears, so was then able to control them, recognising his anxiety was seeded in his bad experience as a child. By developing new triggers and skills, he managed to neutralise his fear, no longer dwelling on it or blocking it out with alcohol.

When people are in an anxiously depressive state and accumulation of racing, excessive, black and scary thoughts take over the mind, constantly there day and night, without any way to switch it all off, the thoughts become relentless, causing the overproduction of adrenaline. Anxiety is basically excess adrenaline and this needs to come out somehow. A usual route of escape is through irrational thoughts, where everything becomes magnified, extreme and very uncomfortable, often resulting in panic attacks. It is very clear without self-confidence, fear can cause severe deep feeling of failure, so when a situation occurs out of the blue like you find yourself under pressure because your rent is overdue and the bills are piling up, it can all get too much to bear in the moment. This accumulation of events, the excessive thinking happening too close together, compounded with the fear of failure and what others will think, courage goes out the window and thoughts of suicide can take over. This is the flash flood of emotions, the danger zone you must avoid at all cost because once you are overwhelmed, buried under a huge wave of fear and negative emotions, it becomes impossible to breathe, relax, or be rational; it's too late.

Once again becoming an objective observer, standing away from yourself and the behaviours you do automatically, based on your false beliefs, then questioning the motives behind them, helps you to see things from a more realistic perspective. If the bills are piling up, the tax man is coming to get you, your world is closing in on you, standing back from it all gives you time to breathe, then problem solve over letting anxiety and panic push you beyond your limits. Fear of failure, fear of being judged, fear of the unknown, fear of making a mistake all stem from what is going on in our subconscious or unconscious mind, depending on where we are in our lives. I am convinced emotional fear occurs simply because we are not living with life but living in our minds. Fear is always about what is going to happen, which often never does, and if fear is non-existent, then it lives only in our imagination. If you are lost in your imagination, this is the basis of your fear. If you are rooted in your reality, then there is no room for fear.

I guess we must decide when it comes to fear, this imaginary but very real feeling, whether we are living the experience of life or avoiding life, understanding it is not always about what could go wrong in the future but is planted by what is wrong from the past. Fear is not a product of life, it is a product of the mind, which is focusing on the past, ruining the future. You can plan tomorrow but you can never live in your tomorrow. Fear is a universal experience.

During our early stages of development as children, we are self-centred, our thinking is self-centred. We cannot distinguish what is objective or subjective, physical or psychic. All our experiences and emotions are inherited from our caretakers, our environments and our circumstances. Socially intelligent people know their own importance. They always work towards improving themselves. They have a mature ability to understand they are not the centre of the world without losing their self-importance. I believe this is what happened to me. I matured quickly, was self-confident, had to fend and find out for myself, becoming socially intelligent early on. I was open and receptive without the need to steal the opinions of others. Fear for me was never irrational, made up in my mind; it was always about assessing danger, using my instincts, remaining alert and watching my back. Growing up in a scary volatile environment with potential danger lurking around every corner, I became very controlled when faced with fear. I put myself in danger many times through being naïve, but my innate inner confidence always saved me. It allowed me to talk my way out of things without freezing or showing my hand. I was emotionally intelligent very early on, and although my childhood was unconventional, I matured well and became a seasoned survivor, something today I am truly grateful for.

A good understanding of emotional intelligence is knowing the differences you have from others around you. When you judge others to further your own opinions and ideas, it stops others sharing things with you. When we mature beyond the opinions and beliefs of our caretakers and other people, learning with respect to express our new core values and individual opinions, our own lives become healthy, productive and peaceful.

What is not real can never hurt you or cause you to ruin your life. Recognise it is the past that is now ruining your future, yet the past is over and gone. What is left with you is an unresolved problem, feeling or emotion repressed in the dark unconscious corridor of your mind. One of those nasty ghosts influencing how you think and feel. I will admit it is quite hard to be a fearless person when we live in such a scary world, especially for those who suffer with chronic anxiety. When we avoid something because we are afraid of it, we experience a sense of failure. Our anxiety gains strength. We lose strength and finally this avoidance makes it impossible to gain the courage and confidence to face what we are afraid of.

The most important part of the mind is the part we cannot see, the unconscious, which comprises of mental processes inaccessible to our consciousness but massively influences our judgements, feelings and behaviours. To be able to observe the unconscious mind at work, the main senses you experience through touch smell, sight and taste as they happen, you must stand back again and watch, identifying your own irrational fear by becoming more aware of it and staying present with it, you begin to put things into context. You begin to function normally over becoming paralysed.

Most therapy for irrational fear will involve like with my case study earlier, gradual increasing exposure to the individual's feared object, at the same time learning techniques to help reduce the anxiety, as a symptom. I am working more on tapping into the unconscious mind to help people overcome phobias, without causing too much trauma through mindful meditation and self-belief, observing the problem as an outsider, not as a victim. Just like the subconscious mind, the unconscious is not a black hole full of fear and pain working to undermine who we are. If it is cleared out and dealt with through humility and compassion, it can transform us into positive productive people. Fear, like any other emotion, is underpinned by physical signals in the body that are critical to the experience of fear, even though they are registered unconsciously.

We are not born with fears, they are learnt. We have acquired them through our life experiences. Just as we are capable of learning fear, we are also capable of unlearning fear, but first we must understand it and what caused it, to overcome it. Based on the people with irrational fear I have worked with, fear is generalised as a form of low self-esteem, often triggered by external factors that then create feelings of self-doubt. They doubt their own ability to complete a set task, let's say like asking someone out on a date. They will give up before they even try. They already believe they are a failure. The basis for this whole journey together is to get to understand low self-esteem and self-doubt are often reflections of how we have been treated as children, the crucial time when we are developing our character.

As children, our mind is the most impressionable. If we are subjected to abuse, criticism, control, or punishment, we end up developing feelings of inadequacy and insecurity. Later in life this translates into our fear, failures and subconscious doubts. A subconscious fear might arise because you have been rejected by your caregiver. This would then develop into a subconscious fear of anticipated rejection later in life; you would likely believe you are unworthy or not good enough to be loved. The key to overcoming this kind of irrational learnt fear is to reprogram your inappropriate fight-or-flight response. You do this, like in my case study, by slowly exposing and confronting the fears you have. There is no other way to do it, sadly. By observing any automatic reactions you have to situations or irrational thinking, attempting to not react impulsively, the subconscious mind can be trained how to respond to things, not react to them. I have noticed with people who seriously suffer from learnt irrational fear, they worry like crazy without having all the information or facts at hand. Their brain fills in the gaps from their imagination and before you know it, they are imagining things that have no hope of ever happening.

A really good way to distract you from your anxiety and worry is to interrupt it by suddenly doing something else, like walking into another part of the house. It takes an awful lot of your attention to think about fear, so if you can remove the attention, you can remove the feelings of fear. How you see your fear situation determines how you are likely to respond to it, so somehow try and reframe your fear and begin to prepare yourself in advance by using visualisation techniques. You can literally rewire your brain to overcome your fear. This I have done myself in meditation when on my deathbed, desperate and more afraid than you can possibly imagine. I had a clear picture in my mind of what I feared. By looking at it closely, I worked hard to reduce the emotional impact it was having on me in the moment. Like I have already said, I visualised it was the end for me. I gave in and watched my own body dead in a bed and as I did this, it became less threatening, less scary, almost producing the ultimate period of calm and comfort. Was this incredible experience for me, an out-of-body experience or a visualisation in my meditation? Who knows what really happened that night but whatever it was, it helped me wipe out my fear of dying, helping me to fully recover without any stress or anxiety.

Once we begin to understand our feelings, motives and decisions are all heavily influenced by our past experiences, stored in the unconscious part of our minds, we begin to see how all this potentially disturbing information could manifest into irrational fear and anxiety. Think about the case study raped by a stranger as a child, then disbelieved by his mother. This dark, disturbing, painful experience was buried in his unconscious mind, too threatening to consciously acknowledge, so he devised a set of defence mechanism such as repression and alcohol abuse to avoid facing his true feelings. It was his unconscious reaction to these thoughts that would start the repetitive obsessing, worrying about unrelated things in the past or panicking about something that may happen in the future. In truth, he never felt safe. It doesn't matter how bad your thoughts and fears are or how much you don't want to think about them, you just allow them and face them. This helps you understand they mean nothing. They don't define who you are; they are just irrational thoughts in your lying mind.

When you can fill your mind with only courageous thoughts, there is no room left for fear. As soon as you can hold the image of your fear within your focus, without giving it your emotional emphasis, you can begin to see for yourself how logically truthful it is, then confidently let go of unconsciously dwelling on it.

Carl Jung, my mentor, said, "What you resist, persists," and this in my mind sums up fear. There are so many different reasons for irrational fear, especially in this current environment, even some new forms of fear and anxiety, so I am going to shed some light on them now, so your own curiosity can be explored some more. Being curious and open-minded, away from the narrow-minded thinking you normally live with, allows for new ways of thinking and is helpful for problem solving. We all have instincts, shadows and drives, the common internal elements we all share that define us. Anxiety and fear are emotions filled with suffering, connected to insecurity and self-doubt, the feeling of living in a world that is not safe. When we look at fear and emotional fear, they both come from the same place, avoidance. We avoid a man with a gun because we fear he might shoot us. We avoid facing ourselves because we don't like and often fear what we might feel. Although we all share the same common internal elements, we all have different personalities based on our environment and our personal individual circumstances growing up.

If we look at fear in someone with post-traumatic stress disorder, like my case study who was abused as a child, the consequences of a prior situation in danger, the rape is relieved in the present, through emotional memories being triggered from the past. Although he knew intellectually he was safe, his brain automatically prepared for the worst to happen. To understand his fear versus his anxiety, he associated fear with the actual event of the abuse and the post-traumatic stress triggered his anxiety years later when he anticipated potential danger. Analysing the unconscious to uncover the root cause of his fear and anxiety making his unconscious conscious was extremely troublesome but by letting go of his resistance to the rape event, accepting it through self-compassion allowed him to finally be free of the event itself.

All our positive emotions come from love. All our negative emotions come from fear. So in my experience, there are only these two important universal emotions and we cannot feel both simultaneously, only one or the other. Anxiety or a phobic disorder exhibited as an unrealistic fear or dread, better known as OCD—a neurosis, a mild mental illness, involving symptoms of stress, anxiety and depression—is very common today. The unconscious part of the mind and how it processes thoughts is inaccessible to our conscious awareness or scrutiny. It is this part of the mind housing any traumatic memories or feelings, threatening anxiety, provoking and unacceptable to the person suffering. By being able to break my case study's pattern of resistance in his unconscious, stopping the desire to run towards worries or fears, he let it all go and replaced his old feelings with self-love and self-compassion. Getting this new focus in his life, no longer using all his energy to deal with the fear and anxiety of the past event, has allowed him to find new meaning, restoring his emotional balance. The best way to understand the difference between fear and anxiety is as follow: fear is a feeling of apprehension that sharpens the senses. Anxiety dulls and paralyses the senses.

Social anxiety, a fear of social situations and interactions with others for fear of being judged, which can lead to feelings of being self-conscious through self-scrutiny, is a huge contributor to depression in the world right now. There are some psychological manifestations that come with social anxiety, intense fear, blushing, heart racing, adrenaline rush, sweating, dry mouth, trembling causing intense anxiety that will not lift or go away in the moment. Although this social anxiety is the irrational self once again, for most people who suffer, it makes no sense to them. I believe social anxiety is all to do with the authentic self, the person under the made-up persona feeling desperate for release and unable to shine or be noticed for fear of being judged by others. When you don't know yourself, the real you, because you have no confidence in yourself, the psychological manifestations, the symptoms take over like a flash flood of emotion. Just like what happens before a person contemplates suicide. If we are always operating in a social situation through only learnt behaviours, never using our unique personality or instincts to connect with others naturally, we end up feeling nervous, uncomfortable, fake and unable to be ourselves. We don't authentically know who we are because we are made up in our minds. This is the reason we feel everyone is looking at us, judging us. We feel we are not good enough, not attractive or accomplished enough. We feel fake, nervous, anxious, sweaty, and just want the ground to open so we can crawl into a dark hole and hide away forever. Social anxiety is the fear of negatively being judged and evaluated in other people's eyes, automatically triggering feelings of self-consciousness with unbearable fear of humiliation or embarrassment. Think about it, if you are an imposter in your own life because you are afraid or don't know how to be yourself, you will always be on the edge, fearing someone will find you out in the end.

Once again, the most helpful thing you can do to overcome social anxiety is to face the social situation you fear. Avoidance keeps the anxiety going. Avoidance of any fear can truly prevent you doing many things like reaching your goals. No matter how awkward or nervous you feel, you can learn to silence those critical thoughts, boosting your self-esteem by being honest and true to who you are. If you don't know who you are, it's time to really think about this. It is not something that will just go away. It is going to plague you until you die. By learning new skills, slowly adopting a more positive outlook about yourself by believing in yourself, you can eventually overcome your fear to become more secure in your interaction with other people, without believing they are watching your every move.

There is no value in overanalysing your thoughts and feelings. The same as there is no value in overanalysing the intentions and actions of others. Learn to get busy focusing on what you are good at, love doing, and forget about everyone else for the time being.

The exact cause of social phobia is not really known. In my experience and research from talking to people with it, I believe once again it goes back to existing beliefs formed in childhood. If as a young child, you are constantly told off, shouted at for something you have done wrong but you have no idea what you've done wrong, whenever you are challenged in the future, instead of being able to look at it rationally, trusting your own instincts, you anticipate a telling off in fear. A straightforward way to explain this negative weak behaviour in confrontation, it is easier if the person in fear says what they think the other person wants to hear to avoid further confrontation and another telling off. You have heard the saying many times, anything for an easy life. It's the people-pleasing problem once again. When children become over compliant, often at the expense of their own wishes and needs, they will fall into the trap of pleasing their caregivers to avoid being controlled or shouted at. This false people pleasing behaviour in children often leaves them as they develop primary targets for bullies, magnets at the mercy of controlling, demanding people, which in turn leaves them with no way of having their own needs met. How children feel about themselves is the single greatest factor in determining their future happiness and wellbeing. Whether they see themselves as high value or whether they see themselves as worthless. When we have deep feelings of inadequacy, we feel inferior, we are self-conscious, embarrassed, feel humiliated, depressed, it feels like things will never be better but cognitive behaviour therapy practice, practice, practice, means we can gradually work on the problems that cause the anxiety in the real world.

When I look back at my own childhood, the emphasis from my mother and those around me in my early stages of development was all about making me feel good about myself, filling me with a true sense of self-confidence. It was this built-in confidence right from the start that made feel positive enough about me, to be willing to attempt challenging activities, make friends, be kind to others and never feel inferior or weak.

Controlling, bullying, demanding parental behaviour towards children, even if it is subtle and from a place of ignorance or denial, often without being consciously aware they are doing it, is not going to make the child feel valuable or safe. The way we are spoken to as children, the words chosen, will ultimately determine how we feel about ourselves as we develop into adults, whether we grow up confident or feeling worthless. It is a fact that small children, even before they can talk, understand what people around them are saying about them. The main reason the whole street where I grew up telling me I was amazing and beautiful, created unbreakable self-confidence in me as an adult. Pointing out negative traits to children in front of other people will produce people pleasers, liars and fantasists later in life. The children will grow up craving praise, starved of when young, and parent pleasers always end up people pleasers. If you grow up feeling worthless, inferior, controlled, bullied and you have little confidence, no social skills, no emotional intelligence and your natural instincts hopes and dreams are squashed, chances are you will develop some form of emotional anxiety. A life filled with unbearable fears like afraid of being rejected, abandoned, preoccupied by what others think, desperate for approval, editing your truth to be accepted and fit in, overachieving, is not what we call an easy life. There is never an easy life, it is always the trembling child trapped behind the fake persona making irrational choices. A rational, mature, centred person immediately stands up for themselves when facing confrontation in a situation they feel is unfair. It is at this stage to avoid future confrontation we start lying, where the lines between right and wrong becomes blurred and we say what the person shouting at us wants to hear, even when it is not the truth. This is the start of depression and anxiety as a symptom. Trust me, there is no such thing as an easy life until you connect back to the real you, the authentic you, the captain of your own ship. From now on, it must be your truth and your truth alone, regardless of what anyone else thinks, and to be honest, if they don't like what you say or what you stand for, why do you care at the end of the day? They are not worth it, are they? If you can imagine because you are afraid to be judged by others, your whole life is potentially a lie, made up to look bigger and better than you really are to impress or be accepted, it is not surprising in social situations your anxiety manifests into your emotional irrational fear. Then add into the mix a lack of confidence, a load of alcohol to keep it all going, it would not be long before this kind of pressure would potentially cause you severe depression and even thoughts of suicide. None of us want to be exposed as imposters in our own lives, do we? I bet all of you reading this right now have told lies or embellished the truth to manipulate a situation or another person into believing your own bullshit.

Social anxiety is the most stupid, ridiculous, pointless mental health condition possible. It is all based on the illusions we create to convince other people we are accomplished and successful, even when we are not. We unnecessarily set ourselves up to fail right from the get-go instead of being relaxed and totally honest about who we are and what we stand for, to me much more attractive and engaging than a fake and a liar. You only know what you know until you know something else. The truth is everyone today is living up to unrealistic expectation and fake beliefs, created by social media and big brand marketing to keep us all buying in. How we feel about ourselves based on what we have experienced in our childhood through our circumstances, traditions and parental care, defines our existing beliefs. If they have made us feel inferior, we will always be easily influenced by materialism and status. It really does not matter what anyone else thinks about you. We are all unique and fabulous regardless of what we have materially, what we look like or where we come from. No one is perfect. No one has the right to judge anyone else without checking themselves out for perfection first. Wisdom has way more value than good looks or material wealth, which can be taken away at any moment and should never be relied upon. An ugly personality will always destroy a beautiful face, so which would you prefer if you had the choice?

Marketing by big brands is the main reason young people today have lost their own identity. Wanting to be someone else because they look better, have more money, appearing to live a better life, is pointless. They are already taken so it can never happen anyway. All these anxieties can easily be treated by learning the triggers, overcoming the symptoms, helping the person suffering focus their attention on their reality, providing wider meaning to what they perceive to be real.

I am living proof it is not money that buys a life or makes you happy. I started out at the bottom, went to top, been back at the bottom and now back at the top, quite a unique position to be in, making me an expert in this matter. I did have a mild dose of social anxiety when I was rich. Keeping up with the Joneses is so much harder the more money you have. These days I rely only on my truth to impress and if others don't like me being real, then so be it; their loss, not mine. I am no longer anxious or fearful of what other people think about me. I am what I am. I do my best to contribute back, adding value to life whenever possible. I am no longer keeping up with the Joneses anymore; I am the Joneses and I expect people these days to keep up with me. I am no longer living in the wake of my mistakes, I have grown because of them. I would always remember this little quote below when feeling emotional fear. It reminded me what I feared was not real, just my imagination playing tricks with me. The thing you must understand to be the truth about your own fear.

False Evidence Appearing Real

I want to bring in another modern-day disorder here also contributing to many people feeling unhappy. They call it status anxiety; the desire in people to climb the social ladder and the anxieties that result from focusing on how one is perceived by others. Would you rather float in the ocean or flourish in a puddle?

When I was rich and had everything money could buy, I would always buy the biggest, most expensive but not always the best. For example, a big house next to another big house in a wealthy area, where looking the part was more important than what I really liked deep down inside. When I lost all my money and found the authentic me without worrying about what others thought, I picked a small rundown cottage set in the vast Leicestershire countryside, my own Gosford Park, and I still live there today. I can tell you for a fact, envy is an extremely toxic emotion, not a core belief. However high you set the bar with wealth, someone else will always outdo you. When I lost all my money in the 2000 stock market crash, I wanted to kill myself. Only briefly did this thought cross my mind but many people who lose great wealth go ahead and do it. Without it, they cannot imagine living. The money defines them. Although I could not imagine a happy life without the money, I had grown up without it as a child so losing it for me was not about the money, it was more about the fear and shame of what others would think. It was this social anxiety that really caused me to attempt suicide. I suddenly realised in my meditation and splendid isolation, working on myself after the crash, I could never be the person who fought so hard to escape poverty, then die a loser who greedily lost the lot gambling. This could not be the story on my headstone. The shame, the humiliation, the guilt, the anxiety, the painful unbearable overload of feelings in the moment caused me to malfunction and contemplate suicide. As you already know it didn't work and for this today, I am truly grateful. Now when I tell people my story of losing my money, being homeless, almost dying, they don't judge me, they are inspired by my honesty, my openness, my vulnerability. It makes me human and to be honest, without relying on credit cards, most of us are only a pay packet away from poverty ourselves. Status anxiety is the fear others will think less of you based on where you come from or what you have materially, but money does not make someone more valued, important, interesting or a good person. It just buys freedom and even that can become a curse. There is no shame in having less so why do we measure ourselves by someone else's standards? The fear of being judged, found out, the lying the status, the pretence can only get in the way of living a true life of abundance. Living in a box, doing what everyone else is doing, conforming to the unconscious ego driven template of life makes you a sheep, always steered to what you think you need to be happy. So how come most people, the masses, have ended up miserable, lost, addicted, in debt or depressed?

We have all been fed the wrong information through brand marketing, TV, the media, and it is this misinformation that's keeping us stuck in anxiety, unable to go against the grain for fear of being isolated, different from the pack. I have always wanted to stand out from the crowd, be unique, be different, and this is down to my unbreakable confidence. I am living proof; with it we can do anything we desire. To find your own value of success is the key. Comparing yourself to others for fear of not being good enough or not having enough material stuff is the greatest obstacle to your happiness and personal growth. What you have does not make you who you are. FACT. When I lost everything materially, it happened very quickly with no time to plan or make provisions for myself. Through this experience, I learned a great lesson. How to be humble and practise humility. When you are starving, you are forced to beg. This is not easy when in the past you have been greedy and ungrateful. You are naturally forced to surrender any pride you have. You mellow with age and experience. You stagnate and shrivel with envy. I guess you need to understand you have no control over what others think or do. All you can do is mind your own business. Other people's judgements only matter if you care about them. The fear of constantly being asked questions like what do you do? Where do you live? What car do you drive? They will always lead to snap judgement and decisions based on trivial information about who you are. It never tells the whole picture about what is truly important about you and, let's face it, most people lie about what they do anyway. If you believe for one second life feels good because you have more than those around you, you have lost your mind and your humility. There is nothing more unattractive than a snob. It is important to be clear what real success means to you. Make sure they are your ideas and not what you have been programmed to believe in your existing beliefs by your parents, the media or a celebrity magazine.

Gaining back control of yourself and your thinking is all down to how you talk to yourself through your inner dialogue. Never criticise yourself or put yourself down in front of others. We all make mistakes and remember none of us are perfect. Humility, like integrity, is a universal core belief, a modest and low view of self-importance, not thinking any less of you, just thinking of yourself less. As we go on this journey together, I am hoping to reinforce the idea of universal core values by encouraging people to replace existing beliefs with a whole new set of beliefs and for this to become a universal moral compass going forward. Humble people tend to have better social relationships with others, excel in leadership, are more forgiving, grateful and tend to be more generous with their time and money. I try and practise humility daily to constantly remind myself what I have failed at in the past, does not make me who I am today. Becoming a kind, well-adjusted, generous person has helped me flourish as a human being. It has become one of my core strengths.

When it comes to fear, our brain likes information it already knows and understands but doesn't like what it doesn't understand—the main reason it is hard to change embedded patterns and emotions. Staying on the long sometimes painful but exciting enlightening path to uncovering your true self and your purpose for being here, your true calling, will be the key to your true happiness, growth and internal peace. This is where becoming your own mind detective can truly transform your life. Once you have gathered all the evidence keeping you stuck, you have uncovered the crimes against yourself, you can start to solve the mystery behind your pain, improving the way you respond to it with more confidence. If your friends, family and loved ones truly care about you, they will want you to be happy, so be brave and let people know you are taking some time out alone to sort yourself out. Sometimes when you are brave enough to look danger directly in the eye, you realise what you are terrified of is nothing more than what you don't understand.

I believe the happier we are, the more content we are. The more content we are, the less we will allow fear and anxiety to dictate our thoughts, feelings and emotions. To have complete clarity when it comes to mastering happiness means understanding; if we have no idea what we really want, how can it ever be manifested? We won't even recognise it. It will pass us by like life. Most of us think we know what we want, usually more money, more stuff, less stress, more free time, but even if you had all these things in place, it would not guarantee your happiness. If you are unhappy with yourself, you will always be unhappy with your life.

Exposure talk therapy will help you to retrain your brain. It won't help you get used to the fear; it will retrain the signals and messages in the brain to stop sending a fear signal when there isn't any danger. In our brain, we have a small almond-shaped thing called our amygdala. This is what helps us to make our fight-or-flight decisions when faced with fear or danger, and it works quickly without us being conscious of it. It is an automatic programmed response. Obviously when we are in real danger, we need to act fast to survive and avoid the threat of death. Your amygdala learns by association, not reason or logic. It just helps you survive danger by quietly sitting back, observing and watching. It learns only from experience. If every time you have an anxiety attack and you run away from facing your fear, your amygdala learns how to trigger you to leave the situation to be safe. Basically, it models the same behaviour you give it. Each time you trigger a false signal of fear in your brain, you shrink your amygdala, your fear centre. This is the main reason you are unable to get back in control of your fight-or-flight response. To change this pattern, so it learns to do something new, you must retrain it by activating triggers through exposing yourself to fear. If you are afraid of lifts, you must expose your amygdala to going into lifts slowly in repetition until it develops a new memory, eventually overcoming anxiety every time you need to use a lift. Whenever we retrain the brain to think in a different way, it takes around nineteen days to break a habit, so don't expect miracles over night without doing the work. Doing the work will pay off and then real miracles will happen. Exposing you gently little by little to understand more about how you work—your fears, your pain, your anxiety, your depression, your emptiness—will help you to see most of it is pretty much learnt, not real. You really need to begin to believe this now and see it for yourself, so you can stop hiding behind the idea your problems are down to other people. You are in charge as an adult.

We all have built inside our brain natural triggers, helping us to operate and exist in the world if we are taking care of ourselves, not clogging ourselves up. Think about your brain like a house with an alarm wired in its foundations. When something alien interrupts and stimulates the alarm sensor, it makes a loud noise to warn you of imminent danger. You wouldn't turn this off or clog it up, would you, because you hate the noise it makes? Fear is part of your built-in alarm system and is normal. It pushes you to escape danger. Learning how to respond to it when anxiety, depression and stress take over, is much harder. The fear is not connected to your survival instinct but to an emotional reaction to something unknown when you anticipate something bad is going to happen. I totally understand when the imagined feeling of unknown fear takes over, outside of the normal survival instincts can feel very real, almost paralysing, to the point it creates further fear and anticipated anxiety, which becomes truly debilitating. The more afraid a person becomes, the more the fear becomes amplified in the mind and senses like if you were on a flight, the plane encounters light turbulence, you can believe the plane is about to crash. This is where mindfulness can really help. By learning to stay in the moment prevents you from automatically rushing off into what is going to happen in the future. You cannot panic in the present unless in real danger. Remember we are what we repeatedly do; excellence is not an act but a habit. Like your amygdala, learning to follow through to the end by imagining the worst-case scenario, as you sit on a fence and observe the outcome, understanding how you are feeling in that moment with that thought, will eventually retrain your brain to understand that your fear is not real. You will begin to see what you believed would happen does not happen at all. It was just anxiety and stress in your subconscious mind, ready to take you down as it automatically does. No amount of worrying, fretting, obsessing, panicking will stop something that's going to happen. This is life. Bad things happen.

What happened to you in your childhood, the way you were treated, the things you were told, the unresolved issues you harbour, have all helped to create and shape certain beliefs in your subconscious mind. Some of these thoughts may have empowered you, but it is more likely many are limiting you today. These subconscious beliefs in your mind will directly influence what happens to you in the future and determine the level of success you achieve in your life. It is so important now as an adult you begin to see your truth and recognise there is no one holding your head under water. You can pull it back up, breathe and walk away from everything that is taking you down. Just remember, the next time you feel scared will be down to an automatic reaction unless you are genuinely in imminent danger and your survival is at stake.

If your imagined fear, the emotional repressed feelings from the past, trigger the fight-or-flight response because somehow you have linked it to your internal pain when you are faced with what you fear, you automatically kick off your genuine survival mechanism. Think about this. You are short-circuiting your own built-in alarm system, creating an abnormal connection between your brain and your body. This is not good. You cannot distinguish between real fear and learnt irrational fear.

We have all experienced feelings deep down in the pit of the stomach, heard that little voice inside our heads telling us our dreams are impossible to achieve. Expanding your comfort zone during these strong gut feelings, to destroy the illusion of their importance, will begin to empower you to take steps towards more self-belief. Remember once again and reinforce your conscious mind, real fear is a response to an immediate threat like a lion coming for you at full speed. Anxiety on the other hand is a response to you anticipating threat or danger. It is an experience of uncertainty which occurs in a totally different part of the brain. I know it is easy for me to say all these things but learning to feel comfortable with change is critical to help you understand the things you fear don't really exist. It was only when I began to read from the experts about how my mind and body worked internally, I started to understand how much control I had over changing things. The next time you notice yourself in a familiar situation, where you normally trigger the habitual pattern of irrational fear, simply notice what is happening. Start to bring mindful awareness to the sensations in your body, your thoughts, remembering in every single present moment that you have the power to choose an alternative way to respond to events.

A solid, embedded in the ground, tree can stand alone, look up to the sky and last forever until its foundation is disrupted or it gets uprooted. You must find this strong stature within yourself, never letting anything or anyone cut you down or put you down. The biggest threat to your safety right now is you with your lifestyle choices, like smoking, alcohol abuse, drug abuse, junk food, stress and prescribed medication. These are all unnecessary dangers to our health and wellbeing, yet we all participate without consciously thinking or facing the idea of potential death and disease. There is an amazing Winston Churchill quote that says it all about human beings facing the truth.

"Men occasionally stumble over the truth but most of them pick themselves up and hurry off as if nothing ever happened."

There are three different ways we think. Either we are action driven—we do what we say and will do it without fear. Automatic thinkers—we go through the motions without thinking or we think via our imagination making it up as we go, or we don't think at all. Which kind of thinker describes you? Action thinking, driven without fear, describes me. If I say I am going to do something, I do it without fear or worry of what other people think. It is my life. It is the strength of your inner foundation, your character, your core values that dictate how you think, but it takes great courage to be honest with yourself and admit you have potentially let your morals slip.

In this current economic climate where funding for talk therapy is non-existent and social conditioning has created mass focus on the external self, rather than internal exploration, everyone is now left responsible for dealing with their own pain. In my opinion, what we need to do going forward as a society is to educate, to understand how simply we all work internally and how our emotions, feelings and conflicts cause us to doubt this miracle. It is a very complicated world we live in. We must learn to recognise emotions and feelings tend to ignite short-sighted impulsive reactions from deep-rooted unconscious insecurities. Understanding why you are in such misery, turmoil, depression and self-danger, is the beginning of understanding why you alone doing the work to change is the only way you will free yourself from the past.

To end this part of our journey, a very important part, we have established irrational fear is the main basis for our inability to evolve. We can hopefully see now that anxiety and fear can only thrive when we imagine the worst. Our imagination is all about projecting into the future so we can plan things ahead of time. But we cannot predict what may or may not happen. Misuse of your imagination will chronically increase your fear and anxiety, so learn to embrace fear as part of your life but not something that stops you living. Once we learn to choose love over fear, shifting our perception to higher thinking, through our new set of core moral values, we can begin to clear and dissolve the painful emotional triggers keeping us trapped and consciously participate in the process of maturing.

The price we pay for being a conscious human being is understanding things change. We all know we will die but we have no idea when or how. It is just the way life is constructed. Therefore, the truth is simple. We will never be safe. Once you begin to trust yourself through practising mindful meditation, you will see for yourself for the first time how much of your negative behaviour is motivated by your irrational fear.

Your Life Purpose

The need for your purpose is the defining characteristic of any human being. We all crave purpose. We intuitively know we want it and can suffer serious psychological problems when we don't have it. Purpose is a fundamental element of a fulfilling life.

Long before I found my own purpose, before I made all my mistakes and had my near-death experience, I always knew I wanted to be rich, successful and powerful. I realise now why the mountain I was climbing to success was, in fact, the wrong mountain to begin with. It was an escape from me; I was doing it for all the wrong reasons. Drive, ambition and determination are all amazing qualities to have when it comes to creating material wealth, what we think we need to be somebody worthy and accomplished. For me, I was left empty, unhappy, unfulfilled with zero spiritual development. I have been lucky enough to get a second chance at living my life. The life I deserve and since my crash, worked hard to create. The insight I gained through my life experience I now want to share with the rest of the world. This has become my purpose.

Living with a fast-paced, impatient, focused, fanatical mindset, permanently fixated on all the wrong things, in the past left me with a limited ability to travel and advance to a higher level of thinking. I had self-belief without question. I had work ethic. I had unbreakable confidence. I was thinker. I even had guts. But I had no real idea about who I was deep down inside. No thought ever went into anything other than a compulsive driven mindset. I was going to survive against all the odds. I believe this drive, this mindset to be my truth. I wanted to create the life I believed would make me happy but the life I created never really belonged to the authentic me. It was a life designed and structured around my survival as a young child. Losing all my self-made wealth, status and almost my precious life pushed me to a spiritual awakening, an altered state of perception, a knowing beyond knowledge. It allowed me to be open to examine my existing beliefs, let go of the past and take better care of myself spiritually. It is quite hard for me to define what this awakening was. I have never been religious or spiritual in any way. I just instinctively knew getting another shot at life was a huge gift I could not ignore. Once I separated my old ego self from my conscious mind, handed myself over to doing good work during my recovery, gave up all my addictions and distractions, I began to focus only on nurturing healthy patterns and disciplines. This is what happens naturally when you truly value your life.

My life today and life itself, I know now is a true gift, and purpose is somewhere embedded in this idea, hidden somewhere inside all of us. To gain access to it, we need to climb to a higher place spiritually, the not-so-easy bit. A simple way to think about this kind of empowering self-development is to imagine your challenge in life to reach a higher level is like playing a computer game, where your goal is to role-play as a superhero through increasingly difficult tasks. You must learn to play the game of life by beating the odds before it ends and time runs out. A game of life where you decide who the winner is, not your circumstances, past experiences or negative mindset.

Recognising consciousness is always awake and infinite in its potential, allowed me to reach a true state of realisation beyond my unconscious ego. I was grateful to be alive. Enlightenment and growth for me happened instantly. We all have own specific unique calling. The greater purpose is to share knowledge with everyone else to keep it alive. Knowledge will never limit or deceive you. It is a universal truth and can be relied upon in times of personal turmoil like where you may be right now in your own life.

Your purpose with me is to prepare yourself for a greater understanding of the world you live in, so you can begin to decide, then learn how to change the negative thinking keeping you stuck into mindful thinking that one day will set you free. Once your life is fulfilled, it becomes justified. The world does not seem such a difficult place to exist in. Life is not about punishment and pain; it is about pleasure and personal empowerment, the two vital ingredients eluding you right now in your depression or misery. Your purpose is never to escape this world but to understand why you have come into it, and it all begins with the preparation of small milestones in your personal development, like learning to breathe, the mindfulness and the meditation.

I have learnt through my own personal development, and remember, I felt lost like you do, once upon a time. We are all here for a specific purpose: to contribute and make the world a better place to live in. We are not here for our perceived reasons. We cannot rely on those, can we? They change. I promise you, with a greater awareness will come an even greater ability to cope. Greater knowledge and wisdom will take you into fresh territory, beyond your old boundaries and assumptions. It will give you a brand-new way to look at things from a better place of understanding. How can you understand what a Frenchman is trying to tell you if you cannot speak French? The truth is you cannot. So, if you want to live in France, you must learn to speak the language to thrive and survive. Without preparation, you will never achieve anything substantial or life-changing. This is a fact. I understand how hard it is for you to motivate yourself in preparation for substantial changes when all hope is lost, everything seems pointless because you are consumed with fear. Remember, the concerns are real but the fear is not. You need to begin to develop longer-term goals, even if these goals just get you through until tomorrow. Preparation means you must start somewhere, the beginning, so your first step is to prepare you for freedom from your mind.

A journey of self-discovery with determination to prepare to discover your true purpose in life and why your life matters is going to take enormous amounts of self-honesty, something you are not open to right now but will come with preparation. Understanding self-honesty takes you acknowledging both the good and the bad in your life, admitting when you have made mistakes, finding time to reflect not react. You must learn to pay more attention to your feelings through ultimately practising integrity without doubt. Honesty is the only route to your internal peace of mind, which will fulfil a real sense of justice within you. This then means other people will begin to respect and listen to you because you learn to choose your words carefully as you command respect through integrity.

I have learnt through greater knowledge to have compassion, humility, grace, to be open to others who have different ideas from me. I have learnt to be non-judgemental when confronted by things I don't understand or want to tolerate because I think I know better. The truth is none of us know anything really. I now look to nature for my inspiration. The beauty and power of how it all works perfectly leaves me astounded and in awe. I look at the complex way fruits and vegetable need soil to grow, the soil needs water for the fruit to flourish, and we need water and vegetables to stay alive. This makes me feel like I am part of something whole, something bigger than me. I have dissolved the illusion I am separate from the universe. I have also realised since my awakening, just how limited my thinking was back then. Once you recognise you are part of something greater than you, you suddenly wake up. This profound experience of finding clarity within offered me a clearer understanding of what is real and what is an illusion. I began to let go of the old fake me, the person I believed I was without even blinking an eye as soon as I realised the person I truly wanted to be, was nothing like the person I portrayed. Today, I am very different person. I mirror image my thoughts with my actions, my ethics and my heart.

Life is a journey, never a destination. I want to reinforce in you no matter how long you prepare for and practise mindful thinking, you will never get there. Learning and growing never stops. It just keeps getting better and better until you are prepared to give yourself over to help other people and the world. Once you manage to let go. When you stop worrying and obsessing about yourself, you will begin to forget about your own worries, then embrace the world from a different perspective. Once you manage this, you start to feel whole and purposeful in the bigger picture and you start to belong, rather than believing you are lost at sea alone without a lifeboat. Today, I always focus on a long, straight, narrow road with no end. I call this my determination satnav set in stone, with only one instructional voice inside my head, advising me to keep moving, never tempted into thinking I know better, veering off on to dead-end roads. Although these side roads always appear inviting, when the long road seems endless and pointless, when your patience runs out and you feel like you are not getting anywhere but believe me, every time you veer off, it will be that dead end you eventually face and return from, always on the back foot. You must keep going no matter what, in times of both happiness and despair. You are here for a reason, so accept your journey will be amazing. With this dedicated mindset and hard work, you will begin to bypass all that made no sense to you, revealing all that is meaningful and permanent. You will start to see the truth about what your life really has to offer, outside of the box.

Right now, you have been following your destructive satnav down one of those side roads, ending up at a dead end. Literally, you have become afraid of your own reality and stepped closer into a fantasy world. You must now learn with honesty and trigger when you recognise this happening, to immediately turn around and change direction, back on the straight and narrow, to get your determination satnav back on track and continue your journey. I am well on my way now on the journey of knowledge through self-determination, discovering inner power and wisdom through self-study, daily practices in preparation for my work and contribution back to the world. I knew I had to write something real and passionate about what I have learnt on my own life journey, so I could pass it on, helping others without hope and nowhere to turn get in touch with their own reality and purpose. Once you hit upon the secret to working yourself out because you have suffered, learnt something new yourself, dropped your ego in exchange for telling the world your truth, you genuinely strive to spread the word. When you hit rock bottom and you have nowhere else to turn, understanding where to turn is crucial. It stops the feeling of hopelessness in the moment. It leads you inward to find the authentic answer to the reasons your life matters, beyond the cruel world where the illusions you believed have let you down.

As we learn and explore together the layers in your mind, how it all works internally, we will clarify what the purpose of identifying its functions are, the first one being your unconscious ego. This first layer is the one that helps create all your false perceptions and pretty much controls how you think, without realising it. Our mind influences all our main senses and helps us to see the external world through these senses. It then uses this information to form a conceptual understanding to accurately determine the reality or circumstances of a situation. As we begin to understand why it is important to train the mind to be free from the negative unconscious ego, to stop it controlling our lives through negative impulses and uncontrollable reactions, we find freedom from letting it go. Once we identify the unconscious ego is the reason for our dark, impulsive, ignorant reactions to our thoughts and often our confusion inside, we break free from its power over us through increased self-awareness. We can suddenly and confidently stop hiding behind it. When I talk about the unconscious ego, I am talking about something we are not consciously aware of but something we use to appear more confident. We rarely feel safe in life and it may not always be obvious, we are protecting ourselves from getting our feelings hurt. This is called self-protection, our defence when we perceive we are being mentally attacked and need to defend ourselves. This is your unconscious ego's primary job and often this built-in self-protection strategy can be way more powerful than even the truth. Your unconscious ego has encouraged you to lose touch with your authentic self. It is a defence tactic which means we don't really know ourselves and when we don't know ourselves, it leaves us unaware of what we are projecting.

Any defence self-protection strategy makes it almost impossible to deal with or reach our deeper feelings, those repressed in the unconscious that menacingly influence all we do and think. The main reason we are not conscious of these repressed memories, feelings, situations influencing our behaviour is because part of the memory is suppression itself. Returning to awareness will come from the regular practice of your meditation, finally making what is unconscious, conscious again. For us to deal with our internal conflict, the unconscious ego will employ a range of defensive mechanisms, operating at an unconscious level, to help ward off unpleasant feelings and emotions, like anxiety, fear, stress, anger and so on. Repression is the primary way the unconscious ego protects itself in childhood. Distressing, painful, uncomfortable feelings and memories are always kept from your consciousness. Unfortunately, these feelings and memories can be triggered and surface in adulthood when the psyche is ready to handle them better. The main problem with defence mechanisms, basically your denial, the uncomfortable thoughts and unpleasant feelings don't just go away— remember Jung here, 'what you resist, persists'—they intensify and unconsciously continue to influence your decision-making process.

The developing brain in childhood can take a knock through adversity. This then becomes long-lasting emotional and psychological spiritual damage following us into adulthood, unconsciously impacting all our choices. For us to heal these knocks that have becomes our internal wounds, even if we believe we have had a normal childhood, we have all experienced some level of adversity trauma or mental distress, we must be open to revisit it so our inner wounded child can share these feelings with a wiser more mature listening self. This allows us to understand openly and honestly with compassion, we are not to blame. We are good enough. We are safe. We can be loved and finally be in control of how we feel.

The purpose of your mind is not to be controlled by negative ego entities, planted by past circumstances and experiences, it is to understand the bigger perception of your true reality, behind all your false fears, anxiety and depression you live with without question. The true nature of the real you behind your consciousness. All the made-up rubbish currently controlling your life is not found anywhere within your internal soul self, the part of you that takes you to your heartfelt feelings. It is only found in your lying mind. When we live life as our false self, it is an ego defence designed to protect the true self. We are often working from a place of anger, pride, intolerance, self-denial, materialism or blame, stirring up drama, living in the past. When we begin to live life as our true self—our mature, authentic, honest self—we work from a place of self-acceptance with sympathy, wisdom, peace and gratitude. We begin the accept things, situations, circumstances, taking personal responsibility through focusing on living only in the present.

It is important to understand, once the unconscious ego gets too attached to the persona, the false self, we lose all sight of who we really are, taking on various roles, acting in a pre-determined way according to what is expected of us, rather than how we truly want to live our lives. I don't think anyone really understands how hard it is to act like everything is OK on the outside, always being strong, rose-tinting the truth, when in reality on the inside we are on the edge of a cliff ready to jump. Once we give up our individual original self in favour of the persona, basically we become part of the template, we believe we will no longer feel anxious and alone anymore, but it comes with a huge price. We lose who we really are inside. If you want to live the life you dream of having, deal with the inside of yourself first. It will then manifest in the outside world. Recognise you are wasting precious time holding on to things preventing you from discovering your true purpose. Once you learn to focus your thoughts on what you truly want, resisting all temptation to seek comfort when at first you don't succeed, creating this space in your mind will allow you to receive what you need. Basically, only tell your subconscious the things you want to come true. Your only responsibility is to love yourself, be yourself and know you are good enough, making sure the game of life is structured in your favour. Trust me there is no greater agony than holding onto the pain you harbour inside. Getting your untold story out on the table or into a journal means you are a blank page, ready to write your real story.

After years of pretending to be something you are not to please other people and not yourself, various negative unhealthy symptoms like depression, anxiety lack of meaning, even physical problems will manifest. This is where I found myself during my different stages of psychological development. Uncovering my true self behind my unconscious ego, the trapped, unhappy, wounded child within, allowed my true self to shine beyond the mask, without the need to feel insecure, ashamed or empty. I finally stripped away all the layers, exposing my soul-self for the world to see, without fear. This is what happens when you reach the bottom and you have no choice. It was an amazing experience which today I am truly grateful happened.

Once again, I will repeat, I am in no way religious. Religion is to believe in and worship a superhuman power, a personal God or Gods, which for me is difficult to define because it is not a one size fits all model. It means something different to many people. I always come to the same conclusion when I look at different religions, how they often end up causing conflict. Although they all pretty much follow the same message, 'my God is better than your God' gets in the way. The message gets lost in this conflict. Religion is a very complex human phenomenon, part of the human condition used in ritual prayer, faith and belief. A supernatural interaction with God or Gods will happen in the hope of salvation and guidance and are all unique. I am of the idea that prayer, regardless of whom or what you believe you are communicating with, is a good thing and will continue to exist until the fundamental problems troubling humankind are treated. We all need someone to listen to us without judgement in times of trouble. We all need a chance to face our demons steering us to the repeated cycles of trauma, stress, anxiety or depression. It is true for someone living with a troubled mind, the idea of God could be used as a psychiatrist, just like a priest where in prayer the person suffering can privately offload their problems. Can there ever be a practised religion where the believers don't believe they are practising a religion? I guess the Muslim community would call their religion a way of life. Buddhists would say theirs is a practised philosophy. Christians may call it a relationship but whatever it is, the word religion itself conjures up preconceived taught ideas I cannot personally buy into myself. My only religion today is doing something good religiously whilst I am on this earth to feel better and improve my life, always grateful, humble and useful.

Spirituality is the quality of being concerned with the human spirit or soul, as opposed to something material or physical. Again, like religion, it is a context with room for many perspectives like searching for the meaning of life, a personal relationship with the higher self. There is no single definition of the word spirituality. Its meaning has evolved over time. In my mind, I prefer to think of myself as a teacher of life. I have resolved my own mental health issues through my own experience and not from listening to someone else. When I was drinking, smoking, drug taking, shopping, eating meat and not practising any disciplined mindful thinking or taking care of my finely tuned machine—my body, my health—I was too clogged up and detached to feel any connection back to myself. I had no connection to anything deep and meaningful beyond what I believed I wanted to make me happy and be accepted by others. I had some good core beliefs and values, but it was difficult to bring them into practice, when making money and success was my only goal. Spirituality for me has been a boundaryless dimension of my own human experience, influencing me on a deep level, changing rapidly the way I thought about things and encouraging me to behave in a way that has become useful to others, the world and my purpose. This unfamiliar territory of vast endless possibilities has allowed me to extend myself and grow after a deeply personal experience with tragedy and near death. None of us have any idea what is awaiting around the corner. Praying for money, a miracle hoping one day everything will just fall into place is not going to happen. All the luck in the world will not change how you feel inside. This will only come from you recognising you are not invincible and never free from danger.

I told you in my own story at the start of this journey how I had seen myself outside of my own body in a flash before my eyes. This proves to me something does exist beyond human understanding. Who knows if this experience was real, my unusual event on the brink of death? It could have been a dream, a hallucination, but I am more convinced it really happened, the more I grow and continue my spiritual journey towards higher thinking. Whatever happened back then forced me to become a blank piece of paper today, ready to start a new life. To arrive at this place of spiritual maturity, the place where you accept full responsibility for all your mistakes, you learn who you really are by facing the darkness, then committing to grow beyond your pain.

I was forced to accept my circumstances and trust me my situation was more dire than anything you could imagine. I had to stop the blame game and look at my mess, hold my hands up and accept that I created it all myself. When you realise you have completely lost control of your own life, ending up dying alone in a hospital bed, after losing all your money and status, surrender is your only option. It was at this time I realised just how irrational fear can be. Although I was being told very clearly that night back in LA I was dying, it did not immediately sink in. My very first major concern after the flash flood of unbearable emotions and fear of death, I was more afraid of having the blood of a total stranger pumped into my body. All I could focus on was contracting HIV. It is amazing to think now, the doctor telling me I would die without a blood transfusion, yet the idea of dying from HIV was more fearful than the idea of impending death for real. This is just how irrational the mind can be when it comes to the idea of fear. The doctor in that hospital that night was brutal. He told me there was no time for irrational fears. I needed blood immediately, and although there was a risk of HIV, there was no choice in the matter, so I closed my eyes and prayed. And this, my friends, is what real fear feels like. It was at this point I realised there is no safety to be found in anything physical. The only safety we have is in a connection to the soul self. Everything else is just an illusion.

They told me later that night my body had rejected the first transfusion for some reason, and this kind of blood rejection I have since discovered is quite rare, so I am grateful and lucky to be alive today. It turned out after all the panic and pain I had an eight-pound fibroid in my uterus. I had been bleeding for almost a year. My blood count was low, so low my heart had given up on me. I had pretty much bled to death. It is hard for me to understand today how back then I could have let things escalate, but trust me, when you have no money, no medical insurance and your whole life has just fallen to bits, subconsciously dropping dead is not such a bad thing in the bigger scheme of things.

During the next few weeks before I was evicted and moved to the homeless shelter, I was bedridden, weak and can honestly say I didn't feel like me anymore. The idea of having the blood of someone else running through my veins was a truly scary, unnatural concept. The intense fear of being taken over by a stranger in my own body was horrific. The best way to describe how I felt is a bit like, if you can imagine, waking up from a deep coma. You have no idea where you are, who you are or how you got there. You are just there inside a body looking out from behind a pair of eyes.

I lived by the ocean and my windows were always open. Often during that time, the room filled with a powerful smell of violets so overpowering, it made me feel sick. To this day, I cannot really explain what happened to me back then, but once I got home to the UK and the NHS saved my life, putting me back together, I decided not to see it as an unexplained phenomenon but as a miracle. I never find myself going back there. Today the past is truly wiped from my mind, resolved and finished with, almost like it never happened. The reason why I know letting go and surrendering is the key to your own freedom.

One of the most amazing and fulfilling things I did, once recovered, was to volunteer my services in Oxfam two days a week, which got me out of the house and my small world, back into a bigger, wider community. I began to really enjoy this slow move back into the world of work after being isolated for so long through ill health. It encouraged me to join in, feel valued once again and be part of something good and purposeful. This was such an empowering feeling after my brush with death. The action of doing something meaningful got me results.

It made me realise I wanted to do something good to help save those less fortunate than me. It gave me hope, a brand-new perspective on my own situation, outside the isolation felt during my recovery. They say in all those self-help books, once you find your true purpose, your whole world changes. Everything becomes clear and aligns perfectly. I am living proof this is true having had the experience for real myself. My advice for you because you haven't had this experience, when you read about purpose it will be hard to imagine, so don't wait until it's too late and your depression and misery has taken you down, go for it today. Do something to change things now.

You will find once you switch from listening to your mind, your heart is the place you access and discover your true passion and purpose. When you are fully in tune with your happy self, inspiration flows from your heart and soul. You will naturally become more joyful both inside and outside of yourself. Today I have discovered I have many passions in my life. So many new things to keep me excited. Never get bogged down or lost by thinking you will never find your own purpose. It could be many things you become passionate about, as you begin to explore unfamiliar territory, outside of your comfort zone, the place you believe you are safe, but in truth you are stuck. I love doing good simply because it makes me feel good and when I feel good, I produce my own happy endorphins, something you will never enjoy if you are clogged up and closed off, alone in a bubble. Before you go to the idea in your mind that I am a born-again, reformed, goody two-shoes, retired from what is perceived as a good time, think again. I am more alive today than you could ever imagine, open to everything, closed off to nothing. I let things happen naturally without interfering or conning myself anymore. It's a hard dream to sell to others. People are pre-conditioned into believing that getting drunk or high, broke, in debt, aspirational, desperate for a boob job, consumed with consuming, are all the things that guarantee happiness. You only need to look at how many people are suffering in silence right now to see the reality. I don't sell it, I live it, and trust me, I am not boring or bored, showing off or preaching any gospel. I am building an empire working towards my goal, creating something powerful and useful to change the world. A long list of things that make me happy, beyond the idea of money and greed.

I am a free life coach these days. My degree in life gives me the insight to help others find what makes them happy and fulfilled, especially those who have given up on life. I am a talk therapist and modern-day mind detective having studied my own mind and the minds of others, using my life-changing experience combined with the theories of Jung and Freud. I am hopefully proving what they left behind, their life purpose, truly works in practice. I am a businesswoman once again and make my money from an ethical fashion business supporting made in England manufacturing, my passion to bring British back. I have left capitalism behind me where it belongs. I have learnt money is no use if it is not a shared experience for us all to enjoy. I support charity shopping and buy all my designer clothes second hand. This keeps me focused on looking good, doing good, saving the planet and saving money for more important things, like helping others in need. I practise yoga and meditate daily, plus I find the time to have a brisk walk, keeping me healthy and on top of myself physically, focused and positive mentally. I meditate and practise mindful thinking outside in nature. The world always seems calmer when you walk with the elements. Finding things that make you truly happy, filling up your time to be productive, develops happiness. When you are productive, you get things achieved, making you feel worthy and empowered, not depressed or hopeless. It is all well and good to stay in bed all day looking at social media, magazines, watching movies, believing you have a full exciting life in your imagination, but this is not reality. You must help yourself every day by getting closer to your authentic self, no longer being a fake or imposter, going through the motions of a life template set out in stone, living a lie. The feeling you constantly have that something is missing in your life will totally disappear when you get your head out from under the duvet and connect back to your real life. The life you deserve and no longer dread.

Very few people know instinctively what they want to do with their lives, so don't worry you are not alone. I was the same. I thought I wanted to be a City of London high-flyer, but in the end, it turned out to be something totally the opposite. I found my new business passion and purpose by thinking about what I truly loved, what I was good at and what was needed in the world. Three crucial things needed to create a fabulous profitable business I am proud of and love working at every day.

Our emotions are what make us human. We cannot push them aside to find our purpose and passion, we must get in touch with them to achieve personal mastery. The process of learning to positive self-talk with mindful thinking must come first before anything else will ever manifest inside. Remember, no one is perfect, and working on yourself is not about being perfect, it is about being true to you, the good the bad and ugly, accepting all of it without shame or blame.

If you truly want more desire to discover your purpose in this life, you must empty your mind of all the false things you have learnt from others, including the idea you don't have a unique purpose at all, because you do. We all do. It's a fact. I can tell you with clarity, discovering your purpose is the easy part. The difficult bit is keeping it with you daily, working on yourself to the point where you become that purpose fully, without doubt. If you imagine for one moment the idea of living a convenient life with everything you dream about at your fingertips, a convenient world where what you want can be purchased to make you happy, take a long look at yourself right now. Have you found the answer to happiness yet? It is unlikely if you are honest with yourself. The truth is, you would not be reading this book if your life was filled with joy and passion, you'd be too busy living it instead, spreading the word like I am. Any passion is about what you love to do. Purpose is what you should do. Talent is what you can do. Change is what you need to do. I am living proof that making money and doing what I love ethically is possible, even in a world where greed and money rule.

If you spend your whole life worrying about what you cannot change, these negative thoughts in your subconscious will manifest into your reality. Start thinking about what you can change, then you will change. It's simple. Depression is a vicious cycle. It manifests the feeling of being powerless.

Reclaiming your power when you feel powerless, especially for those who believe in inevitable doom and gloom, will be the biggest challenge you face when you try and change. The main key to facing and then eradicating your depression is to understand why you are feeling bad in the present. You have let the depression become part of you like an unwanted, unhealthy growth in your mind. You accept it without ever questioning its purpose or where it came from. It changes you. It takes you over. It makes you sick, unsociable, not grateful for the good times, the light times, the people close to you.

It is true most of us compromise ourselves when it comes to who we think we are. We cannot accept fully who we are because we are not prepared to be honest, to look at the things we don't like about ourselves. The more you accept where you are today is never going to change, the less motivation you will have to change things in the future. When we are doing what we are supposed to be doing, not what we have been forced to do by others, circumstances, addiction or depression, we are more connected, joyful, loving and purposeful. Try and make a note of the times you feel like this, even if it's just a glimmer and hold on to it for the times when you are back in the darkness.

We all have built-in instincts and the subconscious mind does have a way of letting us know when we are heading in the right direction. The reason you need a clear mind to notice these signs. Try and connect back to something outside of yourself. Take a walk in the park, take a breath of fresh air, take up yoga, talk to strangers who smile at you for no reason. There are so many things out there in the light that make this life amazing, so much talent, so many gifts left behind by geniuses, the art, the music, the culture. The universe is full of signs. You just need to be open to explore your mind in order to see what is right before your eyes. When I started to notice these signs through listening to my instincts, I would see things I never noticed before. I have seen the statue of David in Florence many times when I had all the money in the world to travel. I had never really taken in the genius or significance of such a wonder. When I revisited this genius work in my meditation, during the dark times of my life falling to bits, I began to recognise we are all just slabs of stone that need slowly chipping away, until the real beauty emerges from underneath the façade. I did the work necessary to chip away. I let go of all my mistakes. I forgave myself. I rekindled my passion and before long just like David, the real me emerged, solid, strong and finally released from my old self-destructive lifestyle.

I know it is hard for you to imagine your life could change so radically like mine did. It all seems so overwhelming right now. Your purpose may not be immediately obvious. You are much stronger than you think behind your existing belief system. Remember that negative inner dialogue you have with yourself is designed to keep you back inside the shell you have grown comfortable living in. It is what you have been programmed to believe automatically and subconsciously by your lying mind.

Our purpose together in this book is to get you to understand this part of your mind fully. To recognise by learning how to make the best of combining your conscious thinking with your subconscious power, you will gain more control over your emotions. It is a fact whatever you plant in the subconscious mind and feed into with repetition will eventually become your reality. Our beliefs are formed on repetitive thinking in a certain way, the repetition of the same thoughts over and over for a long period of time. If we consciously focus on positive thinking repetitively, over and over, eventually things change in our belief system. If you plant positive seeds within your conscious mind like I am depressed, but I will get better, I am open to change, your subconscious mind will obey these thoughts and grow into your new belief system. You can decide, make the choice and be in control of what thoughts you plant in your own mind. You have the power to tell your subconscious how you feel. Your subconscious has the power to provide you with the right response or reaction, depending upon how you talk to it through your words. Ask yourself this question. Do you want to grow healthy, colourful vegetable in the garden of your mind, or do you want to grow deadly nightshade that will continue to destroy and strangle your positivity?

I spent a long time stretching myself from the comfort zone of everything I had stored in my subconscious—the patterns, the beliefs, the traditions. I knew I had to feel uncomfortable and uneasy to grow. It took many failures and awkward feelings. I am growing more and more every day as a result of working on my mind to finally understand more fully who I really am. Many people, including me, will choose a life of self-betrayal rather than a life of fulfilment. They are simply too afraid to step out of their own comfort zone. Don't let this be you. Understanding how your mind works, in my opinion, is a personal thing. We all think differently. We all have our own way of coping with things, how we see things, how our personality has developed and obviously how we have been raised as children.

Sigmund Freud's theory divided the human mind into three levels. The conscious part of the mind occupies approximately ten percent. We can give it orders but we cannot do the work it takes to see them through, unless everything is in our control in the rest of the mind's remaining ninety percent. Think about your conscious mind like the CEO of a company who sits at the top in a big office, sending out instructions to the workforce, who are left to carry out the orders and do the work to the boss's satisfaction. Unless the CEO is sure his staff are all on the same page, working hard together to carry out his instructions, it is likely the company will fail to be successful and nothing will get done. Our conscious mind talks to the outside world and to our inner self through speech, writing things down, or physical movements. It is what other people associate with who we are. You may consciously say to someone and mean it in the moment, you have made the decision to give up eating meat. You take the pat on the back for making the decision, then later that day in a restaurant smell a sizzling steak when considering a small salad. Unless you have trained your subconscious mind to believe you have given up eating meat, you have changed the habit, the smell of the sizzling steak will override your one conscious decision and you will be stuffing your face, looking like a liar. Think about this and then think about how much work and discipline it takes to give up eating meat. We don't just consciously decide to do it one day. It takes hard work. We must replace the old habit with a new habit, focusing all our attention on being mindful to resist the meat, until the new habit is in place. There are two functions of the conscious mind. One is the ability to direct our focus. The other is the ability to imagine what is not real, a bit like a scanner perceiving something, triggering a reaction to it then depending upon its importance, storing it in either the subconscious or the unconscious.

Your unconscious mind is the central place where all your thoughts, feelings, past experiences and memories are stored. All the ones repressed through either trauma or things you have simply chosen to forget about. Freud gave this level of the mind approximately forty percent capacity. These unconscious repressed thoughts, feelings and memories of a disturbing or unacceptable nature are made unconscious by the conscious because they have a potential to hurt or affect us. We hide them away to forget about them. Although stored in the unconscious, they still have the power to influence how we feel and what we do subliminally. They never go away. They just get stored as mental unconscious memory. Freud concluded unacceptable things were rejected by the conscious mind because they were the things that could potentially make us mentally sick. If you think about this, approximately forty percent of your mind is permanently occupied by things you potentially don't feel good about.

The unconscious mind is different to the subconscious mind. This is the part of the mind that stores information continually and sends out emotional reactions based upon recent experiences; basically our short-term memory, constantly in touch with the resources of the unconscious mind. It the part of the mind that remembers and pulls information out, even when we are not thinking about it, like a pin number or a phone number. Freud gave this level of the mind approximately fifty percent capacity. So it is the most amazing memory bank and very powerful when we need to recall information. If your subconscious mind oversees your recent memories, think about your conscious mind telling it you are going on a diet. It says back OK great, I'll remember that for you, then you move on to the next thing you are doing consciously, like cleaning your teeth. You feel empowered in the moment. Pat yourself on the back but immediately unconsciously forget about the diet commitment in the moment. Your mind has wandered on to your next thought. If during the day, say at lunch time, your subconscious mind has spent the morning dragging you back to the place where you are reminded through your internal dialogue you hate your job, you feel like a failure, unless your subconscious mind is trained to reinforce the belief you are on a diet, you will fail and turn to comfort automatically without thinking—the autopilot. Think about all the times you have read a self-help book to try and help you change your bad habits and inspire you to win, how positive and easy it all sounds in the moment. Now think about how you start the changes you make with gusto but always end up falling back at square one, returning sheepishly to your comfort zone in guilt. Unless you work every second of every day to heal your unconscious mind, forgiving the past with compassion, you will always fail to change anything because your emotions won't remain stable.

When people have therapy or counselling, it is the unconscious part of the mind that first needs healing. Without sorting out what is making you mentally sick, unhappy or depressed, there is no hope of training the subconscious part of the mind to help you be a winner. Now if you think about mindfulness, you will begin to see why focusing in the present, on the things you do consciously, then reinforcing them positively in your subconscious memory bank, will eventually change your automatic thinking. You can train your brain to remember your pin number or phone number without any bother, basically because you repeat it over and over until it is embedded firmly in your subconscious, your short-term memory. You need to do this to ensure you can get money out of a machine when you need it, the desire is there, so if you can train your brain to remember a pin number, you can also train your brain to remember anything, you just need a good reason and enough desire.

We don't just wake up and work properly like a machine. We are complex creatures with complex wiring. Understanding how your mind influences your emotions is critical to making changes in your behaviour. To recap, your conscious, ten percent of your mind, takes in information, basically you read a self-help book and decide to make a change. Your subconscious, forty percent of your mind, your short-term memory stores your conscious decision, so it can be easily reached to help you act out your intention. Your unconscious, fifty percent of your mind, your long-term memory will be the reason you fail if you are harbouring unresolved negative issues from the past. Once we understand and begin to recognise what we consciously think is no use without focus, we stop spending most of our time using our imagination to believe what is not real or true. Think about when you have daydreamed or imagined a fantastic happy date with someone you have not yet met, based upon a photo or profile. You wouldn't consciously look at the picture and the profile, then decide it is the one for you. Instead, subconsciously you start to daydream, imagining this is the one for you. Will you get a kiss? Will he ask you to marry him? Before long, your expectations are high, all based on nothing but an idea inside your head. You will have told your subconscious all the wrong information based on imagining the date and it will have given you back the wrong feelings. Now think about pitching up for this blind date for real with high expectations and anticipated feelings, only to discover the person you have decided is the one turns out to be nothing like you have imagined. Your expectations are immediately shattered. You feel unhappy, depressed and all based on nothing but a pre-determined idea in your mind. Think about having the positive feeling from the pat on the back for giving up meat before it was your truth, then the shame and disappointment you experienced when you could not resist the smell of the sizzling steak and you looked like a liar. This lets you see just how powerful the subconscious mind is and why it is important to understand it cannot distinguish between what you imagine and what is real. Enjoying positive, happy feelings before the hard work is done to get there will always make you fail, leaving you depressed and unfulfilled. What you tell yourself and your subconscious about anything must always be honest and real. If you told it the wrong pin number every time you try and take out some cash, you would end up with a big problem. It is only fear that stops you from working yourself out.

In this book, I am trying to help you understand how your mind works so you can be mindful to begin the process of rewinding it for a healthier, positive outlook. We don't just work like magic and we cannot have our cake and eat it, if we want to be happy. It is simple. Living vicariously through your imagination, daydreaming and making up stuff in your mind to make you feel better or convince you, you are happy and accomplished, is why you cannot feel authentic. You are not living in the real world; you are living in your mixed-up mind. Never convince yourself of anything in your mind until you have all the facts on hand. Never have high expectations until you have all the evidence at your fingertips. What you expect to happen is realistically achievable based on fact, not fiction, desperation or your unconscious ego convincing you.

As you know, I had a massive life-changing event that forced me to alter everything. The feelings I had towards myself back then made me cringe and break down. I imagined my way to the top, believing money would make me happy, arrived, accomplished all the success with all the money in the world, all without facing what I had emotionally endured to get there. It is not going to be easy for you to change what you consciously think in the moment. You already know this. You have tried a million times in the past to change. Understanding it is your subconscious that obeys what you tell it is a good place to start the next time you consider embarking on anything new.

I changed my own life at the core not on the surface by uncovering what was lurking in my unconscious mind to help me change on a deeper level. I did this by understanding forgiveness not just for me but for my parents and siblings, too. I found compassion, humility and grace all waiting inside for me once I kicked out all those ghosts festering in the closet. I then focused with these core beliefs to take charge of what was influencing my subconscious mind. I started letting go of the past to live purposefully in the present. Going through this spiritual awakening was one of the most challenging, incredibly enlightening experiences you could ever imagine. I finally got to see beyond the lies, the illusions, realising there was nothing external that would produce happiness for me. I began to crave something more substantial, more genuine and lasting. I wanted to feel complete, satisfied, whole and above all be part of something more powerful than me. I suddenly woke up to my life, free from my catatonic coma, getting to see with clear eyes there was so much more to myself and my life beyond what I had learnt during my childhood.

For you to grow out of your comfort zone, you will need to be prepared and willing to feel awkward and uncomfortable when you begin to do new things. Basically, you are going to be unlearning pretty much everything you have been taught and that is not going to be easy. Once you manage to unravel yourself, face and forgive the past with compassion, you can start aligning your needs and desires with your consciousness. As this work progresses through your meditation with love and self-acceptance, you will start to like yourself more. You will start to gently heal at a deep level connecting you back with your soul.

Your subconscious mind has the power to heal you inside out, at the same time giving you a greater sense of empathy for yourself and others. A subconscious belief in yourself starts with a conscious decision to master your negative thinking through your inner self talk. Remember, you are the CEO in charge of your own mind, so be brave enough to give it the right commands, expecting amazing results in return. Our beliefs are the things we accept to be true which often is not the truth, hence the reason we must recognise this before believing in them, ensuring any new beliefs align with our truth, not our imagination.

Someone who has a mental health illness does not always distinguish between reality and imagination in the same way a healthy person does. The conscious and the unconscious mind begins to make things up instead, in order to make the person feel happy, accomplished or escape their reality. Our conscious mind uses language for our thinking and our unconscious mind uses no language for our thinking. It is just aware of what we are thinking without words. We are less skilled at becoming aware of things when we think without words. It takes a lot of practice through the silence in meditation to become aware of non-thinking language, your autopilot inner dialogue. The ability to make considered decisions, to come to sensible conclusions, is what it takes to succeed with your mind. Good judgement comes from experience, and experience comes from bad judgement. It is simple. I want to talk here about addiction and why so many people use drugs and alcohol to mask pain, preventing the subconscious mind being able to store the correct information necessary to help the person suffering function more positively. If you think about being drunk, it is unlikely you would remember anything you have said the next day, so whatever you said becomes stored in your subconscious memory. It is not going to be of any use solving your life's problems when you are sober. Alcohol diminishes our ability to hold onto information like your pin number but your subconscious is with you all the time; you would not be able to function without it, so understand being drunk is an altered state of consciousness. If the subconscious mind remembers everything, it may not solve our problems, but it will remember we enjoyed getting drunk and encourage us to keep doing what we think we enjoyed doing consciously. How many times have you come home from work, opened a bottle of wine to relax or unwind? How many times does one glass of wine to help you relax turn into a bottle and then two, putting you from a relaxation stage to a vegetative state where you are no longer conscious of how much you are drinking or what you are thinking? At this stage, you would be off with the fairies in your imagination either feeling depressed, sad and not remotely relaxed or dreaming about a feeling in your subconscious that once made you happy.

Alcoholics—and I am sorry to be the bearer of bad news, but if you cannot go a day without a drink, you are addicted—are not drinking for the experience of pleasure or relief, they are addicted to the experience of the moments they feel free from pain and anxiety, the invisible misery inside. People commonly believe when we release dopamine, we feel a pleasure reward, when in fact it is a learning transmitter. The alcohol hijacks the dopamine telling the brain what we are doing in the moment is rewarding, therefore worth repeating. Alcohol is a mind-controlling substance in the moment but long term if we become addicted to the reward pleasure dopamine rush, our subconscious mind learns to store all our lies and denial. This keeps us stuck, unable to connect the dots consciously to create a happy picture of who we are and what we stand for. Once again, recognise you are not a machine and you don't work like magic. Blocking out your feelings does not mean they have gone away. It just means they are repressed in your unconscious and will come back to bite you when you least expect. Alcohol is not the answer to combat your fears or your problems.

I used drugs and alcohol many times in the dark times to help me believe I was having a good time, forgetting about my problems, but the good times only ever lasted past a few vodkas before I was talking complete rubbish to anyone who would listen. When we are drunk, we will embellish our truth to look like we are more interesting and exciting to others. Lying and making up stories, memories that don't exist may make you look good in the moment, but you will look like a liar when you are sober and don't remember, so what's the point?

Alcohol is a depressant that helps trick the mind into thinking you are having a great time, when all you are doing is opting out, choosing to forget your reality. This is not good for your soul or finding your purpose. It is more likely to kill you in the end. If you ask someone to film you when drunk, then play it back when you are sober, you would cringe beyond belief at the crap coming out of your mouth and be quite shocked by someone you wouldn't recognise or relate to in any way. When we are drunk, we don't make sense. How can we? We are not conscious of what we are thinking or saying, we are allowing our subconscious thoughts to run riot, creating a picture of who we are. Think about it. If you are depressed, unhappy, full of misery and negative thoughts about yourself in your subconscious, then you get drunk to forget about it, feel better or have fun, you will not be spouting happy fun dialogue, you will potentially be mean, angry or depressing to be with. A few drinks can be a good thing to loosen you up, make you feel more confident, give you a little boost but to go beyond this stage, it is unlikely you will ever feel strong and confident, you are more likely to be ashamed of yourself instead.

As a non-drinker now because I love my life, my thinking and enjoy being in control, it is a real eye-opener when I find myself in a social gathering with drinkers. I get to see how people change. How their personality develops during the getting drunk process and how they turn on each other or themselves to deflect from their own flaws. Once you get to a place in your life where you are awake, engaged, thinking, being mindful, curious and open, you will have no desire to escape yourself anymore. You will master yourself and your mind by listening to what you are thinking, then working out what is real and what is holding you back from being real. The truth is your body is the home for your soul and must never be abused. We were born to eat healthy food to ensure our bodies remain in full working order. It is only outside influences that have led us to be unhealthy.

Fast junk food and alcohol are making big businesses rich at the expense of your poor health and wellbeing. You are what you eat. If you are contaminating your body with processed convenient fast food, full of preservatives and poisons, you are drinking too much alcohol or consuming fizzy sugar-rich drinks excessively, it's no wonder you don't feel good inside anymore. We are not here on this earth to spend our lives at the doctor or the pharmacy, looking for ways to stop us having a headache, burping, indigestion, bloating or diarrhoea, being overweight or hungover. Eating healthily, taking care of your body so the above is not ruining your life, is the number one change that must be made if you want to get on the road to personal happiness and fulfilment. The degree to which your conscious desire expands is the degree to which you will understand yourself better. Detoxing your mind and your body is the most interesting exercise you could ever imagine. You get to see just how bad you feel inside.

Think about visualising a dirty, smelly, festering house never cleaned, full of rubbish, rotting food, blocked up drains, sinks and toilets where nothing works properly, unlived in for years, nobody going near it except germs and illness. Now think about your body like this house, visualise switching all the lights on, having a massive spring clean, flushing out the blockages, scrubbing the floors, opening all the windows, decluttering, making it spanking brand new again. A beautiful clean healthy place where greedy germs have no desire to visit. The intensity of perception is often experienced as an openness to experience things in a different way, like opening the curtains in a dirty old house. By doing this, more positive light and impressions can come into your mind, totally changing how you feel and think about things. When you experience a spiritual awakening, you are cleaning out your own house and your whole inner world will change, creating massive shift in how you feel inside. You have been in a coma, clogged up for years and although the shift will be slow, I can promise you eventually you will feel like a new person with a clean mind and a new body.

The need for a purpose in life is the defining characteristic of all human beings. We all crave a purpose, the fundamental component of a fulfilling life and as you know with your unexplained depression, not having one has caused serious psychological difficulties. Recent studies have shown people who are contributing to a higher purpose in their lives automatically have a happier, healthier outlook, becoming more resilient and more capable to cope with stress, anxiety and trauma. Maybe if you look back to a time when you did something with real purpose, you did it with real determination, it made you happy inside and want to get up in the morning, you will recognise without it now you feel empty and lost. It is important to understand, purpose will be unique for everyone. What you eventually identify as your own path will be different from others and will shift and change throughout your life journey, in response to evolving developments and changes. Once your authentic purpose becomes crystal clear, you are then able to share it with the rest of the world which becomes your contribution, your gift back, your part played out in the bigger picture of life. This, my friends, is what we call true happiness and progress.

The key is to live the best life you can in the moment by actualising your true purpose and passion in the present, rather than putting it off into the future, the unknown where anything can happen without you even being involved. If you dream about being an actor, engage yourself in this possibility outside of your day-to-day essential stuff. Find the time to discover ways to open doors, creating the possibility of making it happen for real. I want to make you think about your own life in a new way. We only have a short amount of time on this earth and we never know when this time is up. Understanding this will help you believe in leading a bigger, fuller life, outside of your inner demons and dark depression. If your true purpose is never focused on or uncovered, you will find yourself scattered everywhere, lost out of sea without a lifeboat, thrown all over the ocean by the deep unchallenged currents of your circumstances and life dilemmas. I can tell you, with purpose comes your core values, an integral part of your life. The rules and guidelines we follow, to help define integrity, steering us to stay on the straight and narrow road toward one end goal, to ensure we leave this earth having achieved personal growth and success. Your heart is the only way to access your true potential, purpose and passion. Ask yourself today what it is you truly love, then begin to take small steps towards doing what you love by loving what you do. If at this point you have concluded you love to drink, smoke, eat, shop, have sex, you are not listening to your heart but your mind still and need to go back to the beginning of this book to start again. You are back on a snake heading downwards. This is not progress, it is depressing.

It is very likely you have good reasons for being depressed and unable to retain positive information. You may feel like an outcast. You might be being bullied. You might just feel empty or have demons dictating how you feel but whatever the reason, there is always a solution. I know someone who was very close to committing suicide. One day when these feelings took over his rational thinking, he managed to pull himself outside into the fresh air into a park to have a walk, close to where he lived. During this lonely, painful walk, he suddenly came across a dying fox that had the misfortune to be run over by a car. The poor fox had pulled himself into safety in the bushes to die alone in pain. This friend of mine felt enormous overwhelming feelings of compassion and empathy for the poor fox so decided to take it to a local vet close by. The vet was kind but sure the fox's life was over, so set about putting it out of its pain and misery, the only kind thing to do under the circumstances. This random experience on his lonely walk that day completely changed him forever. He suddenly realised no matter how alone he felt in the moment, there was always someone out there who would show kindness and empathy to a life in trouble, even a fox. He realised by pushing himself outside, away from the overpowering desire to self-harm, changing his surroundings, away of his own turmoil, there was a purpose for him to put the fox out of its pain, forgetting his own misery in the process.

Talk therapy is an amazing and effective way to control anxiety and negative thinking. It helps break down and reshape the beliefs and judgements that contribute to the anxious concerns in the first place and helps us avoid acting on impulse or doing something I believe we would all regret after the event. Your life has so much to offer the world. You must be willing to wake up and open your eyes to it without judging, blaming or self-harming. Recent studies have established a clear association between alcohol abuse, drug addiction and a lack of ultimate meaning in life. This research found that little spiritual dimension appears to be the most significant factor affecting depressive symptoms and any treatment needs to address purpose, giving the sufferer something to live for. Many people believe there is no intrinsic meaning to life. The main reason humans created religion to offer an easy solution to a mass problem. Recent study has also shown that the possible negative consequences of looking outward for happiness found those people who place all their value on being happy, ended up with more mental health problems, including depression. Finding meaning over happiness is the key. I can confirm this from my own experience of having it all materially. It did not make me happy and losing it all gave me my purpose, making me truly happy. Change the way you look at things and the things you look at change.

Your purpose throughout this journey together is to bring all your memories and repressed unresolved issue to the surface of your conscious mind, so you can begin to experience what is holding you back through mind awareness of your emotionally triggered pain from your subconscious. You need to dig deep inside yourself to find out what it is that has hurt you and left you feeling depressed, anxious, unable to be happy, fulfilled, unique and individual. Our goal together is to heal your pain and stop your emotional triggers keeping you trapped in fear, feeling unsafe, unsure, forever escaping the reality of your truth. To change your negative patterns, you are going to need to see them first, not deny them, the hard bit. We are going to find the inner observer in you to help you feel safe again, cleaning out the pain inside your body, triggering you to feel depressed, miserable and unhappy. Carl Jung, my mentor and inspiration during the most challenging and difficult days, taught me a great lesson that changed my life and made me realise, discovering my own purpose was the key. He said, "If you are a gifted person, it does not mean you have gained something; it means you have something to give back to the world. The picture you create in your mind of what you believe to be real and true, creates the behaviour you express."

All I can tell you from my own experience, when you are fully focused on what you are doing in the moment, your conscious mind is in control and you will feel safe. Once you take your finger off the button and start to drift off thinking about something other than what you are doing in the moment, your subconscious programming kicks in to keep you thinking you are safe. Most of our subconscious programming is formed in the early stages of our life, even before birth. We soak up everything we see, feel, experience, like a sponge. We learn subconsciously how to act in certain situations—what makes us angry, what makes us cry, how we express love, interact with and respond to others. All this information then creates our automatic thinking patterns about our reality. As we develop and grow into adulthood, we continue to subconsciously develop new patterns, but under the surface, the ones developed in early childhood will be most dominant. We will always return there when making our choices and decisions later in life. The purpose of your meditation before you go to sleep is to help you clear out your mind, making space so you can override these subconscious fixed beliefs through the practice of repetitively planting new thoughts and actions. You are not a victim of anything other than what you have subconsciously been programmed to believe in childhood.

When it comes to purpose, remember stress and fear will close off your heart. This will make you judgemental and critical. The main reason your life feels empty and meaningless. As you become more present, more sensitive to your own feelings, natural kindness and empathy towards yourself will begin to ignite. This amazing experience of change allows you to be fully conscious and present in your own authentic life. It will allow you to let go of the blaming and resentment plus anything else interfering with your mental and emotional wellbeing. Once you can begin to listen to the silence behind your thoughts, experiencing yourself as you really are, a conscious operating human being without the baggage or fear, you will enjoy emotional and spiritual harmony inside. You will have finally mastered the art of letting go.

Why Suffer in Silence?

Meditation is an amazing practice to help you clear out the mind, but it is not the only key to changing your self-limiting beliefs. The real key is developing self-awareness. When we become aware of the structure of our negative beliefs, they naturally collapse in front of us. This is what happened to me. The consequences of the compulsion to keep going to negative thinking can and will endure because it is an emotional habit of the body. If we continue to constantly be aware of it in the present as an observer, eventually over time, it will diminish and be replaced by new positive thoughts and patterns.

The first step in any change is cultivating awareness. The moment you are aware of your life, you begin to go through it using your conscious mind to know and understand everything around you—the good, the bad and the ugly. Awareness forces you to ask questions like "why am I like this?". Your subconscious, when you ask this question, will dig deep and search into your past, giving you the answer to why you feel the way you do based on your past negative belief programming. If you ask yourself questions like "why am I full of joy?", your subconscious will dig deep, searching through your past life to bring the answers with joy. By asking yourself the wrong questions with negative energy and thoughts, you will automatically produce negative answers. As we have already established, we all have negative voices in our minds, our inner dialogue, but hopefully by now you have understood we have control over what we let in. You decide who has the power to tell you how to think and feel.

It was only when I was committed to shifting out my own pain through self-awareness, no longer denying it, I began to experience true emotional freedom. I found the courage to look within to find out what was causing me to feel anxious and unhappy. Although I knew consciously losing all my money and finding myself on my death bed wasn't helping, I had to face through being honest with compassion; it was all my own fault. Not easy when you have lived your life believing you are fantastic and invincible. I can confirm without doubt, running away from your pain and your unresolved issues will never make you feel better. Like I say, examining it is not easy and likely, you unconsciously have no idea it is logged in your mind. Our memories are deep-rooted and often not real or remembered fully. Until we begin a journey of awakening, these memories will continue to define you. They are your pain and the cause of all your fear-based reactions. The reason you always feel stressed. Although these feelings and emotions feel very real to you, they are in fact unconsciously triggered by negative thoughts, existing beliefs and memories from your past.

By clearly understanding this, you can form a new perspective of your consciousness, then letting it all go will happen naturally.

I have shared some of me with you. I hope it has been helpful. I believe talking openly about things, especially feelings, discussing it all without fear, can be very helpful, not morbid as some might assume. You may not be able to ask for help or even admit you need help right now but that does not mean it is not wanted. I don't think you want to die or give up on yourself. You just want to stop hurting or self-harming. I want to clarify here what I mean by self-harming. Many people believe only the truly depressed or suicidal self-harm, but this is no longer the case in this current environment, believe it or not. Most of us are self-harming in one way or another without consciously realising we are doing it. If you are over-eating, over-drinking, over-indulging, using fixes for comfort, are addicted, unable to control your habits, your health and wellbeing is suffering and as a result, you too are self-harming. It is important to understand by abusing your body, in denial, believing you are sick or because you think it is hereditary and nothing to do with your lifestyle choices, this is not that different from committing suicide, you are just doing it to yourself slowly. I know this may sound harsh and not what any of you want to hear but with self-awareness must come pure honesty. Once you are fully aware of what you are doing to yourself subconsciously, your denial and negative belief system collapses and you are forced to take back control of your choices. Most of us if we are honest will agree, all we seek is inner peace and calm with less chaos, less stress and less internal conflict.

To those people who are not depressed or in despair, it is hard to understand what drives another person to want to commit suicide or give up on life. You never know what is going on inside the heads of other people. Not all of us with mental health issues, depression and anxiety have contemplated suicide. We all have different levels of coping. People with depression and anxieties find it exhausting to constantly try and explain how they are feeling. Listening to well-intentioned friends and family is not always a helpful cure for the problem. The people around them often have no idea what they are even talking about. The depression doesn't allow the energy to talk to others about it openly. It's hard enough to get through the day when nothing interests you, not even what you normally love and enjoy. There is a massive stigma when it comes to talking about mental health. People feel weak when they ask for help. Really, the opposite is true. It is courageous to talk about how you are feeling. Facing your problems and issues through seeking professional help is the first step to getting better. Talking is the most important thing in helping reduce the stigma around mental health, to help others understand what and why. Getting the thoughts out of someone's head and putting them in the cold light of day, so the person feels less alone and more able to cope, beyond the chaotic confusing chatter in the mind, is critical for healing the soul. You are never alone, no matter how much your depression and misery say you are. Your mind is lying to you. Once you start to look at things objectively, separating yourself from the reaction to the feeling, you can begin to get rid of self-doubt and move beyond the pain. Misery loves company. There is something comforting to know there are millions of people out in the universe all facing the same struggle. So in this sense, it shows we are never alone, even if we feel like we are in our minds.

People with depression tend to make everything their fault. It is like they twist everything, something they cannot help doing and sometimes for no reason other than having a bad day. They will have no idea why they are depressed until they are not depressed anymore. The normal healthy sense of optimism we should feel about life and our purpose for being here is diminishing slowly in this cruel, unhealthy environment we live in today. Mass depression has become an invisible illness many don't understand. A massive black hole that sucks away all the meaning and purpose from our existence. I had a friend many years ago who described the feeling of depression like a feeling of disappearance in his appearance. He suffered alone for years in silence, always telling me it was ugly, it was painful, it was rotten, it was like a living death, being dead but still alive. He had mood swings, some days of happiness in between many days of depression. Always without warning, the blackness would swoop in and suck out the light without mercy. He would suddenly for no reason become detached and adrift, unable to connect or communicate his feelings. He would want to fall to sleep and never wake up, sometimes sleeping for the whole day like being in hibernation, a state of subconscious shutdown. He told me sometimes getting out of bed was like running a marathon. On good days, he would talk about the obtrusive, unwanted thoughts pushing him into a mental prison. He started to eat more as a coping mechanism, until he was addicted to the food. The food gave him comfort but made him gain weight and this vicious cycle made him even more depressed and isolated. The destructive combination of weight issues and depression forced him to turn to self-medicating, using recreational drugs like marijuana, wine and painkillers to try and ease the increasing chaos he was experiencing inside. Obviously, everyone's experience of depression will be different, but this case study shows how easy it is to let one negative thing lead to another, until subconsciously everything becomes negative and not manageable anymore. Now think back to the way we negatively talk to ourselves through our inner dialogue. The questions we ask ourselves dictate how we feel. This makes it easier for you to see how your own subconscious programming could cause complete havoc in a depressive episode. The truth is, you can talk yourself into anything, just like you can talk yourself out of anything.

In a way, depression is a symptom of the way you have programmed your subconscious mind to behave. You tell yourself you feel like a failure, you have nothing to live for, you hate your life. Your subconscious digs deep and searches for the answer. Because you have let the depression define you, now you have a built-in belief, potentially planted in childhood, dictating how you feel about yourself. This belief can then be triggered by various things that happen, like a setback, a rainy day or an overload of emotions, all in one go. People who suffer depression will remark how they remember little of the event after the episode is over and coming back to normal feels a little bit like having your emotional system switched back on short term, until it malfunctions again. Regular deep depression is a repetitive negative wired-in state of mind based on unconscious negative beliefs and negative feelings repressed from childhood, not faced or healed. These feeling are continually played out then reinforced by the subconscious. Most of the people I have worked with who have suffered depression have experienced some sort of challenging trauma centred on violence, abuse or caregiver control. The subconscious mind in these cases has plenty to throw back when the person is depressed and starts the self-sabotaging thoughts. You are what you think, remember. If you think you are nothing, you will always feel nothing.

I am talking more about depression here because I believe in this current culture of self-sabotaging behaviours, whether it be overeating, binge alcohol consumption, reckless sex, drug addiction, purposefully skipping out of life, most of us are suffering depression in silence in some form or another. We are all becoming bipolar based on our crazy emotional up and down state of mind, often feeling like we are in a hole we cannot be pulled out of. We are all walking on a tight rope above our consciousness, the state of being aware. We are not being responsive to our surroundings or circumstances, unconsciously participating, going through the motions of life in denial, not evolving spiritually beyond our mental agony. Most of us don't have to live in total denial, to not be personally impacted by the current chaos of mass human pain and suffering. The truth is, mental health is now out of control. War, famine, poverty and persecution have become so normalised, we almost dismiss it as fantasy. This denial tactic only breeds more deception inside. Just because we believe something terrible is not happening on our own doorstep, it won't happen to us, we will be safe, it's not a priority to our own survival, does not mean these dark forces are not impacting our spiritual wellbeing. As a world we seem to have adopted an infinite appetite always yearning for more, yet never understanding what more is. Depression is self-serving, absolute apathy, the best state for the human brain to be in. We don't feel a thing. We don't want to break free from the life template we have created because that means dealing with our emotions and changing. We prefer instead to continue battling in silence, praying we will either one day win the lottery, a miracle will occur, or the universe will provide all we need. The universe already provides all we need. As human beings, sadly, we just don't appreciate it. Our life is washed away with too much detail, so my job with you is to help you simplify things down by becoming fully aware of what you are doing and why you keep doing it.

Depression is often misunderstood as sadness, but it has nothing to do with sadness, it is to do with numbness to our emotions. A real feeling of being killed from the inside, an emptiness that cannot be explained and I think this sums up pretty much how most people are feeling right now. We cannot choose what life throws at us. Life is not fair, and your mind may have betrayed you. You may be abusing your life. Your resistance may be shot to pieces. You may believe money and beauty buys you freedom but whatever you believe, you are wrong. Whatever you are feeling in the reality of your life, behind the illusion, the façade, the addiction, the painted smile, things will never improve on a bigger scale unless you are more open-minded to become more self-aware, it is potentially you causing your problems.

In this demanding culture of high technology, increasing competition, our so-called noble society is stressed out, causing unwanted pressure on the earth's natural resources. If this mass depression is not faced soon, it will spread and contaminate everything like a cancer cell that destroys every other healthy living cell. Becoming more centred, open and honest by looking closely at your own situation, your own behaviour will give you the wisdom to help you see why you are simply not happy. Blaming other people who may have hurt you or betrayed you, only serves to make you the victim, magnifying your suffering more. Listening to your own thoughts, like I have said before, is the most important element to being present. It opens you up and allows you to hear the truth. You begin to experience being a conscious awake human being, the essence of humanity. Looking at the bigger picture helps you to see you have compromised yourself, your needs, your happiness in the pursuit of perfection, money and aspiration. Although we are not all clinically depressed, we all seem empty and numb to the idea of meaning and purpose. I would always choose compromise for all the wrong things like money, security, advantage, approval and social acceptance, losing all contact with who I really was deep inside. Suffering in silence, feeling like a fraud, always looking outward in the pursuit of happiness left me looking like such a failure to my family with all their high expectations of me.

Today, in my enlightened state I know I had to fail in my old life to enjoy new opportunities and beginnings in this new life, where I never seek approval from others, compromise myself or worry about what other people think of me.

There must be no more suffering in silence and until you reach this turning point in your journey, gaining more self-knowledge, as you travel on the straight and narrow road, you will still be living only a small part of life. Changing anything is a process. It happens in stages, with small steps, never over-stretching yourself, never berating yourself. Your mind has been doing that for way too long. Making mistakes is an important part of gaining great wisdom; the bigger the mistake, the bigger the growth. If you survive the pain and disappointment you feel and don't kill yourself, you will begin to learn what is real and what everyone else experiences too.

The problem today is the stigma attached to mental health. If you have a physical health problem, you visit the doctor, he prescribes a pill based on your symptoms and diagnosis, but with depression, you don't always need a pill, you just need a change of lifestyle or someone to talk to in the moment. Often just a good night's sleep can change the whole perspective of someone feeling anxious or depressed. I don't want to sound like a speaking clock, but a healthy lifestyle will always lift all kinds of moods, as well as help conquer obesity, diabetes and all the other associated problems from self-harming behaviour. If you have not been compassionately honest and authentic with yourself, crystal clear in your communication with yourself and you have been making fear-based decisions, allowing your unconscious ego, your desires and needs to rule your thinking, you may now have to accept there has been something unpleasant going on inside your mind.

As you practise mindful thinking, meditation, breathing, sitting alone quietly with no outside influence or stimulation, you find the time to discover your real values, your priorities, your own unique desires, not those you have been conditioned to believe by others. Every single day you will climb further up that mountain towards a higher level of thinking, breaking all those chains holding you back, one by one. If with courage you keep going through the pain barrier without fear, you will cross over into new territory, understanding finally what freedom from your thoughts really means. We live in a very loud scary place and internal peace is not easy to find these days. We all get sad from time to time. This is a normal part of life but when the sadness is persistent and all-consuming, it becomes increasingly hard to carry on, so we end up looking outward through various fixes and comforts to help us feel better.

Suffering in silence, and by this I mean never facing yourself, is very different to being alone. Sometimes being alone is the most powerful thing you can imagine when it has a purpose and you are using it to develop your self-esteem and self-worth. Begin to authentically declare your intention from your heart not your mind, resolving your pain, misery, depression, anxiety whatever it is holding you back from being open and honest with yourself, then commit to serve only your healthy inner desires. You may not understand what I am talking about just yet. You have become so used to taking direction from the cruel critic living in your mind, constantly pushing you to fail or make bad choices. During this journey of self-discovery on the straight and narrow road with no bends, no side roads and no dead ends, it is important you don't explain to others what you are doing. Just tell them you are working on re-evaluating your life strategy. You don't want to be influenced by others and their opinions ever again, unless they align with your own. Until you have cleared out and healed your unconscious, then reprogrammed your subconscious in your favour, always work alone on yourself in the silence and safety of your meditation.

Inside of all of us, there is a great power if we can tap into it and learn to listen to it. It will guide us and take us to a higher level of thinking beyond the unconscious ego, so we can benefit from all the unlimited possibilities in the future. This power is nothing to do with religion or God. Believe it or not, it is to do with you. You are the power. My goal as a talk therapy guide and mind detective is to hopefully stop you giving up on yourself and push you back into thinking straight again. In the old days, they would use Edison's medicine, electric shock treatment to help get people thinking straight after a nervous breakdown. Thank goodness today we have moved on from this. In my experience, there is nothing other than forgiveness and compassion to heal the problems of a sore mind.

The world has never been in such a chaotic challenging time where religions are in competition, poverty is leaving half the world starving and greed leaving the other half with grave health issues, like obesity, addiction and anxiety. Is this the kind of world you want to live in? Most people have given up on the search for greater meaning. To embrace change, you must first do the work necessary in preparation to gain the knowledge that leads to your purpose, ultimately creating the happiness you deserve. The more of us who are operating properly through being mindful, working together for the same purpose, to contribute back to humanity not take from it, the more monumental things can happen collectively with mind-blowing results, impacting us deeply.

Depression, a symptom of loneliness, is not a weakness. It is an illness of the mind. It impacts the lives of millions of people every day. Globally, it is estimated that three hundred and fifty million people suffer from depression, so you are not alone here and have no need to feel ashamed or the odd one out.

Committing suicide is the worst-case scenario for someone with dark depression yet frequent thought of suicide and self-harm are very common with mild depression, the people who think about it but don't act on it. The thing I have discovered with depression and anxiety is everything we know about them is pretty much wrong. Most people who suffer are not experiencing a chemical imbalance, where anti-depressants will solve the problem. The reality is, they just suppress their reality. Understanding the root cause of where the depression started, then digging it out like a cancer growth, is the key to overcoming it.

There have been many studies carried out showing the problem is getting worse, not improving. More than half the people prescribed anti-depressants are depressed again within a year of coming off them. The dark truth sadly is the only people benefitting from this misery crisis right now are the drug companies. In my own experience, depression and anxiety are down to the way we carelessly go about our lives. We have become so disconnected from our authentic selves and from our purpose, our core values, we have lost sight of the power of our connection to nature and other people. We have created a society based on all the wrong values and our way of surviving is no longer safe or secure. We have become addicted to everything, whether this is food, drugs, alcohol, shopping, sex, gambling, with no real connection beyond what we believe we want. Instead of acknowledging what we need, healing our past childhood traumas, our unresolved issues, we have callously pushed ourselves beyond it all, disconnected from it mentally, ignored it, pushed it inside and now we are all suffering in silence because of it.

The best cure for depression and anxiety is not to take a pill. It's about coming together as a society, recognising we all need each other, we cannot fix this problem alone. We all naturally have a strong desire inside to reconnect with what really matters in life, beyond the power of money and greed. I understand some people need pills for mental health issues, the majority do not. They just need a steadfast constant voice that inspires, understands, relates, sympathises, educates and on occasion gives people the kick up the bottom they need. You may have guessed by now this is my job. If we take pills to suppress the emotions we feel, making them unimportant in a way, rather than facing our issues head on, the minute we stop, the problem is still there only much worse than it was to begin with. A sleeping pill might help you sleep short term, but the quality of the sleep will be poor. A happy pill might lift your spirits short term, but do you really want to rely on something potentially addictive to make you feel happy? Trust me, the continued compulsive search for the instant fix to put your life back together is a trap. You will end up caught up in the net, in the darkness, imprisoned and disconnected from any joy or purpose you deserve. In a way, like I said, we are all addicted to something. We are all the same underneath the layers of life's pain. Working on ourselves, understanding, untangling our subconscious thinking, facing the dark demons that relentlessly emerge from the shadows, will ultimately help us understand why we became depressed in the first place. If we can learn to stay on that straight and narrow road through hell until we reach the other side, we will begin to understand what is on the other side beyond what we perceive is keeping us stuck.

I suffered in silence myself for quite a while after losing my money but because I had built-in self-confidence from childhood, once I got beyond hell, I found the strength to face myself, take myself on with the kick-up-the-bottom cure, which although brutal, worked for me in the end. I had to accept the dark place I found myself in was my own greedy fault. I wanted to blame my broker, my bank, my accountant, the stock market but the truth was simple. I thought I knew better instead of cashing in and walking away. I was addicted and gambling became a vice I couldn't live without. The stock market is like a casino with pretty much the same odds. You buy low, sell high then get out when you are ahead but just like the casino, if you stay too long, the house always wins and you end up broke.

Self-awareness for me during this horrific time was the key to better mental health. Looking inward and asking important questions like "Who am I? How do I feel? What do I want from my life?" and most importantly, "Have I become the person I can be proud of?" got me to the place where I realised I didn't know the answers. This experience shocked me but showed me how little I knew about myself in truth. When I first started to meditate, I just couldn't do it. I found myself being aware of the strangest random thoughts, some so random like I say I was shocked. I had no idea how busy my mind was, how little time I spent on self-reflection. The more I tried to relax and empty my mind, the more I noticed how much unconscious activity was going on in it. It was at this point I had to learn to not get emotionally involved but stand back as an observer with my giant imaginary tennis bat, hitting every unnecessary thought out of the space until my mind was clear.

You cannot imagine right now what bliss feels like. You are still too consumed with your past but trust me there is nothing more life-changing than an empty healthy mind. You won't like what you hear once you begin to take notice and listen but stick with it, even if you are crying your eyes out because it is your truth, and if you don't like what you hear, make this the incentive to change things for good. You may have to face the fact you are not the amazing, intelligent, fabulous person you have pictured in your mind, and of course, this is going to make you feel bad. Remember when this happens your unconscious ego will give you the perfect excuse to delve back into your illusions. Learn to tolerate this short-term emotional discomfort by exploring the feelings. When you are feeling uncomfortable, ask yourself what it is you are feeling. Stay with it, own it, accept it, ride that wave until it passes over you and it will pass. It is true we will do almost anything to avoid having to face ourselves. We lie as self-protection. We exaggerate to protect the image of how we see ourselves, but we all know what happens when we lie. We end up feeling bad. It is this willingness to stop self-deception that stops you feeling bad and finally sets you free.

Once you begin to relax into a deeper comfy cloud of safety in your meditation, you will start to want to be there more times than not. The new place you want to hang out in. The white soft comfy cloud, your new safe bubble. The safe place in your mind where you can be completely free. When you start working on yourself in this comfy cotton wool cloud, reprogramming your subconscious in your favour, you will start to be aware that your unconscious ego has prevented you from doing the important work on yourself; remember, it hates change, it only knows how to get more out of who you already are. If we let the unconscious ego take charge of our new self-improvement project, we will fail. It has its own agenda, the main reason we feel uncomfortable when we try something new.

Our habits are a mental or physical behaviour we repeatedly play out in our lives without being fully conscious. For example, you might believe you need a cup of coffee before you can get out of bed in the morning. A habit you have adopted and repeatedly do without ever giving it any thought. The truth is there is nothing to prevent you from getting out of bed without having your cup of coffee other than you. You can consciously program your subconscious to believe you are getting up without the coffee until this becomes your new habit.

I can promise you if you are looking to transform your own life in a deep and meaningful way, there is no self-help manual, transform-your-life book to help you do it. Your unconscious ego will always stop you succeeding in the end. You must learn to disarm it by changing the simple habits like the morning coffee, slowly building up to changing the more difficult habits like your more dangerous addictions. We can all work on ourselves with self-help of course. We can work on personal empowerment, get fit, improve our confidence, change jobs, travel, see new things but we will never realise true happiness until we have sorted ourselves out internally and engaged in some new core values, like humility, gratitude, compassion and integrity.

When I was dying, I asked for help from a greater power than me. It was instinctive and happened outside of my unconscious ego state. I had a deep connection with the divine part of myself within myself, the thing some people call God. When you are listening in a deep state within yourself for the answers, you are forced to put your own personal agenda to one side, the difference between listening to something inside of you and praying to something outside of you. When your mind is completely empty, free from any negative thoughts and personal agendas, you too will hear this voice in the silence. It is not your unconscious ego, the cruel critic, berating you anymore, it is your soul speaking from inside your heart. This happened to me. I humbly asked for help and waited with a clear empty mind. Once I realised I had my life back, I discovered the true value of pure gratitude in my heart. How could I not be humbled and grateful in a situation which I believed at one point I was never coming back from. This is how I know now I am the voice inside my mind. It is me, not what I have been programmed to believe, not the negative bias, not the opinions of others, not the automatic, cruel, fear-based sabotaging critic, not a man in the sky, just one simple secure voice, my voice.

I have learnt gratitude is the most important link to my mental wellbeing and without doubt the most valuable character trait I possess. Practising gratitude has increased my cognitive functioning. It has helped me sleep better, in turn keeping my moods balanced and stable. People who learn to achieve this deep level of meditative state can tap into the deepest dormant levels of brain function, which results in huge success in personal development. And the good news is we can all do it.

Today when I meditate, I feel like I am outside of myself watching myself, but it is never completely external, like the feeling I am outside of my body. It is not that kind of disassociation. It's more like a disconnection from my conscious mind, but I am still aware. This is the exact same feeling I had with my near-death experience when I saw myself at the end of the hospital bed. It proves to me there is something more powerful inside me than my actual physical body, something unexplained yet familiar. Once I got to grips with this, I planted compassion in my subconscious, focusing only on the beauty and the power of nature. I set my mind free from any attachment to the things I could no longer control. The mind is like a parachute. It only functions when it's open, so now I always have an open mind when it comes to examining things I don't understand.

The hardest part of this journey, and we are halfway through now, is going to be you attempting to break your bad habits, especially those geared towards your self-sabotaging behaviour. So let's break it down. There are four steps you need when attempting to break a bad habit. The first step is to identify the routine of the habit. The behaviour you want to change. As an example, let's say you want to stop smoking. The second step is about the reward. Most cravings are hard to see. Experimenting and using different rewards helps us to figure out if the craving is about the smoking or an emotional distraction. Basically, we need to find out the real reason we reach for a cigarette. The third step is to identify ahead of the pattern and behaviour of the smoking habit, the triggers that leads us to the habit. Why we need to smoke. The fourth step is about having a plan of action to change the habit/pattern. Once you have a plan, you can shift and change the habit by anticipating the trigger, changing to a different routine that delivers a reward. If stress is the trigger that leads you to smoke, instead of reaching for a cigarette to relieve the stress, leave the packet at home and go outside into the fresh air for a walk, your new routine. This will lift your stress, giving you mental relief—your reward. We will never fully eliminate our bad habits but what we can do is try and replace them with healthier ones.

All the difficulties you have, all the problems you battle, all the experiences you face, all the pain you endure, all the bad habits you covet, exist quite simply because you do not want to grow up. When we rely only on external sources to fulfil our needs, we automatically forfeit our responsibility for getting our needs met. Essentially all life as we perceive it is just an illusion. It is only nature that will remind us of the qualities we admire and cultivate within ourselves beyond our addictions and habits. The power of the ocean, the beauty of the moon, the resilience of the trees, the consistency of the changing seasons. This consistency and resilience within nature and the universe is the perfect framework for a happy healthy life, filled with peace and purpose. The real key to diminishing your unconscious ego and fake persona comes from understanding you are not alone. We are all pebbles on the same beach and flickering flames in the same fire. We are all part of nature.

Making the Right Decisions

If you are still with me and have not given up, you are now ready to wipe the slate clean and begin to set yourself some practical goals, so you can sort any immediate worries, obstacles getting in the way of mindful thinking, becoming a better you in the future. Imagine for a moment you are sitting on the edge of a ledge on a tall building, you are contemplating suicide because you can see no way forward or any way out of the situation you find yourself in. Now imagine I am sitting right next to you on that ledge. You don't know me. I am talking to you and asking what you are doing there. It would be most likely you would tell me you didn't want to be here anymore. There was no point to your life. You would tell me the painful hopeless feelings you have are real, you didn't ask for them, you cannot change them, you wished it all would just stop, go away and disappear into nothingness, without you having to face your mess. This scenario is potentially how most people feel at some point. Not all of us are on the edge of a building contemplating suicide but we have all felt completely hopeless and overwhelmed when faced with stressful things we believe we cannot change. When those black clouds come over you with that overwhelming rush of negative emotions, no matter how well you think you have been coping, at this point you would have reached the end of your tether. Unless you have a miracle and someone steps in to talk you down, the risk for you ending your life at this point is extremely high. Once you are in the turmoil of that emotional overload, it is too late. You have already let your irrational destructive mindset take over your rational conscious thinking. There is a big difference between the people who suffer deep depression, those who have struggled for years without getting on top of the problems, and those who get depressed because life is not providing the joy they believe they deserve. This difference in our cruel, self-obsessed environment today is closing the gap, as more people disillusioned with life consider opting out through addictions or committing suicide. Mild depression is on the increase, as life becomes tougher and the mind becomes contaminated with irrational fears.

It is important for those suffering with mild depression to examine their priorities, adjusting their expectations. Depressed people often falsely believe they will never be happy without certain things, such as material possessions, more wealth, more romantic relationships. Changing these negative perceptions, negative thinking patterns through understanding acceptance, is the best way to improve the quality of someone's life. It takes a truly strong person to identify and accept where they are going wrong, then move forward with lifestyle changes to put things right. I want to focus more in this chapter on mild depression in the majority. Those who choose depression and misery over making better choices in their lives, not the people prepared to sit on the edge of the ledge when it all gets too much.

If we get a little niggling worry or a parking fine and we ignore it, hoping it will just go away, the worry might go, another emotion can change the mood, but the parking fine won't, unless you act immediately to sort out the problem. Basically, if you don't immediately sort it out, it will be too late, like sitting on the edge of the ledge for someone deeply depressed. Most people when they find themselves at the end of their tether, not just those overwhelmed by their emotions but in everyday life, often pray to something separate from themselves for help. Please God, just let me win the lottery and I promise I will change, I will be good, be kind, even go to church if that's what it takes to get the miracle I believe I deserve. This built-in conditioning in the subconscious mind telling you to forget about the parking fine because either God will pay, or you'll win the lottery, is a false comfort blanket you live under in your imagination. I know this for you is your comfort blanket. I know the feeling that you can hand over your mistakes, your problems, your mess to someone else who will sort it out for you, is real to you. If you really think about it logically, there is no imaginary person in the sky to help you sort out a tangible parking fine or help you to win the lottery, only you oversee your choices and decisions—fact not fairy tale. Having a fantasy person, someone to offload your problems on, so you don't have to take personal responsibility for the mess you find yourself in, is simply you in denial. I just won't open this letter—the parking fine—and deal with it, even when I know it's urgent and needs my attention. If I do this, it means it's not real. I can ignore it or pray it goes away. Like I have said a million times before and will repeat here again, there is nothing external that can sort out your problems. It all comes from within. Once you can let go of the fairy tales, the dogma and the pain, all the pretence that comes from never growing up and maturing into an adult with integrity, you will begin to understand the rules of a happy fulfilled life.

Turning inward for anyone who has not cleared out their mind mess is very dangerous. We will only hear the truth about ourselves once we have faced the problems exist and have healed from them, forgiven ourselves for them and then moved on from them. Detachment is a healthy alternative to obsessing about your problems. If you are forever overwhelmed predicting the future, wrapped up in knots, convincing yourself there is no way out by detaching emotionally, you become less over invested in your internal chaos. When you are over attached to your mind chaos, you become fixated, over-worrying and dwelling on the negatives. Recognise this pattern behaviour is completely dysfunctional, controlling and prevents rational problem solving.

Being mindful of your fear, your anxiety, your depression, allows it to become your teacher, giving it a purpose to what is otherwise meaningless and pointless suffering. Remember, fear shuts down your intuition, your instincts, your gratitude, your humility and narrows your vision. All common sense goes out of the window. Learning to skilfully work alongside your depression, fear and anxiety is an essential decision you need to make to move away from the pain of your past. As you learn to deepen your spiritual connection through mindfulness, you can slowly encounter your fear through being curious and open to your unwanted irrational feelings, the uncertainty about yourself, and begin to awaken inside. When this happens, you can separate yourself from what you believe to be hopeless and overwhelming, clearing the black fog, catching a glimpse of the light at the end of the tunnel, becoming open to change the way you look at things.

I love the saying: we cannot see the wood for the trees. When you think about it, you cannot have a wood without trees, but you can have a tree without a wood. The saying means you cannot grasp the main issue because of over-attention to the details. If you cannot see the wood for the trees, you cannot see the whole situation, the bigger picture. Your narrow-minded vision only allows you to see your negative beliefs and feelings. We can all see a tree without the wood. It stands alone, tall, strong, connected firmly in the ground, separate from the wood. We can see it more clearly and rely on it to be real because it has been there a long time and weathered the storms of time. Using strong visualisation and body language like imagining you are this tree, separate from the wood, will send a strong message to your brain you are showing unbreakable strength. Practise standing tall whenever you feel small and insignificant, so your brain can reinforce that it believes in you because you are strong, not weak. The biggest challenge for people deeply depressed or contemplating suicide is finding this firm centre like the tree, away from the wood, the middle ground between hope, fear, avoidance, compulsion and the hopelessness. The one conscious voice of reason. You need to find a way to separate yourself from all that is challenging and taking you down, through finding the strength to face the real world, not retreat into yourself (the wood), the place where you can avoid your problems, get lost or escape into your imagination for some temporary relief.

It is much better to understand and know a few things more deeply than have a million opinions about everything. This wisdom and knowledge will help you understand more about yourself, facing your truth, outside of the misery in the moment. Achieving one small task at a time, like opening the letter, the parking fine, making a call, paying it or asking someone else to help you pay it, even getting some free advice on how to pay it, will leave you feeling more accomplished. A problem shared is a problem halved. The more you do this, the better you will feel and the more manageable your life will become. You learn with confidence to turn away from your avoidance, running away from things, taking personal responsibility instead. Running away from taking personal responsibility for anything only happens when the person running has an immature mindset. Anyone centred would not get to this place in the first place. They keep on top of problems, like paying a parking fine.

Mindful thinking begins by understanding that the secret to life is to be happy with what you have, not yearning for what you don't have. We always pay for our mistakes in the end. Look what happened to me. The decision to nurture gratitude is a real tonic for your wellbeing and mental health. You should always count your blessings, not your troubles. I understand gratitude is hard to find when your thoughts and feelings leave you scared, overwhelmed, draining all your positive energy, making your life not worth living. I also understand most people can keep these feelings at a distance but when depression takes over, it is not possible to stay out of the chaos. I believe we must fail in life to be able to succeed in life, and if we fail again, we must keep on trying, no matter how big or small the challenge is. This is how we develop our confidence. Once you give up, it's over and once it's over, you either let it go because it was not right in the first place or you allow it to define who you are in your mind, a failure.

Our minds will always perceive our negative thoughts much easier than our positive ones. This is sadly because we are wired this way often in childhood. Happiness is something we discover for ourselves. This for me came from understanding and experiencing true gratitude for my life at a time when all the fake happiness and money in the world let me down. Feeling gratitude will never come from a negative mindset. What do you have to be grateful for? The truth is, you have your life to be grateful for. The most amazing gift, yet most of the time we take it for granted.

Becoming aware of what is important to you, regardless of your unconscious ego mind, is your intellect. This helps you to balance things more appropriately, to act in harmony with your needs and not against you. Self-awareness is a conscious knowledge of our character and feeling. When we focus our attention on ourselves, we begin to evaluate and compare our current beliefs to our internal moral standards and values. In other words, we become self-conscious as an objective evaluator of ourselves. This is a major factor when we begin to understand self-control and we learn to be honest with ourselves, deciding if what we are doing mirror images our morals and personal standards. You cannot say you love animals and then eat them.

Learning to focus and develop self-awareness like everything else I am teaching you, is never easy when you have already given up on yourself. When you next find yourself stuck in a negative emotional pattern, i.e. you feel that hopelessness coming on, give it a name like black dog, then practise how to separate yourself from the experience by choosing a new name to replace it, like white dog. If the black dog is hopelessness, the white dog becomes hopeful. Just by changing what it means to you, the emotion you feel will change. Your brain and thoughts in your subconscious towards it will also change. Your subconscious obeys these changes and gives you the right feelings associated with the two dogs' names. Walking and exercise have been proven to change moods. When you exercise, you produce endorphins, so my advice, take the white dog out for a long walk and leave the black dog—the old habit/pattern—chained firmly to the back door until you are ready to return and face it all in a better frame of mind. Eventually, the white dog will become your loyal friend and companion, your new positive pattern/habit you can rely on, to get you out of the house—thinking, not sinking. The black dog will eventually break free and run off.

Any habit is easy to form and difficult to break. Think about when you first started to swim. You would give it your best shot through trying and trying, again devoting lots of energy to it through repetition and confidence; once you became comfortable in the water, swimming became second nature every time you got in the pool. Healthy eating, walking, swimming, exercising and all other positive habit-forming activities pretty much follow the same behavioural pattern. The more we practise, the better we get at the desired activity. Remember, you are the CEO of your life, sitting at the helm, consciously driving the mind in the direction of where you want to go. Your unconscious and subconscious mind will do what it is trained by you to do. Think about how many times you have had a scary nightmare, full of mixed-up things you could make little sense of after the event, yet you can wake up feeling stressed and frightened, glad to be in the safety of your own bed. This would potentially never happen again if your unconscious repressed thoughts and fears were erased and replaced by a tranquil Garden of Eden. If every night before you went to sleep, you informed your subconscious you are having a wonderful night's sleep because you were happy and loved yourself, you would never have a nightmare again. Once again, I will reinforce here, it is you that oversees, directing your subconscious mind by only giving it clear positive instructions. If you say you cannot swim because you are afraid of the water, your subconscious mind will make you feel physically stressed every time you envisage swimming. It's simple. If you say I cannot swim but I am going to give it my best shot and learn, your subconscious will give you the feeling of courage and encourage you to jump in at the deep end.

Let's go back to fear here, the main reason we find it impossible to change. Most of us have no clear definition of what fear means in the context of our lives. What I call fear, you might call anxiety; someone else might call it panic. The main reason we must examine what we are feeling outside of the stressful event. Much of what we are experiencing is amplified by hidden fear, past trauma or buried emotional wounds. We cannot keep running away from fear and anxiety reactions anymore. We must decide to start looking more deeply at our perception of our debilitating feelings to finally reclaim some spiritual freedom away from them.

Our irrational fear represents physical, mental, emotional and spiritual bondage. It enslaves us, destroying any chance of light clean energy coming into our consciousness. It hijacks our subconscious, destroying who we are in the end. Being courageous enough to start the process of facing your deepest darkest buried fears, being open and willing to overcome them without letting anxiety step in, will allow you to develop a higher spiritual consciousness.

Many of us have real difficulty accepting ourselves as we really are. This lack of self-acceptance has a huge impact on the soul. When we lack the ability to accept ourselves as we are, we become unable to make meaningful changes. Once you understand clearly that the worst of all our enemies is ourselves, the cruel critic inside the mind, predicting the outcome of our lives, we discover what true acceptance means. I recommend you start to write a list of all the things the mind critic challenges you with every day, then practise taking one of these things each week and examine how much of it is real, pushing you out of your comfort zone into unknown territory. If it tells you, you are ugly, a failure and will never get anywhere, stand back and ask yourself why. Then write down what you believe is ugly about yourself. Write down what you have failed at and then see if it is the truth or if it is just something within your existing belief system. Once you can accept the challenges you face, your reality, you will feel much calmer, therefore think more clearly, pushing you a little bit closer towards confidently believing in yourself. When you think too much, you over-analyse details, and this makes it harder to accept your reality, so practise detaching from overthinking by becoming a doer, not a slave to the self-critic.

Making changes in your life, especially those who have already given up all hope, is never easy but you must make the decision to retrain your brain to understand what you feel is positive and permanent, regardless of your emotional state. Self-awareness is at the centre of our emotional intelligence. It is our ability to monitor our feelings and emotions moment to moment and doing this helps us to understand ourselves much better, beyond the unconscious ego's control. It is often a shattered sense of self that brings about a habitual sense of suffering, driving us to addictive behaviour or dark depression, altering our sense of identity. The immense pain never resolved from childhood will always halt the natural development of the soul self. Your soul is way too sensitive and developed to participate in the painful self-sabotaging behaviour of a lost tortured child, projecting blame on others for the way things have turned out. Many of us are completely unaware of the connection between past traumatic childhood events and current behaviours. Time alone does not heal our pain but having awareness of it give us hope.

Many people who fall into depression will turn to alcohol, drugs, food, or try and commit suicide because they want to escape their past, their failures and disappointments, the things that haunt them but escaping never works. Most of the time, we are operating on autopilot, not conscious of how we are feeling or what we are doing. Our chaotic minds are always wandering from the past to the future, never experiencing the present—life's biggest mistake! You must learn to know your own truth in the moment by being more honest and aware, then responding to any challenging circumstances immediately with clarity and confidence, developing better coping skills through practice and patience. If through your mindfulness you can learn to stop reacting and ask yourself how you are feeling in the moment, you will start to notice real things, not your imagined pre-determined emotions based on comfort or your pattern behaviour.

Next time you unconsciously reach out for a big calorific fat-filled burger and chips out of habit, try and consciously stop to ask yourself how you are feeling before you scoff it down. Work out if you are reaching for it because you are hungry or wanting comfort for a hangover. Is it to feel false pleasure or numb pain? Next time you convince yourself you are going to get drunk because you deserve it, ask yourself how you are feeling inside to find out what it is you want to block out, what you are potentially running away from facing. By consciously understanding how you feel at any given time through being mindful, you will create the time to decide if what you are doing is automatic, without thinking, is the right decision for your health long term. You will be able to work out if you are doing it out of habit or to heal something you are unconsciously harbouring inside. If you do not develop this self-regulating skill and you do not respond appropriately, big life changes will have a devastating impact. You won't see it coming or be able to handle the consequences. What you think is acceptable behaviour will become an addictive, uncontrollable problem. The development of your coping skills will allow you to regain some emotional harmony, especially when dark depressing thoughts and feelings unconsciously take over your healthy thinking. Creating coping strategies through either talk therapy or positive self-talk will help you to break through damaging negative patterns, so you are able to build a healthy resilience against future episodes.

Nobody consciously chooses to feel depressed, miserable or full of anxiety. It is not a passing phase but deeply embedded in your psyche. As you become more skilled at acknowledging your feelings, emotions and behaviours, you will improve your mood swings until self-control becomes a natural part of your everyday life. The reality is we should have learnt this as children. A good example of using triggers to help inform you, you are about to go over Niagara Falls, is to buy some post-it notes and write some positive reinforcement messages, like I can do it, well done, I feel empowered. Stick these all over your living space and imagine it is me observing and talking to you. If overeating is making you depressed and you are spending more time with the fridge than your family, put a note on the fridge door saying it's over, I don't need you anymore. You are dumped. Goodbye, fridge. Dumping the fridge and starting a new relationship with exercise, water and a healthy balanced diet will be a real challenge to begin with but like any new relationship, the more you work at it, the easier it will be to master. If you are drinking too much and have become dependent on alcohol to wind you down when you get home from work, put a note on the bottle saying "Think before you drink me", and go out for a long walk instead. Once you are outside walking, your train of thought and internal dialogue will change automatically. You have changed your routine. The post-it notes are your conscious instructions and they will remind you what you have decided to do in order to change your subconscious thinking until you create your new healthy patterns.

In my own life when I was working on changing my own unhealthy habits and patterns, the addictions, it took around nineteen days to change from one habit to the next. This was being focused with discipline, so it is possible to do if you can consciously remind yourself you are committed to changing. The bad mood or unrelaxed feelings you have when you come home from work, driving you to push your head into a bottle of wine, are triggers to let you know you hate your life. Staying the course and changing is the hardest bit you are going to have to face because your unconscious ego thinks it knows better. It is important to remember these bad habits you have become addicted to, your pattern behaviour, are all things you do automatically without thinking. They are always triggered by how you feel emotionally. Do you really want to be someone who lives their life doing things without thinking? Can you see how out of control you are when it comes to making choices? How much are you just not consciously participating in your own life?

Most things we do, we do on autopilot, like driving the car, rushing around the supermarket, rushing to get the kids ready for school, rushing to work with a million different thoughts, always ahead of ourselves. We are either planning or predicting what will happen for the rest of the day. With all these thoughts and plans, combined with our many different emotional reactions to these thoughts, it's easy to see how stress, panic and forgetfulness at the end of the day would encourage us to numb it all out with some form of comfort. Anything we do with our mind operating on autopilot, distracted, only partially aware, is the perfect example of how we miss the moment.

Mindfulness is the opposite to autopilot. It ensures we deliberately bring our attention into the moment to consciously focus on what we are doing and why. It encourages us to be present in our lives, helping us to cope better, get more done, feel better about ourselves and take back control. Your autopilot is your inner dialogue with yourself. The cruel critic you live with and listen to without realising it. During these times when you are distracted, only partially aware of what you are doing, thinking, it's the perfect opportunity for the cruel critic to slip in and push you further over the edge. For example, you are rushing around making breakfast, feeding the cat, running a bath, cleaning the toilet, feeding a baby, arguing with your partner. The baby suddenly throws food on the floor, you react, shout and scream out of frustration without thinking. It is not the baby's fault you are frustrated, over-worked and stressed, wishing it would all just stop. The baby just happened to get the brunt of your pent-up negative thinking and you reacted in the moment. Now think if you had been relaxed, happy with no stress, consciously enjoying the moment, in control of your internal chatter, the food on the floor incident would not have happened. The baby would have had all your attention. Of course, it is hard to stay focused when you are multi-tasking to keep everything together but if you truly want to get back in control of how you think and feel so you no longer emotionally react, you must learn to be mindful in the moment. Remember the subconscious mind takes in every single conscious command, including all your negative thoughts and as the pressure and stress builds up, a small thing will always push you too far. In these situations, you will always react and never respond. Like I said, the poor baby just wanted your attention. Everyone and everything else wanted your attention but you are not superhuman, so allowing your anger to produce feelings of guilt, convincing yourself you are a bad parent, is not your truth. The emotional reaction from feeling guilty about something that is not true goes straight into your subconscious, reinforcing your feelings of guilt, based on the idea you are a bad parent. The information is wrong, so the reaction is wrong. You are not a bad parent; in fact, you are a multi-tasking genius who can manage to do it all. Unfortunately, when it comes to the mind, multi-tasking is tricky. Remember, the CEO, the conscious mind, has only ten percent capacity to decide. It relies on delegating the other ninety percent of the mind to help finish things off efficiently, so the outcome is positive and productive. Everything you think unconsciously about, related to how you are feeling—the autopilot—is stored in the subconscious part of your mind. If you are rushing around like a stressed-out, windup toy, in chaos, trying to do ten things at a time with many different negative thoughts in your internal dialogue, unhealthy stress will automatically build up inside. Chances are you would be repeating and reinforcing through your internal dialogue as you are rushing around—I hate people who don't put down the toilet seat; I hate the smell of bleach; I am dreading today; I hate my boss; I hate my job; I wish I could just have a drink right now. All these thoughts of hate are then stored at the forefront of your subconscious mind and would eventually become anger, fear and frustration, not about what you are doing but about how you feel about yourself and your day ahead. You enter the kitchen full of anger. The baby throws food all over the clean floor. You have a major emotional reaction, not based on this one thing but all the other negative things you have been projecting on yourself on autopilot. You reach a peak in your head, you explode in moment when tipped over the edge and, before you know it, your whole world crashes in, you hit boiling point and explode.

When we look at other examples of autopilot thinking, only partially participating in what we are doing, it is easy to see how it would be impossible to achieve anything without beating ourselves up when one little thing goes wrong. Think about all the times you have consciously decided you want to lose some weight. You go on a diet, easy; it just needed you to make the conscious decision. The next step is about your motive. You need to lose weight because you hate your body. You hate yourself for eating the fridge. Every time you say you hate your body, you are sending messages into your subconscious that are totally wrong. You don't hate your body, you love it because without it you would be dead. You just hate the way it looks, what you have done to it through being out of control. Start saying to yourself instead with compassion and gratitude, I love my body because it keeps me alive, but I get upset with myself when I cannot control my eating and drinking habits. I am unhappy but I am not sure why. Being kind to yourself, asking yourself consciously how you are feeling with self-compassion, is way more realistic and positive than hurtful, damaging non-truths in your imagination. If you consciously keep saying you hate your body when you don't—without it, you would be dead—your inner dialogue will automatically keep reinforcing negative thoughts during your autopilot unconscious eating binges. Your emotional reaction back to this behaviour will remind you, you're a failure that hates their body. My advice is try swapping your unhealthy existing beliefs and feelings of greed, gluttony and guilt for more graceful, healthy values, like gratitude for your body and forgiveness and compassion for putting it through unthinkable pressure to give you what you think you desire. In other words, to put it bluntly, you are the police in charge of your own bad behaviour. No one has a gun to your head, forcing you to eat the fridge. It is your own lack of self-esteem, self-worth and self-control holding you hostage. Remember, you grow through what you go through.

How you talk to yourself unconsciously through your inner dialogue, the words you use to describe what you think of yourself, informs your subconscious memory what you think about yourself. Ask yourself now, is what you are repeating to yourself in your mind words used by your parents, other people, or is it what you really think? Our subconscious mind is crammed full of unconscious ideas and beliefs we don't realise we have, and they guide our behaviour, many times holding us back from being the people we really are deep down. As we have already established, most of these beliefs and ideas are either planted by our parents early on in development, or they have come from other people's opinions about how we should look, behave or be. Understanding the subconscious takes finding out where your beliefs came from in the first place. If your sister called you fat as a child, it was her opinion and not a fact. Your subconscious mind may have believed your sister's opinion back then when you had no choice, but you don't have to believe it today, you now have your own mind and opinions. Only your opinion counts. This is where being a mind detective kicks in. You must go backwards over all the evidence, to discover where your autopilot negative self-talk began, then decide if it is real or just a bunch of unimportant opinions planted in you from other people. This truly is an enlightening experience, bringing the conscious mind closer to the subconscious memory and the only way you will ever get to know yourself better.

Whatever you have going on in your mind will play out in your life. If you waste any more time continuing to do and say negative things because you are stressed or need the approval of others, you will always be comparing yourself to something you cannot live up to and sadly, you will never be happy. How you feel about yourself, how you talk to yourself, will always dictate your behaviour towards yourself. If you consciously keep repeating through your inner dialogue, looking at yourself in the mirror—I love my body because I am grateful for it, it keeps me alive—your subconscious will hold this fact and over time, you will swap the feeling of wanting comfort for gratitude instead.

Comfort is not pleasure. When you are automatically eating the whole fridge believing it is satisfying, you are not feeding your body nutrients, fuel or energy, you are feeding your negative emotions instead. They will never be satisfied until you consciously sort them out by resolving unresolved issues from the past. Reprogramming your thinking takes a great deal of practice, the reason processing and repeating things like I am doing throughout this book is crucial. It keeps you moving forward with small steps, consciously keeping on top of what you are doing and thinking, until eventually you process the idea that all change starts with you.

I suggest you look up the meaning of the words you are using to describe how you feel about yourself, words like hate, an intense dislike, then ask yourself what it is you intensely dislike about your body. Then look up the word love, a strong feeling of affection, gratitude, being thankful and appreciating something. Now decide which you prefer to believe about yourself and your body. If you have an intense dislike for it, that is not good, is it? How does this make you feel? I would imagine quite bad, so you need to change this round to appreciating and being thankful for it. Start telling your subconscious mind something different and see how much better you feel. Being thankful and grateful for your body because you need it in your life will begin to replace the feelings of hate and eventually you will find its purpose. When something has a purpose, you take better care of it. It's simple. I am trying to make you recognise when you make better choices, you let go of fear and don't allow other emotions to confuse how you are feeling. The problem with hating your body, it will always be followed by deep feelings of guilt. You will know deep down inside you are committing a crime against your health and this leads to internal shame, painful humiliation and before you know it, you will need something nice, like the cream cake or the wine—the comfort—to make you feel better. See how it works. It's a vicious cycle.

Loving something, on the other hand, is usually followed by intense feelings of great pleasure. A deep feeling of happy satisfaction and fulfilment. Understanding the words you use to describe how you feel, does not just apply to how you think about food and your body, it applies to everything you think about yourself. You are what you think. If you keep consciously saying you feel bored, fed up, jaded, sick and tired, ask yourself how you feel about this. Being jaded is about a lack of enthusiasm. A lack of enthusiasm means you are physically tired and exhausted. Is this how you see yourself? Get on board and recognise telling yourself you are bored will make you sick and tired. Sick and tired means you need a rest from yourself. Start telling yourself you are not feeling fulfilled right now, satisfied or happy. Your subconscious mind will then give you what you need to help you face this and then help you change it.

Your unconscious mind comprises mental processes inaccessible to your consciousness but will influence your judgements and feelings. It is vital to understand that your motives, feelings and decisions stored in the subconscious are strongly influenced by your past experiences. Talk therapy is all about being open and brave enough to look deep in the mind to pull out painful repressed memories. It is an opportunity to look at your problems in a different way with someone who won't judge you or compromise you. Meditation is a powerful brain retraining method and helps us regain our core values and authentic beliefs, changing the way we think about ourselves. Basically, if you can forgive yourself and the past by letting it all go, tell yourself in humility you have nothing to feel guilty about, be grateful for your health and your life, love yourself, see yourself as authentic with integrity, your subconscious will process this as your new reality.

Your heart is the main organ within your body that truly needs to be cared for now to keep you healthy physically, not always stressed with permanent unease. This will by default sort your mind out. You will be giving it all the right messages from your instinct and intuition, not from your imagination. When you listen to your heart, the central most inner part of your being, the place your instincts live, the way you behave will never go wrong. To receive your instincts from your heart, it must be healthy, happy and full of joy, not clogged up full of unease. It needs to be open and honest, working efficiently to not only keep you alive but to fill you with the love and comfort you are desperately seeking. If everything you are doing today comes only from your conscious mind, the element of you that helps you be aware of the world around you, your experiences, how you think, it is important to remember this only works at ten percent capacity. I would be more inclined to listen and rely on my heart and my instincts for guidance over a tiny part of my mind that only allows me to have one conscious thought at a time. Your heart will always tell you the truth deep down. Your mind, on the other hand, lies. You can manipulate it through your imagination. It can create fake happiness when it suits you, to help you stop having to face your pain, shame, guilt, depression or personal misery.

Listening to my open heart in an open honest way, instead of being challenged by my mind, has changed me dramatically. I never make rash impulsive choices anymore based on my need for comfort, believing it is pleasure. I am disciplined and focused on living my life. I have managed to change an extensive list of unhealthy habits, giving up smoking, drinking, impulsive spending, becoming more frugal, sex, drugs, meat, caffeine, creating a healthier lifestyle being more organised and focused. You will be thinking right now how did I manage to give up everything in one go without difficulty? I must be superhuman. I am not superhuman, I just truly value my health and my life more than anything else these days. This is what happens naturally when you face death for real. You change your attitude and perspective, and start to value the things that truly matter. How would it be possible to smoke a cigarette again when I value my heart? It is my information source and helps me to feel happy. How could I value money over my happiness when I already know money did not make me happy? How could I eat an animal when I have empathy, the ability to share and understand feelings for another life?

Once I reached the bottom, I connected with my divine self, the authentic me, through compassion, grace, humility and gratitude. Smoking, drinking and sex all seemed futile, pointless pursuits, not good for my health, my soul or my happiness. I automatically swapped my negative beliefs, thoughts and habits for some self-respect, self-esteem and healthy positive feeling of gratitude. I began to evaluate my priorities, resulting in more meaning in my life. A wonderful experience I will never forget. I no longer con myself these days into believing I'm having a good time. I truly am enjoying my life for real. I am happy, centred, balanced, healthy, honest and grateful. Nothing ever throws me off or tempts me to believe I am invincible. I now know I am not.

Giving up sex, becoming celibate—eighteen years now—has been an amazing journey. I have discovered I don't need the validation or even the connection of a man in my new life. I have many male friends and enjoy their company, but I no longer feel the need to have sex anymore. Like any other thing you do without really thinking, like eating meat or shopping, with time and honest internal dialogue with yourself, you start to think less about the fix and more about why you do the things you do. Once you become connected with your divine self, your soul, you understand empathy, compassion, you gain more knowledge about life, the planet, the universe. It becomes impossible to do things like eat animals or have risky sex. The desire fades naturally. You recognise if you had to kill an animal yourself, you wouldn't be able to do it. Once you connect to this powerful place inside and begin the process of understanding love from your heart, not your mind, you don't need anyone else. You naturally enjoy being self-sufficient.

I have naturally deconstructed my old self and reconstructed my new self through having a peak experience, not a creative artistic one, but a life-changing spiritual one. This has opened me up to my true talents and creative expression. This kind of massive experience will not happen for most. We rarely have such life-changing things happen, but it is possible I believe to change sufficiently to reach the divine self by rewinding the mind, facing ourselves openly with faith. By faith, I don't mean anything religious. I mean believing in ourselves.

You may think your life would be boring or no fun if you had to give up your bad habits. You might even conclude it would be impossible to be happy without sex, drugs, rock and roll, but you would be wrong, trust me. The kind of happiness, peace, joy, love, excitement and personal growth I am selling to you is magnificent and beyond your wildest dreams. I am hoping to get you to become a fully functioning human being and although it may take me a lifetime to convince you to change, I am never giving up. I have all the time in the world. I am going to devote the rest of my life to help people realise their full potential, which today is my purpose and payback to the universe for giving me another crack at life.

I will try and help you to at least begin the process of recognising your existing beliefs, then breaking them down, showing how the negative bias implanted in your memory, keeping you stuck, believing you are happy, is not the truth. If you were happy, you would not be reading this book. To recap, if you have a wonderful, happy, honest and fruitful garden growing in your unconscious mind, you keep telling your subconscious mind for nineteen days you don't like wine, you prefer water, you will eventually beat your bad habits, desiring fruit and water over chocolate and wine. I can imagine what you are thinking right now. This sounds impossible but I used to be a chocoholic and a borderline alcoholic, so anything is possible with the work and the desire.

This journey of change is all about developing long-term goals you will cultivate over time. You must learn in stages because you grow in stages. You will begin to see with more clarity as you start to master your mind and negative thoughts, just how the past has tricked and deluded your awareness to be able to act, when action is required.

A simple way to let go of the past, the pain, the mess, the addictions, the guilt, the old you, is a visualisation experience that will feel quite empowering when you do it is as follows: buy some balloons, blow them up and tie them individually to a piece of long string. Use a black felt pen and write on each balloon whatever it is you want to let go of. If it is an ex, write their name; if it is your anger, write anger, and so on. Once you have written all you want to let go of on the balloons, take them to a beautiful spot you love, somewhere with space in nature, like the top of a hill, and let them go into the atmosphere, watch them drift away into the distance until they disappear. Once you can no longer see the balloons, psychologically, the past, the pain and the things you have held onto for so long will have left you for good, never to return. Letting go is about being free and being free means you can start afresh. The past is the story of your life. If this story does not mirror image how you see it because you have painted the wrong picture of things in your mind, discovering your truth will put all this right in the end. The balloons are a symbol of your past pain and letting go of this pain means you can replace it with something new and positive.

Life can easily get on top of us. I have found the best way to combat mental health is to spend time alone interacting with nature without question. It is a fact that the quality of our thoughts dictates the quality of our lives. We have between twenty-five thousand to fifty thousand thoughts per day, so imagine how busy your mind is at any one time. Now imagine if most of these thoughts are negative, how easy it is to understand why depression and misery has become normal. Can you now begin to imagine how potentially you have spent your whole life to date never challenging your thinking? How many times do you automatically think the worst or assume you will fail, blaming yourself when something goes wrong? What you have been taught as a child has kept you stuck in the child state. As an adult, you have not been free or confident to make your own choices based on your authentic needs. The main reason many are plagued with depression and misery today. We have followed the pack, listened to all the wrong information, craved validation and connection, bought into marketing, the pull of materialism and status, never once stopping to reflect or rewind. How many times have you gone through the motions of doing something deep down you know you cannot afford or don't believe in, just to please others or not be left out? Through self-analysis, asking yourself questions, you will begin to unravel what the truth is and what is a lie. This will provide you with the only permanent solution to your suffering.

Beginning a journey of self-exploration through your meditation to uncover the root cause of your depression and anxiety will help you to see change as it happens, giving insight to help you overcome your immature ignorance. Basically, as you unblock your mental blockage, you will discover the root cause of your pain and suffering, like I have said many times before does not belong to you. It belongs in the recycling bin. Once you learn to define your own unique strengths and you use them for a greater purpose, beyond your needs, like I am doing right now, you too will begin to contribute and make a difference in the world.

Fulfilment in your life can only come from living in alignment with who you truly want to be—your authentic self—and what you genuinely hope to achieve. There is an important factor to consider when it comes to changing your whole life, especially as you begin to recognise you are not the fabulous, truthful amazing, good person your unconscious ego has had you believing all these years and this is a sense of humour. Believe it or not, laughter has incredible psychological and emotional benefits. It stimulates a chemical change in the brain, helping prevent stress through releasing endorphins, lowering blood pressure, lifting moods, soothing depression and misery. It helps release tension in the physical body, all that stress and pain buried inside, keeping you believing you are sick, when all you are missing is having a good laugh at yourself. When implementing new habits and behaviours going forward, remember to always have a sense of humour and self-compassion. As you approach change, take one day at a time. This approach will help relieve stress and keep you motivated. Compassion means being open to recognise your suffering and be supportive of your pain. A sense of humour means being open to see the funny side of things, something you will need in abundance when you take on your mind, trust me.

Is Your Life Just a Template?

Hope is an amazing contributor towards being happy and secure. Drive is the key to ambition and success. Learning is about memory, and your personal circumstances often dictate the outcome of your life.

As you know I had a very positive start in my life in terms of being instilled with enormous confidence, the circumstances around me on the other hand were not so positive and helpful. My built-in determination and desire to succeed prevented me being stuck with my lot. To accomplish success as we develop, through learning different skills—with me it was sales—we can discover our unique drive, ambition and achievements as we travel the journey of life. If we want change, we must be that change. Life will always hit us hard and often we will fail. We must learn to get straight back up and fight. Nobody else can be responsible for your failure as an adult other than you. Everyone is fighting their own battle deep down inside but not everyone has the courage to show it. When you hit the lowest point in your life, you are at the bottom end of the curve. The only way back is up, but at least the worst is over, if you survive yourself.

My upbringing, once the first eighteen months were over, was a downward spiral of poverty, pain, loss, danger, isolation exposure to alcohol, misery and confusion. Not the best start for a happily-ever-after ending but I was never controlled, abused or bullied. I was driven, self-aware, with an inner desire and passion to succeed I never really understood. My mother leaving was tough in the beginning. It kept my father working all hours to pay the bills. I was pretty much left to my own devices. I had to learn my life lessons the hard way on my own, but my gift of unbreakable confidence, given before she left, was a godsend on reflection, the only one solid thing I could rely on to get me through it all. At such a young age, I found myself alone in charge of my choices, and I made all the wrong ones as you would imagine. You only know what you do until you know something else and with no one older at home to model on, I made it all up as I went along.

I always wanted to stand out. I had the confidence but standing out meant being different and being different meant being alone most of the time. I soon got comfortable being my own boss. I loved the freedom it bought me. I made many mistakes for sure—some major ones—but I always learnt the hard way, my way, and my mistakes became my blueprint for success. My life of pain always ensured I never gave up trying. My mistakes included skipping school for smoking and fun, going to town in the evening to meet boys instead of doing homework and buying clothes without being able to afford them, often stealing the money from my dad's pocket without him even knowing when he was tipsy. I soon learnt how to survive by lying and creating a made-up version of my truth, to get me from A to B, without being noticed by the establishment, my school head and her rigid rules. She was one person who truly put me off ever wanting to live a life inside a box.

I began to drink and enjoy alcohol early on. Everyone around me including my family did it, so to me it was normal to do the same. Sex became a way for me to feel wanted, needed, and gave me the power to escape myself and my internal pain—for a while anyway. I can never remember being read a bedtime fairy-tale where the handsome prince comes to save the day, sweeping the girl off her feet to a castle with a white picket fence and a happily-ever-after ending. I see this today as a massive plus in my enlightened state. Once you grow up and recognise these stories never tell you what happens beyond the happily-ever-after ending, you realise this is because there is no such thing, unless you are your own happily-ever-after first. I am not saying people are never happy with their choices, some are. What I am trying to show is how the choices we make, based on the information we are given as children, must be useful and productive not based on fantasy or sentiment, otherwise we end up disappointed as adults. If the centre for educational neuroscience concludes most of our learning occurs in the first three years of our life, the critical period for brain development, in my mind filling a child's head with all the wrong information, believing you are protecting them when in fact you are lying to them, is fatal for emotional development.

In nature, if a songbird does not learn its own species-specific song early on in its development, it will never be able to communicate properly and survive long term. As human beings, we must learn emotional intelligence skills early on too or we will never learn them at all and just like the songbird, be unable to communicate how we feel or what we need to our fellow human beings. We learn to think at the same time we learn to use words. We have already established not all our thinking is a conscious act. We have a conscious purposeful use of talking to ourselves through our inner dialogue. We also have many automatic unconscious thoughts that become mixed up and scrambled with no purpose at all. This internal automatic inner dialogue, that cruel critic, happens fast and gets confusing, as we negatively argue with ourselves, berate ourselves, planting more negative ideas and thoughts in our subconscious that are just not true. This often comes out in words without thinking and ends up being a reaction not a conscious thought-out response.

Think about how many times you've been in a bad mood because of how you are feeling, then been horrible and taken it out on someone else who has nothing to do with your rage or frustration. You end up projecting your misery onto them. Sometimes we can be aware of our internal dialogue but more times than not, we have no idea we are doing it. The reason mindful meditation is critical to help us hear this negative chatter. The same goes for what we do consciously, automatically without thinking. In this chapter, I am going to be talking about events and traditions created in the ego-driven template of life and how we celebrate mass events like Christmas automatically, even if we don't really want to.

I never remember happy Christmases beyond a few token gifts. Money was tight, alcohol-driven fights and fallouts created my memories, this was real life. I always knew what to expect and it was not aspiration, debt, fairy tales and fluff, just one different day from the rest of the year. If you think about this, you see how big brand marketing, money and greed have driven us all into celebrating for months ahead of the event through compulsive shopping, eating looking forward, completely missing the point of the present. This shows me just how unhappy people are, when they spend time and money they don't have to celebrate something for months that has no purpose other than gluttony and materialism. I believe having family time is a good thing, celebrating something is a good thing, cooking a nice meal is a good thing, but Christmas isn't about this anymore, it's just another addiction. Christmas has become something we are driven to do because everyone else is doing it. If you take away the money, the materialism, the getting drunk, the cooking, the present buying, the fake illusion of a *White Christmas* DVD and ask yourself what you are celebrating, it will become clear you have no idea unless you still believe in the reincarnation of Jesus. I grew up not putting much value on something that today lasts for months. I don't ever look forward to Christmas. I dread it and always have. This is because I don't like doing the same thing over and over every year, like everyone else. I like to be different and do what I want to do. This works for me.

We are all capable of observational learning. You have heard the saying, monkey see, monkey do. What we see and learn especially as young children will have a pro-social or anti-social effect later in life. We model, we copy, we repeat. If you want your children to read, you must let them see you read. You need to have books around the house, talk books, live books. If you want your children to be grateful with humility, you must model this behaviour yourself, teaching them values and morals; what they observe, they learn. If as a child you grow up in a situation where you are abused and witness your caregivers dealing with anger and frustration, acting out violent behaviour, you are likely to learn things in the same anti-social way. You copy the same actions with the same reactions because it is all you see.

All our learning as children occurs by modelling and copying on our caregivers, parents and siblings. What we see them do, what they say, good or bad, by simply observing their behaviours, is the reason many families mentally get screwed up. I was one of the lucky ones. At the beginning, I modelled on amazing things and by the age of nine, I was pretty much alone, learning things for myself through experiencing real life, not copying a life already mapped out for me. Obviously, I do have some memories from back then. I knew instinctively the life template filled with traditions and regular events was not for me. I can remember births, deaths and marriages. They were all the same format; dressing up to celebrate life or dressing down to mourn the loss of it. I never had a proper relationship with my mother after she left. I never really saw her except from time to time after she remarried, usually in the pub or at family gatherings, created to celebrate these births, deaths and marriages. We learn from one another via observation, imitation and modelling. It's a bit like a bridge between behavioural and cognitive learning, encompassing memory, attention and motivation.

I learnt very early on the fairy-tale life template, the traditions, events and copied behaviour patterns, was all about people escaping their life. I had no interest in repeating what everyone else was doing. I instinctively knew there was more to life than what I could see with my eyes. Growing up in the fifties was all about muddy puddles, handmade toys, imagination, making perfume from rose petals, hopscotch, skipping ropes, rhubarb crumble and bubble and squeak. In the current environment today, things have moved on but not for the better in my opinion, based on the misery I see every day. Christmas lasts for months, children are spoilt, debt is out of control, the streets are dangerous places and the mobile phone has replaced real conversation. We all have our own reasons for doing the things we do, day in day out, but sometimes when you look at things from a different perspective, it can be a truly enlightening light-bulb moment. Much of what we see today is an illusion driven by money, greed and status. Poor mental health is a byproduct of out of control, self-indulgent, materialistic treadmill of repeated expectations. This has left many of us at the mercy of our own ignorance, with mental problems, unexplained anxieties and mass depression. The truth is, we are all mental in some way. Every one of us has had something happen growing up that has influenced or moulded us to become the grown-up people we are today. The template of life we have all been conditioned to follow has become our only road map to happiness in life through copying, following events and instructions from big brand marketing and family traditions.

From when we are born, we are immediately exposed to certain times during the year like Christmas, Valentine's, Easter, bank holidays, summer holidays, bonfire night, Halloween, father's day, mother's day and back to Christmas to start all over again. In between this list of calendared events, the rest of the year is filled with birthdays, weddings, christenings, anniversaries, births, deaths and marriages, creating new families. This life template we have all been forced to be part of is fine; some people fare better than others in terms of where they start out, either in poverty or privilege. Whatever background you come from, a template life is restricting and suffocating to personal spiritual growth and evolution of the authentic self. It is hard to change when others are not changing with you. You will always struggle to turn right when everyone else is turning left.

I never wanted to or felt comfortable blindly following others. I have always been a leader not a follower, and this is from having tremendous self-confidence, never needing validation or permission to be me. I have never seen my need to be unique as anything other than a true gift, a miracle, something that helped me overcome my difficult, challenging start. It helped me get to the top, fall from the top and rebuild my life the best possible way today with a new purpose and no regrets.

In the first three years on this earth, I learnt to love myself unconditionally, believe I could do anything, was never spoilt, overprotected or fed made up fairy tales. Life was all about survival, getting on with it, never complaining, always with high expectations, often disappointed but never feeling like a loser. I knew I was a winner right from the start.

The brain develops further after the first three years of life, constantly changing through to adolescence where further dynamic brain activity occurs. Learning emotional stability at the start of life is crucial to being able to manage and survive the difficult parts that come later in life. To become an outsider, go against the grain, you must first become self-reliant, clear minded, be in total control of your thinking, actions and emotional reactions. You will need to be conscious of your every word, regardless of what is going on around you at any time. When you begin to do things differently, outside the template of life, through mindful thinking, you will be living only in the moment, always preparing for the future. Your past will no longer haunt you and before you know it, what you thought you wanted from life will completely change. When you are living in the moment, your past cannot overwhelm you. All your attention, your awareness, is focused on things more immediate and more significant to you. As you learn to escape the past by engaging in the present, the next step is preparing for the future, your future, not what is expected of you or what you have learnt. As children, our reactions to various feelings and emotions will have a massive impact on our belief system, our thinking, our choices and our behaviour. How we cope and enjoy life as we develop and are exposed to different situation, our emotions become more complex. Developing the right skills to manage these emotions is a critical step for emotional wellbeing. Everyone is different. We all learn in different ways. We all have different ways of expressing how we feel, based on what is regarded as normal in our family environment, tradition or culture, creating a cross-section of opinions and beliefs. Some families encourage their children to express their emotions openly, some discourage expressing emotions at all, like anger or pride, and this influences the way children regulate their emotions growing up—like I said, either pro-social or anti-social.

Imagine if you grew up knowing nothing about Christmas, every year at that time you went to sleep until it was all over. You would not miss it and certainly not waste months of your life looking forward to it. Knowledge in my opinion is so much more valuable than memories. Of course, some memories are wonderful and valuable, the positive happy real ones, but to grow spiritually and mature, you must sacrifice your illusions and become more focused on your reality in the present.

Childhood is an extremely influential time. Events that happen when we are developing, even insignificant ones, will have a direct impact when we reach adulthood and truly understanding this, is the first step in the process of maturing. The first emotions we recognise as babies include joy, sadness and fear. As we develop further, we begin to have a sense of self with more complex emotions like shame guilt, shyness, empathy and embarrassment. Our first important

155

relationship we experience in life is with our parents—our primary caregivers. The quality of this relationship determines our social development, as we learn to manage and evolve our social personality, conflict and bargaining skills. It is a very complex time. What we pick up emotionally as children from our parents and their circumstances, will help mould us and manifest in the way we act out as adults, through our emotional memories buried in the subconscious or deeper in the unconscious. Go back here and remember what you have learnt about your subconscious, being all-knowing, storing everything you have ever learnt or felt since your childhood. This has now become your existing belief system, the road map you automatically follow without question or reason. If you can interrupt this short-term memory, your subconscious, by one year doing something completely different at Christmas, the following year you won't be automatically triggered into complete mayhem when you hear jingle bells.

The life template passed onto you so you can pass it on to your children, does not have to be the only way you navigate your existence. We all have the power of choice to do what is right for us, outside the rigid rules of the template and the human condition. They say Christmas today is just for children, but in truth, most adults are still these children, passing on their own subconscious memories and experiences from their own childhood, even if these memories have become skewed or blown out of proportion.

To develop spiritually into maturity through self-awareness, you must be prepared to trade in the old you, the manufactured you, for an upgrade, to someone more curious, open, less focused on the outside, the fixes, the fluff, the past. I can hear you all saying now in protest, you could never give up what you know, what you say you love, what you are looking forward to, but let's remember you are reading this book because you are miserable, depressed and desperate to feel happy. There is no cake and eat it here. When you change your perspective about the things you do automatically, it will change you. Your family will change, your actions will change, and your self-awareness will grow. Life outside the template is where the real action is. Most of us never get to think about this, let alone experience the feeling it brings. The fear of change gets in the way. Think about it now. You have probably never questioned what you do or why you do it. You just do it without thinking, convincing yourself you're happy but how many times are your high expectations met? How many disappointing Christmases do you have to experience or debts to face before you recognise you need to change the record?

The template of life, the traditions we follow, are in my opinion the main reason for the human condition. They keep us stuck in rigid patterns with unrealistic ideals and expectations that never live up to our expectations or imaginations, leaving us constantly disappointed in a state of either looking forward or getting over. This state is followed by tremendous misery. The blame game begins as we descend into the depths of despair, until the next template highlight occurs and we are pushed to participate once again. If you truly think about your own life template patterns right now, you will start to see your own personal patterns of either looking forward to something or getting over something, completely missing the moment. Once you have made big life choices, based on what you think you want because it is expected of you or you have seen it in a TV ad, there may be no escaping the consequences. You will find yourself stuck forever, wasting your life away, wishing you were someone else or somewhere else. Life should always be moving forward and to be happy and fulfilled with your purpose, you must also keep moving forward with it. Circumstances and feelings are constantly changing too, so gaining more knowledge and curiosity is essential to keeping up with these changes. Traditions make a culture what it is, but we need to face sometimes they outlive their usefulness or reason for existing in the first place, which can hinder progress, the very thing I believe is happening in the world right now. Living life in this template, a constant cycle of shopping, eating, drinking, spending, struggling, often spending money we don't have to keep up with and please others, it is no wonder depression has become a symptom of keeping up with the Joneses, the pressure to compete.

Most people would say they love these traditions and life wouldn't be the same without them, it's what they do. Others may have cultural and religious reasons to continue doing them but what if this repeated cycle of tradition and pressure to keep up with the Joneses has becomes the main reason many of us end up in debt, depressed and unfulfilled. The constant pressure to have stuff we believe will change who we are—if you buy this new car, your life will change, even if you go into debt to buy it—is just another form of addiction. How many times have you truly believed you wanted something and still wanted it once you'd bought it? There is a new anxiety taking over in our culture today. It is called FOMO—fear of missing out. My advice is start really thinking about what it is you believe you are missing out on.

Any kind of automatic mentality, nurtured by big brand marketing and the media, pushing us towards a constant desire for money and status, our external needs, is causing us to malfunction as an addicted, greedy society. The truth is, and I know because I have been both rich and poor, money and stuff will never bring you true happiness. You will always be left competing with people you believe have more than you but remember they are probably doing exactly what you are doing, looking like they have more than they do to impress you. If you live your life through self-satisfaction, believing what you have materially makes you who you are, focusing on outward pleasure, not your real needs, you will be missing the point to your life. You may read in the newspaper about celebrities on the outside who look like they have it all, money, success, stuff, exotic lives yet have ended up killing themselves out of the blue for no understandable reason.

As a society, we seem to have lost the point, the purpose, the reason why we are here. We have been steered towards the idea money and fame is the way to go. We have lost sight of what truly matters, beyond what we see materially. If poor mental health is on the rise and depression is affecting pretty much everybody, including celebrities, then we must look to the environment we have created to find the answers, not just keep going through the motions without questions. The constant voyeurism into the way other people are living their lives, takes us away from how we are living our own lives, fuelling feelings of envy, judging and escapism. Many young people believe how they look is the essence of their existence and without it they are nothing. Living your life on your phone makes you paranoid. This has become one of the main reason suicides in young people is on the increase.

Did you know red is a colour used by big brands to market and attract your attention online? It triggers signals in your brain to alert your reward system, encouraging you to buy something. Subconsciously when you see a red sign, it immediately tells you, teases you to grab a bargain to reward yourself. Many times you will buy in, rewarding yourself with say a little treat because it's cheap, even when it's not something you really want. On social media platforms, you will be alerted in your notifications when you have a 'like' from someone. This is also in red, alerting your reward button, but for many young people, this does not always have a healthy positive outcome. If you are spending your life waiting for the little red reward light to appear, informing you how many likes you have and the likes are not close in number to the likes you got the day before, this can create a feeling of not being popular or liked, basically irrational paranoia. This intense insecurity translates into self-scrutiny. Maybe they didn't like what you were wearing, saying, where you had dinner, and this then leads to depression and anxiety, feeling like a failure, based on nothing more than how many likes you have or don't have. Who cares how many likes you have? The truth is you can buy likes, and this is probably what most of them are doing to look more popular than they really are. The real point to your life is about learning to like yourself. Not being reliant on the fake idea everyone likes you because you look more popular. It's not real. It's just an illusion created by the mind and the business behind the platforms.

If you only get your information from social media, reading the newspaper, celebrity gossip magazines or brand marketing, what you are learning is not the truth or useful for producing a healthy positive mind, it's fake news. A recent study has shown that teenagers who engage in social media during the night are damaging their sleep patterns, increasing their risk of anxiety and depression. Sleeping well without interruption restores our energy and motivation levels, two vital ingredients in making us happy and positive. Let's go back here and think about the subconscious. If before we go to sleep, we are on the phone feeling stressed because someone has made a negative comment on social media, this will play on the mind, making us anxious. The reason we cannot sleep. The last thought you have in your subconscious before you go to sleep will dictate how you dream and how you feel when you wake up, so make sure you feel something positive and real.

Many parents are looking upon these huge waves of change in the young with horror or denial, yet they are not recognising self-awareness must be modelled early on. If children are watching their parents live their lives played out on social media and the phone has become all about anxiety and stress, you cannot be shocked when children copy this dangerous behaviour pattern.

When we live on the surface of life, it can be calm or it can be turbulent. It changes from day to day, just like our moods, but there are deeper, calmer feelings and forces buried beneath this surface. If we can connect to the power of intention and purpose of our instincts, we begin to experience deeper meaningful thoughts, beyond the rubbish we are buying into externally. If you always see yourself as a weak person, trying to survive on the surface, have stuff in your life to be happy in the moment and avoid anything new along the way, hoping at some point things will change, this is surface living. If you use mindful thoughts to help you get to a deeper level of thinking, it will stimulate and encourage healthier, more productive thoughts beyond your existing beliefs and comfort zone. Thinking outside of the box, this template life, is a truly scary concept for those who believe they would be nothing and miserable without it. I say the opposite. Life would be everything, and the misery you are buying into would subside. Happiness does not come from events or pastimes, not long-term happiness anyway. It comes from inside of you. Mindful thinking will eventually help you to have more mature thoughts. The healthier and more balanced you are, the tree that stands alone, the one voice within you, the true person you want to be, the less conflict you will find going on inside.

I always believed before my own life-changing experience, I knew myself and my personality. I foolishly believed I was invincible, nothing could touch me but how wrong was I. You never know what is around the corner. If you are not working on yourself, chances are, like me, you will not be ready for change when it happens. When preparation meets opportunity, you get luck, so I say always be prepared. You cannot spend your life going through the motions, dragging yourself from one experience to the next, pretending you are happy, without at some point reflecting. This I know to be true. Had I stopped and been mindful about my own behaviour, I would have seen the Tsunami coming way before it took me under without mercy.

The road, the straight and narrow route to happiness, fulfilment and hope, is where I am heading today. I have left behind me all the unexplained chaos and confusion to focus on what is important to me and for the good of others. It is an exciting life and much more worthwhile than constantly looking forward or getting over. I know it all sounds amazing on paper, if only you had the motivation to work on yourself, but if you have found yourself at a dead end standing still, with your head buried in the sand, you will never get anywhere but more depressed. Instead of going through the motions of thinking what I am telling you sounds amazing, but you cannot imagine it ever being right for you, ask yourself why. Surely trying anything is a good thing, if everything else in your life has failed?

The human condition, even with all the new research, better psychology and more advanced science, is worse today than ever before. Are human beings nature's biggest mistake? Although human beings are capable of great love, we also have an unspeakable history of brutality, especially towards ourselves. We often have a destructive nature, are competitive, selfish, aggressive and unkind, so much so, we have almost destroyed ourselves and the planet in the process.

Socrates once said, "An unexamined life is not worth living," and I agree. The human mind has been programmed to live on the surface of existence in a superficial way, often escaping, overlooking any deeper meaning to find a purpose to it all. We seem unable to find a solid reason to be here. Because money is the thing we are all chasing; the idea of a life without it has caused mass misery. To be whole, you cannot escape the side of yourself you don't like, living with secrets and lies, pretending it's not there. We must start accepting we have let greed take over our search for inner peace and wellbeing, inventing excuses to justify why the world is in chaos. We have become aggressive, materialistic, angry, cruel escapists, only interested in what is in it for us. We have forgotten we have a conscious choice. We can be better, never perfect, but always better. We have as a culture invested everything we have in the life template we have created, buying stuff we don't need, to look like we have it all, to keep up and impress others. We are doing all the wrong things externally, causing deep dissatisfaction internally. Our core moral instincts have faded away and the template life we are following has been created like religion to keep us stuck in a fixed mindset going through the motions. We cannot go on looking forward to the next good time or getting over a good time, with the hangovers in between. The binge and purge behaviour we have come to accept as normal is not normal to nature or the fish in the ocean, who are dying because of plastic waste. If we can remember past events, we can compare them to current events, then identify regularly our reoccurring experiences. We find insight in what has happened in the past, allowing us to predict what will happen in the future.

The conscious mind, because it is so limited, has stopped our search for knowledge. We have become egocentric, self-centred, artificial and greedy as a culture. We are living in a world in all its materialistic glory, lacking any spiritual, compassionate understanding of ourselves and our existence outside the life template. We are aggressively competing to prove to each other how good we are, when in fact we are fundamentally bad. I am not generalising here. You just need to look deeply at the state of the world right now outside your own ego bubble to see what a terrible mess we are in. When we have got to the point where what we are eating must be washed in chlorine to make it safe because of the way animals are kept and treated, I think we have to face we have gone far away from empathy, compassion and goodness.

If we were more cooperative, less competitive, more loving and selfless, with compassion and integrity, working on ourselves outside the ignorant unconscious ego life template, humanity may have a chance of survival. This important work to save the planet must begin with you. Working on yourself, not overlooking or accepting as harmless your own bad behaviour. You have to stop pretending to be good when in truth, you are bad or in denial.

Looking at the bigger picture, outside of what you are used to believing, regardless of the consequences, gives you a chance to prevent a catastrophe by planning a new way to spend your time. You can still enjoy Christmas, embracing the joy of giving without it costing you money you don't have. Now there's a concept. A great way to change things around is to wipe out Christmas altogether in terms of your regular tradition, telling your friends and family this time around, you are giving the gift of giving. Volunteering your time to work in a homeless shelter on Christmas Day will not only make you feel good inside but will ensure you have no depression or anxiety when the January blues hit you, along with bills you have no hope of paying. I understand this might sound unrealistic or unattractive right now, but if you have made the decision to start working on yourself to eliminate all your problems, you have to be honest and open about your truth. If you are broke, in debt, no amount of buying gifts, spending money you don't have, will get you further on the journey towards happiness.

We have all been programmed by traditions passed down from others, designed to keep us stuck in comfortable misery, keeping up with the Joneses, trying to be somebody we are not in truth. This has left us depressed, broke and broken, and it's the main reason for mass misery in the world right now. Changing your built-in patterns is never an accidental process. It takes challenging work. In my opinion, the only authentic way to step outside of your comfortable misery, into exciting pastures new, comes from the power of intention. A day without intention is a day wasted. If we never press the pause button in our lives, stopping these traditions we live by, pushing us from one event to the next, pillar to post, we will end up like programmed crazy robots.

Most of the time, our minds are caught up in all these negative beliefs, thoughts, emotions and memories. Beyond all this chaos, there is a state of pure awareness, the space between what we think we should do and what we must do. One of the most effective ways to enter this space is through your meditation, transporting you beyond your unconscious ego beliefs into the stillness of your pure consciousness. This is the only place you can plant your own seeds of intention. It will be very difficult to relinquish your built-in ridged attachment to your habitual patterns and thinking until you learn to live in the wisdom of uncertainty. You are what your deepest desire is, so if your desire is to change, this can only be achieved by your own self, will and self-determination.

Behind every decision we make, there is always a problem we are trying to solve. The way we see the problem frames the decision we make to solve the problem. Making the choice to be unconditionally selfless is the underlining theme of our existence. It holds the world together. It binds us together through love, bringing more meaning to our lives. Most of us have the same problems when it comes to the meaning of life. We are unable to cope with our minds or change things for the better, and this gets in the way of changing. This tendency of avoidance, leaving us with emotional suffering, is the basis of poor mental health. It is the main reason we choose to stay in the life template. It stops us having to reflect and although this is understandable, it's human; it is not beneficial to the soul. Our mental health and wellbeing are an ongoing process of dedicated understanding of our reality, not the unconscious ego, imagination or fake persona. Giving up the old self in exchange for finding genuine joy and happiness is going to change everything you know going forward and it won't be easy. It is unlikely you will get there unless you continually work and practise destroying all your existing beliefs. Once you understand through self-regulating, your inner safety is what will make you feel secure, you will begin to build true comfort and peace inside. Like I have said many times, your fear is the biggest reason you are unable to change your thinking. You must put faith back in yourself now.

If you are the solid tree, standing tall, alone with strong core universal beliefs, like humility, grace, gratitude, forgiveness, integrity, and these become the power behind your thinking, your internal dialogue will become a compassionate companion, helping you to start to be kind to yourself. By learning to slow things down, paying close attention to every aspect of your sensory experiences, you will manifest your new beliefs with thoughts and feelings you never imagined possible. This process through awareness will keep your habits and patterns away from having the final say in determining the outcome of your behaviour. When you have a self-control strategy in place, it will encourage a greater tolerance to your emotional mood swings, educating you to identify and acknowledge the overload as it comes over you, not acting on the feeling but resisting the feeling. Think about all the times you are overwhelmed by your emotions and find yourself automatically, subconsciously turning to food, chocolate, wine, shopping for a fix, to make you feel better in the moment.

We all deserve to be free from the clutches of our embedded existing belief system. The painful memories, the damaging thoughts that come with them, even for those of us who believe the past is not affecting the future. Looking inside and acknowledging this internal pain and misery, created by all the wrong information, is what self-therapy is all about. We are courageously, through this journey, getting it all out on the floor like a giant puzzle, until all the pieces fit together perfectly in harmony. You must imagine this journey as an opportunity to rebuild yourself from the inside out to become a better, more worthwhile human being. Once you can look rationally at what you believe is the truth, recognising potentially it is not true at all, you can begin to put triggers in place to change what the belief is, into something else more realistic for you. You cannot just change negative thinking into positive thinking without changing your whole belief system first. It is the belief that powers the thought.

Talk therapy is not just for those who suffer depression but for anyone seeking a more empowering experience during the journey of life. Once we can go through the pain barrier, and it will be painful, we will hit a home run to personal freedom, away from what has been holding us hostage, finally becoming the people we were meant to be before someone else interfered and changed our destiny. Courage is the main key for you to become your authentic self behind that fake persona. By looking your fear and anxiety in the face, you will dissolve your destructive unhealthy beliefs and thoughts. To engage with courage means you must face some unpleasant feelings first; you have to stand up to these challenges in order to rebuild more realistic beliefs and like I have said a million times, it won't be easy. You might prefer at this stage to decide this all sounds too difficult and facing yourself will be impossible, but I want to reinforce here, there is nothing more miserable than where you are right now, so what exactly do you have to lose. Many of the subconscious fears given to us as children have never been challenged by you. You have become consciously enslaved by them instead. If you continue to allow your fear to control your mind, manipulating your perception, you will never grow spiritually, remaining in the life template until you die, and this is not progress, is it? In my mind, it is a waste of a life.

Through your mindful meditation, if you can begin the process, you will be guided to pay more attention to self-care, self-reflection and contemplation. You will learn to understand, without judging or self-doubt, how to appreciate who you really are. Facing your flaws and weaknesses given to you by the unconscious ego, will help you recognise that we are all the same and we all have a past. Understanding this will give you a feeling of relief and exhilaration. The process of releasing all the negative dirty energy, built up for so long, will lead you to creating cleaner positive energy inside.

Since my near-death experience, I have escaped the life template and work on myself religiously every day from a blank piece of paper. I love myself unconditionally, inside out, which has become a truly attractive quality to others. I focus only on my purpose and never look outward for approval. My cup is always overflowing and sometimes I am so happy, I cannot contain what I feel inside. I have experienced self-love and it has brought me the joy and contentment I doubt anyone else could offer me. I never look back to the past and think of it as a mistake. I just remember it never belonged to me in the first place. I know it will be hard to understand this because you are not there yet. All I can say to you, beyond the ego-driven template life you believe has made you who you are, there is another way to live, beyond the misery, the depression, the self-medicating. You just need to take a giant leap of faith. I am convinced once you become addicted to living, your unhealthy desire to remain stuck will disappear forever. Just by learning to battle with yourself, that inner negative self-critic, you will gain incredible power and courage. Remember, fear creates victims and you no longer want to be victimised. You want to be free. Learn to be patient and have some compassion for yourself. Your habits and fear patterns have been with you your whole life, but they are no longer mandatory or required. All we can do is work on ourselves by minding our own business and by this, I mean taking care of how we see ourselves, not wasting time worrying about how others see us because they are not seeing the truth.

Self-awareness is the backbone to all therapy. The degree to how self-aware you are will shape your life going forward and help you take back control of your choices. You will eventually find a way to step out of the life template to accept your own individual nature and travel the journey to find your deeper moral self. You will get to see the life template encourages your ego self to spend all your time caring only about what others think, which has left you unable to be yourself. Once we look at ourselves honestly, we are likely to see we have become self-absorbed and self-centred. This is the first side of yourself you examine in therapy. You get to see you have invested so much in the idea you need to be perfect. Tackling your shadow self will cause you to potentially feel even more depressed and angry than you feel now. As you build self-esteem and recognise none of your pain matters in the big scheme of things, the hard bit will pass by quickly and you will be on your way to changing things for the better. Just as your body grows and develops in stages, so does your psyche, your soul, something potentially you have never even thought about in any great detail.

During my own period of uncertainty, when my external world fell apart, my meditation allowed me to listen to myself, the authentic me. It was painful, overpowering and made me feel desperate, but I stuck with it and realised very quickly my soul was pushing me to feel this way. Listening to myself began by being interested in healing myself and was sustained by self-honesty and further inquiry, accepting the truth about my mistakes and my misfortune. During this painful process, endless thorns and weeds sprung up in my thinking, strangling any new shoots of hope, but eventually, I managed to get beyond this, by travelling further into my inner world, and these weeds eventually lost their power over me. It is a battle. You will always want comfort over difficulty but keep on asking yourself questions, stay focused and remember why you started this process in the first place. If you can weather the storm alone with your depression and defeat, accept responsibility without judgement, you too will rise from the ashes like the phoenix and fly high once again with wings of courage.

Being self-aware involves being curious to understand traits, feelings and behaviours. It is the ability to focus on the psychological state of where you are, outside the ego template. Research has shown that by becoming self-aware, you can separate from what happened to you as a child. Having a clear and honest perception of your own personality, your strengths and weaknesses will help you to understand how other people see and perceive you. Once you have a better understanding of yourself, you can start to experience yourself in an individual separate way, developing new strengths. Your capacity for introspection, the examination and observation of your mental and emotional processes will give you the ability to recognise yourself as individual, separate from your environment and other people. You are your own key to your freedom. You are free to choose your own reality. When you are conscious, you will expand and when you refuse to be conscious, you will shrink.

The key for me at the end of the day was the amazing journey of exploring my inner world, a million miles away from the life template, my false mental images of perfection, my high standards and unrealistic demands on my soul self. The lesson of understanding self-entitlement, believing I deserved happiness peace and joy, without ever doing any work on myself, was the most challenging thing I had to endure during the exploration of my inner self. This shame and self-righteous superior attitude I now understand was there to defend my unconscious ego, making me believe I was a good person, when in fact I was arrogant and selfish. Developing the courage to face my own suffering, my mistakes, my lack of integrity, educating myself through compassion, forgiveness, humility and empathy opened my eyes to the real suffering in the world. This whole life-changing process led to a direct change in my values and priorities, which ultimately changed my life, allowing myself the time to find more clarity in alignment with my spiritual needs.

Once again, I will repeat, it is going to be hard for you to take this massive leap of faith towards believing in yourself. You have been in a coma for most of your life, imagining one day the lights would just go back on and you would wake up happy. The lights can only come back on when you flick the switch. Meditation is the only way you will do this, observing you automatic thinking and behaviours without judgement, to help your conscious mind see the thoughts affecting your emotions. You will never do this while you are living your life inside a bubble. Your goal with me on this journey to higher thinking and spiritual growth is to learn to align your mental and physical behaviour with your core values, not just your cognition and intent. A part of us will always want to resist change and want to do what feels familiar. We will always be wrestling with the idea we need to change, make better choices and be more open to try new things. I have discovered myself, beyond all this pre-conditioning, living with integrity, clearing away the cobwebs in the corridors of my mind and releasing the ghosts, appreciation and gratitude is a real blessing in my own truth. The truth is, once you choose wisely, you will feel it inside, then you can let out a confident sigh of relief, knowing for sure you have finally achieved what you intended to do: Work Yourself Out.

Addicted to Life, Not Death

"We should always have an open mind to everything and be attached to nothing," and, "As you think, so shall you be." These seven words are the most important words you need to master during this journey of spiritual growth. You will always become what you think about. Your circumstances have very little to do with your fulfilment in life. It is how you deal with your circumstances that makes all the difference. Take what you are, accept yourself as you are. Be the kind of person you choose to be and celebrate everything that comes your way, so the world can become your oyster, not your prison.

With your life comes two huge responsibilities: to take care of your mental health and take care of your physical health. The more you value yourself, your strengths by identifying with them, the more confidence you will have in the face of adversity. I am not talking about the fake confidence you get from drinking alcohol, making you feel better in the moment, the high spirit when drunk to take on the entire world but inner confidence that comes from knowledge.

A healthy body creates a healthy mind, creates a happy, productive life and then creates peace, harmony and motivation. These are the essential ingredients you need to take on the entire world without encountering any more of your self-doubt. It is unlikely any number of drugs, booze, fake confidence or fake spirit will help you take on the world. Navigating life is hard enough sober, let alone when infected by outside influences. Developing a solid respect, through gratitude for this incredible power you have within your mind and your body, is the best thing you will ever learn. Your mind and body both have amazing biological influences on how you think, feel and survive. Try and imagine your body is like your car. You would never put the wrong fuel in there, would you? If you did, it would break down and be thrown on the trash heap. The difference between your body and a car, you can easily replace the car, but you cannot replace your body. And yet most people take better care of their car than they do of their body, go figure. Next time you fill up your car with the right petrol, use it as a trigger to check you have put the right fuel in your own body. By doing this, you will remain focused on what you are consciously supposed to doing, making the unconscious, conscious again.

If you learn to focus, you can improve almost anything. Your mind is the most amazing, complex information-processing system you could ever imagine. The only problem is, it doesn't come with a how to program manual. You must plug into it yourself and do the hard work. Something you may not know about your mind is that alcohol doesn't make you forget. When you decide to get drunk, your brain just temporarily loses the ability to make memories, so getting blotto is never going to help you forget your misery long-term. It is also important to understand that stress shrinks your brain. Meditation, on the other hand, when your brain is in your control, cures anxiety. It helps us reach the part of the brain that deals with ourselves, the 'Me' centre, the place that processes information relating to our experiences. As we learn to meditate deeper, we can begin the connection to this 'Me' centre, especially our experiences that make us scared or anxious. We learn to not react, and our reasoning rapidly improves. This is the main reason I am encouraging you to practise meditation daily, so the next time you experience an upsetting body sensation like anxiety, you can look at it more rationally.

Most of us make the fundamental mistake of searching for happiness outside of ourselves. We believe materialism and stuff is the answer, but happiness is something we are. It comes from the way we think, not from what we buy. When your confidence and thinking is established on a deeper level, you start to realise, your life is not to be manipulated to your own advantage, your self-entitlement. It must be built up of knowledge. We are more than we think we are. It is also important to understand, what goes on outside the body also influences the mind. Think about how different you feel on a hot, sunny, blue-sky day compared to a dark, wet, miserable Monday. The environment you are in can flood the brain with emotions that end up remaining in the subconscious. Once we understand we are all connected in some way with nature, accepting the brain is connected to both the body and the environment, we begin to accept there is more to us than our need for self-gratification. You need to start feeding your mind with fresh information now, changing your existing beliefs and start to believe instead just how amazing your capacity for learning is. We all like a drink for fun now and again, maybe even get a little high now again from drugs. We all like to get a buzz from shopping or have random sex sometime when it is consensual. It is a normal way for people to relax. The problem in this current environment of constantly looking outward for the answer, the kicks and the escaping build up and become all you do. Short-term happiness can come from an occasion or having a few drinks, but if you drink too much, your social skills change along with your moods. You end up getting lost in the idea you are having a good time, resulting in being unable to distinguish between fantasy and reality. People who get drunk lose control then make terrible mistakes from their unhealthy choices. If your whole life to date has been built on sustaining the fantasy belief you are invincible, drinking every night to get through it, your reality will escape you and addiction will take over. We live by the eternal law of effect. If you do something bad, you feel something bad. If you do something good, you feel something good. If you find you cannot operate normally without the need to drink or take drugs to feel happy, the fix becomes your only way to relax and let go. Sadly, when you return, nothing will have changed. Working on you not turning to the desired fix for escapism is going to be one of the most challenging things you try and do.

Gaining knowledge of the unknown in the context of spirituality means identifying and questioning everything to get to know yourself better. We are always anxious for a quick result in whatever we set out to do. We are always focused on the future, the looking-forward-to mentality; you cannot ever be totally in the present. Your constant desire for an instant fix result will end up a distraction from action, so learn to give up your attachment to rewards and focus more on the action of gratitude in the moment instead.

The more we run away looking for an escape from facing what is troubling us, the more we create internal chaos and anxiety. Like I have said before, we can never escape ourselves, so we must learn to face the mess instead. Understanding that addiction is not just for an addict, is important when looking at your own behaviour. There is no personality trait that can predict addiction. If you cannot live without it or go a day without thinking about it, you are addicted to it, whatever it is. People like George Best, who died from drinking through chronic liver disease, and other heavy drinkers will use his chronic condition to justify they don't have a problem themselves because they are not dead yet. There are people who will have a beer instead of wine, or wine instead of spirits to convince themselves they are not addicted, just pushing the problem around to mask their denial, convincing themselves they can give up at any time. More than two drinks every day is too much. This is how a bad habit begins. The daily routine of drinking creates your normality, and before you know it, the two drinks become three whenever something stressful occurs unexpectedly. How many times have you said you are having one or two glasses of wine to relax then unconsciously finished the whole bottle? I have asked you this question before and want to reinforce here, when we talk about addiction, it happens without our say-so, so be careful to not fall into the trap of believing you don't have a problem when potentially you do. If you are unconsciously drinking more than you've planned to drink without stopping and having a serious chat with yourself, you have a drink problem. You might say to me, drinking is not a problem but if I have shown you how only one glass of wine changes your subconscious thinking, you might want to revisit again and give this more thought. You could potentially be trapped in denial, and this is not a river in Egypt but a much more dangerous place to be stuck.

I very rarely drink these days. I am not escaping myself anymore or looking to alcohol to help me relax. I hate the way it makes feel, how it changes my moods and dulls my senses, something you will only notice once you are clean and operating without it. Life is simple at the end of the day. It is only you who is making it complicated.

One of the major functions of your subconscious is to help you define who you are. It helps you make sense of your reality. It uses your emotions, beliefs, core values and memories as a filter to meticulously sift through the chaos of information in your overcrowded mind. What we perceive as our reality is determined by this subconscious filter. It takes control and automatically creates our habits and patterns. Think about driving to work without being able to recall what happened along the way. If you begin to think about the responsibility of your subconscious being in control of all your daily movements and activities, it's easy to see the reason why we must not limit our beliefs. People with unexpressed emotional issues and painful memories, the things they are unable to resolve, will remain stored in the subconscious mind, becoming a negative filter, leading to low self-esteem. Once the subconscious memory is full of all your limiting, negative beliefs about your perceived reality, all these negative emotions build up inside, and will eventually turn into dirty energy in your body, weakening your immune system. If most of your mind is being used to store only negative unresolved issues, the painful memories you harbour, an overload takes place and this dirty energy transfers to your physical body with no way of release. To allow inside positive clean energy, creating healthier, happier thinking and a healthier, happier body, we have to resolve our emotions, working consciously with the subconscious through our meditation and self-honesty. Through your meditation, and you should be quite practised by now, you will start to bond more to your heart connectors, your natural core values, beyond the perceived reality of your mind. This is the place you find empathy, gratitude and awareness to access your consciousness, allowing you to feel real, for real. You have disconnected currently from the most important part of your body, relying only on your made-up reality to guide and influence your choices, feelings and emotions. By focusing only on your external needs and desires, you have forgotten what true love feels like. Love, compassion and empathy for life, not just your own but every other living thing on the planet, connects us in harmony, giving us incredible power collectively to make more informed choices about the world and humanity.

The development of my own heart qualities, my natural instincts and intuition truly helped me to recover my own inner core values. It helped me learn how to really feel something deep beyond the madness and misery of my narrow, overcrowded mind. Once I let go of the addictions, my unconscious ego and the idea I was invincible, I found clarity, humility, forgiveness and a deep compassion towards not just myself but every other living thing around me. Once you begin the journey, living your new life through your heart-based feelings, you too will start to care deeply about the important things and no longer be influenced or upset by taking things to heart. You will begin to develop an open heart instead.

To be happy, healthy, energetic, free and full of life, we must learn to protect our hearts and ourselves from false addictions. If we continue to attack and shut down the incredible power of our physical body by not taking care of it, we impair the ability to create positive cardiovascular function. You have already died spiritually, physically is next.

There is a common misconception that addiction is a choice. All you must do is stop. Sadly, this is not the case. Your brain changes with any addiction and it takes more than hard work to get it back to normal, the main reason it's hard to give things up, even when you know they're killing you. Let's just go back here and remind ourselves, when I am talking about addiction, I am not talking about people who die in pain like George Best, I am talking about using things to change the way you feel about yourself and this is pretty much all of us.

There has been major research done recently showing that the power of addiction lies in its ability to hijack and destroy the main region in the brain that helps us survive. A healthy brain rewards good behaviour, an unhealthy brain punishes bad behaviour. It's important to understand, a healthy brain will be in someone who is positive, exercising, living a healthy lifestyle and will act quickly to move away from something harmful. They will be able to decide very quickly if the consequences are worth the fix or not. If you are drinking, smoking, overeating, taking drugs, have an unhealthy or risky lifestyle, you have an unhealthy brain. The normal hard-wiring in your brain is going against you. Your bad habit of over-indulging, especially with drugs and alcohol, is hijacking your reward pleasure circuit, always leaving you wanting more. No matter how many times you choose the instant fix, the momentary high over your reality— eventually your negative belief that you are enjoying yourself—will catch up with your truth, leaving you with addiction issues, a mental health problem, a physical problem or a combination of all three.

This misery and malaise felt by the masses on a huge scale today is in my opinion, through personal experience, down to a lack of mindful thinking, emotional intelligence, lack of purpose plus what we have been taught and experienced as young children growing up. We have become distanced from the answer to our problems. What matters to us the most in life does not always come easy and when the answers finally do come, and we are forced to change, often we are unwilling to do so. We've become a little bit too reliant and comfortable with our addictive ways, avoiding our fears, our feelings, our pain, as well as avoiding the idea we must do the work ourselves to rise above what is making us miserable. By acting upon the need for immediate gratification, we strengthen our bad habits, the cravings, learning to tolerate pain and discomfort more easily when stressed.

My own childhood was spent around heavy drinkers. I was in the pub right from an early age. The smell of alcohol today still takes me down memory lane to negative associations. I started drinking at a very young age. This was inevitable. We model, we copy, we repeat. I thought getting drunk was acceptable. My whole family did it. The whole estate did it. It was normal. I know now on deep reflection, my mother drank because she was unhappy, unfulfilled and hated the life she created, marrying the first man who asked her after escaping poverty at sixteen. My father was a worker and he used alcohol to relax and wind down whenever he had any spare time from keeping it all going. He loved a few pints at the weekend but was never addicted or used alcohol to get through his misery, unlike my mother. I have three older brothers who all enjoyed drinking and often the atmosphere in our home created a real sense of unpredictability, tension, like constantly walking on eggshells. I never felt truly safe or secure. My unbreakable confidence and self-belief, I am sure now, prevented me becoming an addict myself. Although I used drugs and drank to escape my misery during my crash, I have also had long period, years in fact, when I have enjoyed being totally sober. Being aware of my drive and determination to escape poverty and succeed in business always helped me to stay focused. I wanted to be rich more than I wanted to remain unhappily married, on a council estate, drinking myself to death like my own mother. It's easy to blame others, blame circumstances, blame life but in truth, we only have ourselves to blame if we carry on running from our mistakes when we know deep down facing them is the right thing to do.

Emotional intelligence, the ability to identify and manage emotions as well as understand the emotions of others, allows us privileged access to an ongoing interaction with our deeper selves. It allows us to think over feeling, getting behind the bullshit, the persona, the lies, in order to be balanced when we make our choices and decisions. Our emotions not only reflect and reveal our core values, they also enable us to refine them. If your core values have become distorted, so will your emotions, which will lead you to act against your long-term goals, damaging your brain function and ability to be happy. When we go against our values, our feelings hijack our thinking and self-deception takes over in order to hide the truth. When you avoid taking personal ownership for your choices and mistakes, it prevents you taking personal responsibility for your moral failings. You end up blaming everyone but yourself for your problems.

During our time at school, and we are there for at least fifteen years, we are educated and taught the basic cognitive process of acquiring knowledge, yet we are never taught or given advice about our emotional intelligence. If you think how ridiculous this is when we use our emotions to determine our career choices, our relationship choices, our money choices and so on. So many of us just bumble through life, making huge choices not based on emotional intelligence but partly on materialistic needs and partly because it takes enormous strength of character to change existing beliefs, passed on from others. Understanding emotional intelligence encourages us to think differently. It challenges us to stand up to what others expect of us, reinforcing our emotional stability. If we put it bluntly, we may think we are intelligent because we know our ABC but when it comes to how we think emotionally, very few of us have little idea whatsoever. We believe we feel bad, miserable, unhappy and unfulfilled because that's life and there is nothing we can do to change it.

Facing the truth, the idea your whole character has potentially been based on a lie, is likely to push you away from facing yourself, piling more deception on top of deception because it's easier than having to face the truth. If you truly want to create more meaning in your life, once you have accepted the life you have created is potentially making you unhappy, you need to consciously stop running to materialism, comfort and addictions every time you cannot solve a problem. We all know problems come and go. Problem solving and decision-making is part of everyone's life experience, therefore it's crucial you learn how to manage obstacles to be able to find solutions.

Emotional intelligence is associated with emotional awareness, the ability to handle your emotions, then apply them to your thinking and problem solving. The skills for problem-solving come from you having the ability to recognise the problem when it arises, define it clearly and accurately, then set realistic goals to change it. Let's recap. Fear is the biggest reason we are unable to face the mess we create. It stops us accepting personal responsibility, afraid to face the idea we are the problem. Would you rather have hope and the possibility of change at some point before you die or would you be happy living the rest of your life pretending, wishing you would die?

There are many degrees of personal misery. Some people have better coping skills than others, so the severity of addiction and escapism will often depend on your childhood memories. Remember, what we have learnt as children stays with us forever, until we change things in our subconscious mind. I think you need to start remembering there are unrealistic thoughts and beliefs behind our bad habits and negative patterns, so it's vital to interrupt these irrational thoughts by changing them into your truth, improving your perception of what you are emotional capable of.

It took me reaching near death to face and recognise the vanity and falseness of my own self-deception. There was no room or energy left to maintain the illusions. I had little choice but to change, recognising painfully how much of my life I had wasted. I had chosen to walk the road mapped out from my false beliefs, which turned out to be the wrong road spiritually. Being aware of my own flaws and mistakes, taking full responsibility for them, helped me mature into a grateful solid tree of wisdom, finally seeing a clear vision of the adult I was inside, behind the unconscious ego created by me to fit in. My advice to you after this incredible life-changing experience myself is to stop lying to yourself. Once you have got to the point where you can no longer distinguish your truth from your bullshit, you will lose all self-respect and end up a stranger in your own life. When you are forced to change like I was, you naturally take that great leap of faith, and fear becomes your curiosity. Today I don't fear death or even get upset by the idea of it. I know for sure now, nothing ever dies, therefore I am hopeful and positive about living my life the best way I possibly can. When you recognise you are part of something bigger than the idea of your one-dimensional thinking, you automatically stop feeling alone and insecure.

The main reason most of us fear death is because we have not lived life. We have been dragged along from one catastrophe to the next by beliefs and traditions handed to us from others, convincing ourselves we are happy, fulfilled, good people. We have followed the template to the letter, believing we must fit it all in before we die. I have gone through many stages in my life from a young girl to a young adult, to a middle-aged woman, ending up today at sixty-two, yet my spirit, my energy has not aged at all. This clearly proves to me aging is just a mindset. There is no need to give in to the idea of physical or mental deterioration. It's all down to how you think. If you believe you are part of nature, the universe, something much greater than you, rather than part of a manufactured, outdated, boring template, dreading getting older, you will begin to understand you never die. You are just the vessel that houses your energy.

Take your unconscious ego and reframe it, shifting away from your fear, to finally become curious of what it is you really fear. Start letting go of it all. Get rid of the idea you need to be attached to things. Shift the idea you need to be in control and start to trust in something greater than you. Stop praying to something external for the answer to your problems and start a new way of praying to yourself in your meditation. Recognise your consciousness has no boundaries. You have all the answers inside your heart, so start listening. Start to become truly aware of the bigger picture, beyond the basic linear life you believe defines you. Understand you are a spiritual being having a human experience. We are all connected through love, humility and gratitude.

I can tell you without doubt after my own near-death experience, I almost reluctantly didn't want to come back because I had made such a mess of everything, I found the idea of no longer being here, quite comforting. Today I am grateful. I have become transformed beyond belief. All the stress, worry, anxiety, ego, panic, greed, misery, depression and fear are now gone, and today I am calm with a powerful knowing beyond the past, I am better in the future.

Through this book, self-therapy and spiritual guidance, I am hoping to encourage you to believe in your ability to engage and strive towards one goal that leads you to a meaningful life, no longer restricted by your negative self-deception and existing beliefs. I want to help you build a solid bridge with a safety net below, to guide you between your fake persona and false life, over to your true potential, holding your hand as you bravely cross over. I want you to do this without looking back in fear for validation. There is no point in believing you are a good person if you are hiding your flaws and mistakes from yourself and others. Crossing over the bridge of your shortcomings will give you time to stop deceiving yourself and expose you in glory instead, not shame or blame. It's time now to pull off the mask and step away from 'The Imposter Syndrome' without fear of the world finding out who you really are. To be yourself for the first time primarily, because as Oscar Wilde so rightly said, "Be yourself, everyone else is taken." Once you stop working on yourself, believing in yourself, you are just deceiving yourself, playing tricks with yourself, learn to be addicted to your life which is a blessing. Be prepared to leave this place fearless, flying out sideways, telling yourself that was one hell of a ride.

When I began to work with my own subconscious thinking, to change my patterns and re-evaluate my memories in truth, I realised I couldn't remember any times in the past I had felt happiness or joy. I tried to focus on happiness in my childhood, but the memories were clouded. It was tough losing my mother at eight and I am sure back then I was forced to create different personalities to deal with difficult circumstances. I did not see her for a few years after she left. No one talked about where she was or what she was doing, almost like she never existed. I found out later she had suffered a mental breakdown and was admitted to a sanatorium, where she was given medication. It must have been a truly brutal time for her walking away from her children, to start a new life without ever facing her mess. It is no wonder she never really recovered her amazing drive and spirit, dying alone an alcoholic in an old people's home, full of unease. The saddest thing for me is she was such a driven, independent girl in the beginning herself, leaving the poverty of a Glasgow tenement at sixteen to start a new life somewhere better. When I was working on myself in my meditation during my crash, I suddenly realised how much I was like her at sixteen myself, a strong, independent lass, desperate to escape poverty at all cost. It was quite a revelation and the thing that helped me to forgive her before she died, something that helped me understand real love for another human being for the first time.

With this realisation in my new state of calm, having never experienced true joy, I decided the first seed of intention I would plant in my subconscious mind, my own Garden of Eden, would be to grow more joy and happiness in my new life. This beautiful plant of joy and happiness today has grown in abundance. I never feel sad or miserable. I am just grateful and humble to be here on this planet, no longer escaping life like my mother. I am grateful to her for her drive and I am happy her energy is now free, but I am no longer following the same path she walked down. This is an extremely amazing experience. I can honestly say I didn't know her, even though she was my mother, therefore I cannot blame her for what has happened to me.

It is my passion and purpose in giving to others that has created the most joy and happiness in my life today. My free life coaching work helping the homeless and addicted makes me feel useful and this inspires me to keep growing myself. When I think about it, I never really lived in the sheep mentality template. As a child with a dysfunctional upbringing, traditions like Christmas and birthdays were always basic, so I have little memory to pull from. I always liked being in the sun on holiday at Christmas when I was rich and I would try my best to avoid celebrating my birthday—getting old was not something to celebrate in my view back then. Today, every day is my birthday and every day I celebrate being alive. When you learn to love your life, you never look forward or pretend you are enjoying getting over, you just simply enjoy the moment for what it is. Whatever happened in the past remains exactly there, in the past.

The second seed of intention I planted in my subconscious, alongside joy and happiness, was learning how to love myself. When you feel gratitude over resentment, fear or guilt, you suddenly feel happier and not depressed. Being grateful means you appreciate things. When I learnt to appreciate myself for who I am, without judging or blaming, I learnt to love myself. I have been celibate by choice since my crash. Making a choice to remain single and independent was easy during this time. I had nothing to offer anyone emotionally until I worked out who I was and what I wanted. I had spent almost half my life looking for a man to escape with and help sort out my problems, just like my mother, so giving up sex was easy. I created a blank canvass with the past wiped out without regret or remorse, just gratitude and humility, to see what the future for the new mature me had in store. Imagine now just how amazing it would be, if you could wipe your slate clean, starting again with insight to do all the things you've been afraid to do because that little voice in your head made you believe you are a useless failure. I have no real desire even eighteen years on to embark on a sexual relationship with another human being. Once you learn to love yourself unconditionally, you never feel alone, insecure, under pressure or crave another person in your space. The whole space is already taken up doing, not searching. I am not saying I am closed off to having a connection with another person or even having sex, but for now I am happy, satisfied and way too busy trying to change the world to think about embarking on another person's life journey. They say it is better to be alone than wish you were alone, and I totally agree with this. Another person cannot make you whole. You must do this for yourself. How can you love someone else if you don't know how to love yourself? I have myself. I love myself in humility. I like myself. I am busy doing what I love. I sleep like a baby. I wake like clockwork, always happy. I no longer worry about what others think. I think for myself. Many people would call this selfish and I would agree if it was all done in my unconscious ego state, but I have abandoned that and replaced it with solid core values and beliefs, the beauty of humility, the attractiveness of gratitude and the confidence in forgiveness.

I am a self-actualiser, always maximising my potential, doing the best I can do. I am open, unconventional and spontaneous. I have a true sense of realism, accepting myself and others as they are for real. I am not fearful of things that are different or unknown. I see things logically and rationally. I am problem centred, motivated by strong ethics and responsibilities. I am hugely independent and private. I know what happiness is, an experience in the moment I always appreciate. I prefer the journey over the destination, not bad for an ex philistine capitalist who didn't have clue about life beyond greed.

I hope by now you might be able to see you have been controlled, either through childhood trauma or parental mind control, over thinking for yourself. You have never learnt how to problem solve and this has created a distorted, irrational, fear-based belief system you are stuck with as an adult. With time, understanding and self-awareness, the important steps I have talked about through your breathing, meditating, taking back control, getting a healthier perspective, you too will soon discover learning to love the real you improves everything in your life, including your health, self-esteem and innate ability to manifest what you truly desire.

We are all programmed in the template to believe love from another person is a guarantee for happiness, but we all know fairy-tales are made up in the imagination to help us fall to sleep into the land of happily-ever-after. Think about this. What if your whole life is potentially a lie? Ask yourself what is truly going on in your mind. How much of it is the real you and how much of it is you in denial? So many of us hide from ourselves and die, never really knowing who we are inside. I am hoping to get you to start thinking about your inner voice as your small child inside. The lost unloved you, who never had the chance to grow authentically because you learnt how to think and feel in an environment created by others—family, siblings and circumstances. The negative factors in your childhood, how you think, feel and imitate, have contributed to your inability to develop age-appropriate social skills or learn openly how to self-express. How to feel socially acceptable in a caring, sharing way with others and developing a healthy sense of self is what helps you become a purpose-driven healthy operating adult.

Life is a journey of self-discovery to travel and be enlightened. As we go on the journey, we learn the ability to change things for the better, by understanding it is never selfish to love ourselves or believe in ourselves. I am addicted to life like I said and cannot get enough of it. Every day is new day. Every feeling is a new learning curve and every gift from the universe I never take for granted. I believe every person should feel this joy, not just those who have had a brush with death or those who play with the idea of death. The only sure way out of any pain is to face it, accept it's not yours and get rid of it before it becomes the death of you.

When going into any battle, and facing yourself will be a battle, trust me, the best general always learns to understand and to get to know the enemy well. Rule number one, when you are trying to overcome your negative self, recognise the enemy is you. You must truly understand yourself first to defeat yourself second. This is where keeping a journal of your moods behaviours and thoughts will come in handy. The more you dig down deep inside, the more unwanted rubbish you can throw out of your untidy cluttered mind, until there is a space left for the battle to commence. Keep your goals small to begin with when it comes to defeating the invisible enemy within, so you are not reaching for the moon but able to see the stars shimmering in the distance. Remember, all the answers to all your unanswered questions come from within and by paying attention to your gut feelings. The only true way we can heal is to feel. Once you have the courage in the safety of your meditation to bring it all to the surface, feel it, own it, resolve it, let go of it, you stop triggering inside the way you negatively perceive things in your life going forward. By finally addressing your buried issues causing you constant pain and anxiety, releasing dirty energy, learning to respond not react, you begin to dissolve your automatic negative thinking patterns for good.

Be still, be quiet, be present and in this silence, there will be no thoughts. The awakening process from greed, ignorance and illusion will eventually energise your soul, allowing you to experience the being aware of being aware. Once you become fully aware of the emotional triggers that have led to what has hurt you, the internal trauma event or events, you can begin to reclaim them and start consciously remembering in your subconscious what happened to you in your childhood. The time has come to give up the constant unconscious ego struggle with yourself, increasing your ability to show the world who you are for real. Becoming accountable for your behaviour, choosing higher evolved core values and beliefs, humility, forgiveness, gratitude and compassion, means you can finally stop obsessing over the cycle of painful attachment to your past. You will be free to contribute to the world, humanity and start to make a difference as the person you want to be and not the person you have been programmed to be.

Finally, don't believe everything you think is just electrochemical impulses in your brain. It's not. They all come from your upbringing, culture, circumstances and religious beliefs. These are what drive your opinions. Most of us retreat from being truly alive, awake, grown-up in order to avoid reawakening the unconscious. For some odd reason, we all want to remain fixated on an immature, childlike functioning system. People who tend to approach life from this childlike perspective end up having fantasy connections, reliving their parents' anxieties, making the same choices, having the same beliefs and personality traits. It is common to dismiss what happened to us as children as not that important as adults, but when we fail to deal with things consciously, we end up falling victim to the past, in the present. When past trauma and negative events are never resolved, our brain will not be fully integrated in present-day events; this will trigger us back into the emotional turmoil we expressed as children. We must never allow our thoughts and feeling to define who we are.

What's the Point?

The thing I have learnt more than anything else during my journey with this thing called life, we must build on failure, using it as a stepping-stone, never focusing on the past, the mistakes, never dwelling on anything negative for too long. Letting your pain go, setting it free, will only be possible once you have faced it exists in the first place, so hopefully by now you understand the route to your own personal freedom begins with you and you alone. If we have established this, at this part of our journey together, we can now go on to the next process with hope, courage and confidence.

There are many reasons for our personal misery, some we can explain and some we accept. It is all we have ever known but for whatever reason your misery has taken over your life, it's never too late to change things. Developing your clean energy going forward should fill the space that exists within and as you nurture more positive vibes, you will naturally eradicate negativity. Remember, we always naturally, automatically, unconsciously, return to the negative self-deception, our comfort blanket, over change, so we must repeat, repeat, repeat to ward off defeat.

Once we begin to take risks, we soon discover there are times when we succeed but there are more times when we will fail. Both are equally important. Giving up is the sure way to fail, trying again is the only sure way to succeed. If you never try, you will never know your true capabilities, the power within. Once you overcome the fear to go for it, it will totally change your life forever, even if you are feeling useless, hopeless, depressed and defeated. When you make that one switch in your mind, you take that giant leap of faith and go for it, regardless of the consequences, there's no going back. You will automatically lose what was holding you back and gain momentum to push you forward.

The biggest part of being an adult like we have already discussed is about learning to take personal responsibility for our successes and our failures. We cannot live a positive life blaming other people, being jealous of them. This is negative and damaging. Think about what happens when you first learn to walk as a child. You make mistakes, fall over, cry your eyes out, make mistakes, fall over, cry your eyes out but you never stop trying, until one day you can walk by yourself. Life is just the same as learning to walk, you make mistakes, cry your eyes out, fall over, fail, lose sight of the point, but if you are not afraid to make these mistakes, eventually you will start to succeed because there is no other true way to learn. The truth is, all our conflict starts internally. It is how our mind perceives what is happening. When we escape our reality by giving up or giving in and we refuse to resolve our issues, we become weak, undermining our self-discipline. I understand the feelings of being depressed and hopeless are real at the time they happen, but we also now know feelings quickly change, so with something that is never consistent, we have to find the time in between when we are strong enough to take small steps towards building the bridge to a healthier mind.

Failure in any shape or form is what creates your low self-esteem. If from your childhood you have subconsciously been programmed by others to believe you are useless, worthless, not good enough, then you repeat these thoughts through your automatic negative dialogue; sadly, this is what you will become. I have talked about this subject many times in this book, trying to make you see you often automatically go to the negative bias and not always the positive. This automatic behaviour has nothing to do with your depression or misery, it is to do with how you have been programmed through your belief system, your depression is just an emotional reaction to these negative beliefs. Building your self-esteem satnav, the thing you can reprogram to guide you back to your true self, is all about understanding why you have ended up wanting to fail in life instead of succeeding. No one is born a failure remember, it's not mandatory, it's a choice.

No one on this planet will ever feel comfortable without their own approval. Learning to love yourself, when you loathe and doubt yourself subconsciously, will be the hardest thing you ever achieve but when you learn to do it for real, everything else will fall into place and you will blossom beyond recognition. Self-esteem reflects your overall subjective emotional evaluation of your own self-worth, your attitude, to how you feel about yourself. If this attitude on the outside is confident happy, positive and successful but on the inside you are a crumbling insecure angry defeated mess, you can begin to understand how this inconsistency in your belief system would create misery and anxiety for your poor soul self. You are not showing the world an authentic version of who you are. There is an inconsistency. You look like one thing on the outside but act out something private on the inside. We all need a self-esteem boost at some time or another, even for those with all the confidence in the world and sometimes we need it internally to feel better.

It's obvious when you study the law and power of attraction, if we had an improved empowered self-image, the rest of the world would have a connection to it. When it comes to how we truly feel about ourselves internally, it can take a lot of work. Often, we have spent a lifetime pretending to be something we are not, for fear of what others may think of us. This is not progress, it is tragic. Think about how many times you have talked yourself out of asking someone out on a date, convinced they will not think you are good enough, based purely on your own speculation. How on earth can you know what is going on in someone else's mind or what they are thinking? The fear of being rejected is not connected to being turned down. It is connected to an emotional reaction to an existing belief you have, about not being good enough, probably a learnt feeling from your childhood. We believe we are not good enough because we have no confidence, no self-worth. We convince ourselves we will fail before we even try. This is the negative bias automatically programmed in your internal dialogue, influencing you subconsciously, without you even knowing it is happening. This is the main problem for most people who spend their lives never changing their existing beliefs about who they are. Instead, they are too busy worrying and stressing about what might happen or what other people will think. If you are wasting your whole life predicting what other people are thinking about you, when in truth they have absolutely no idea, this is your own interpretation of events taking place in your imagination, through ideas of your self-doubt. Self-confidence and self-esteem are both directly connected to your ability to give and receive love. Think about what happens when you smile at a stranger and they smile back. The world feels a much happier positive place to exist in, doesn't it?

In this current modern-day world, we have become programmed by negativity to fear rejection if we make the first move, but if we can be brave enough to overcome this fake feeling of irrational fear, the reaction we receive back can become infectious and very powerful beyond the perception of the negative belief. Once the authentic you on the outside mirrors the authentic you on the inside, you become whole and real, attracting the same back into your own life. At the end of the day, we attract ourselves. If we are using our heart to make our decisions about how we feel about who we are, not our stupid minds, we will always attract success. Having little self-regard will only lead you to feelings of depression. We are not naturally meant to fall short of our potential. We don't deserve to accept or want to tolerate bad relationships or abusive situations. We are worth more than that. Loving ourselves not through unconscious ego but through humility stops us having to believe in our failures. Understanding the balance between self-love, knowledge and respect, is the key to understanding self-respect.

Self-respect is when we believe we deserve to be treated right and will not tolerate being lied to or judged unfairly. We cannot have self-respect if we are lying to ourselves and not treating ourselves fairly, can we? The inner conflict of self-torture, the internal battle with the outside person we present to the world and the internal mess we hide from the world, is what is making you feel depressed, unworthy and permanently anxious. To esteem something is to evaluate it positively and hold it in high regard but often as humans we will make mistakes and cannot always win, so self-esteem is different to self-respect. To respect something is to accept it regardless of winning or losing. Self-respect is to accept and evaluate without worry or fear of what others think. It is about taking pride with confidence in who we are, developing a true sense of behaving in the right way with honour and dignity. The truth is a person with self-respect will always like themselves, never based on personal success or material wealth, but because of who they are, not what they can or cannot do. It is so important to understand self-respect when you are working on removing your mask. It will help you to be less prone to your lies, stress, regrets and secrets. It will start to let you know who you are for real and what you will or will not tolerate. It is important here to remember just telling yourself repeatedly you believe you are good enough is not going to work if you are not acting out in a good way. It will take an enormous amount of commitment and work on you to connect back to yourself and develop some self-respect for yourself. No matter how negative your view on your life is, it will not change the fact you are here, so you might as well make the most of the time and opportunities you have, not letting others define your identity or purpose.

It is hard to stop your mind from conjuring up fantasies in order to escape your reality. The mind will never stop using the imagination to escape, until you stop yourself doing it. When you feel the need to daydream, divert your thoughts to the reality of the situation. This stops you avoiding your truth. Avoidance of anything is not good for your self-development. Understanding why you want to avoid change is crucial and a self-protecting belief. When you are forced to face fear, rejection or failure, this physically causes you to feel anxious instinctively, always searching for an easy escape route from it. If you spend your whole life avoiding the confidence and strength it takes, to create the willpower you need, to look fear and failure in the face, it will end up reflecting in how you feel about yourself. The more you participate in this negative vicious cycle, the more you will disapprove of yourself. Avoidance is your built-in defence mechanism, which can be useful in the moment when avoiding feeling anxious but can be truly damaging long term, when it comes to your self-image. Every time you avoid facing yourself and your internal authentic needs, your purpose, your potential, the point to your life, your self-esteem takes a knock. This knock then becomes engraved in your self-doubt, leaving you depressed and miserable, believing there is in fact no point to your life. Once you can find the courage to stop avoiding, by facing, this will stop you acting in a defeatist way, always running away from what makes you feel uncomfortable.

Once you begin to adopt a positive I-can-do-anything-I-want attitude, no longer hiding behind your unconscious ego, through self-belief in humility, you will naturally begin to feel better about yourself and your choices. Next time you find yourself walking down the street, hold your head high, put your shoulders back, be noticed by your smile, then see how many people respond by smiling back at you. Make it your mission to show the world why your life matters, why your energy is vital and why you deserve to be alive. As you begin to develop more self-awareness, you will be less influenced by your negative internal dialogue, the cruel critic, paying more attention to what is real and not made up in your sore mind. Remember, all your feelings, failures, successes and loneliness are connected to your existing belief system, not your core moral beliefs. If you can start to understand how you feel emotionally follows your beliefs—if your belief is you are depressed, you will feel depressed—you can start to change your mindset, developing healthier beliefs going forward. If your genuine belief is you are truly grateful to be alive rather than sad to be alone, how you feel emotionally will change. You will not feel lonely, instead you will feel appreciation and gratitude. See how it works.

When we build self-esteem and boost our confidence levels through changing our negative belief system, it is a fact we will feel kinder, more loving and have more compassion not only for ourselves but for others. My advice is stop being afraid to step outside of your comfort zone/mindset and look deeper inside your heart. When I look back over my own life, regardless of all the mistakes I have made, I always had my built-in self-confidence and self-esteem satnav on track. I had fears for sure. I had worries in abundance and dozens of doubts, I just never let them get in the way of my climb to success. I have always known what I think about myself to be way more important than what anyone else thought about me. I believe this to be the secret to success and personal growth. If you let others decide who you are and what you want to be, then how on earth in common sense can you ever be happy, unique or brave?

There is no shame in being depressed. Most people as I have said before have some mental health issue or another, be it addiction, obesity, shyness, lying, criminal tendencies, sexual hang-ups, past pain or anxiety. To be yourself in a world constantly trying to make you be something else is the greatest challenge we face, especially with social media, where looks are more important than what we offer as unique talented people. Our deepest fear is not we are inadequate, it's that others will think we are. If we can be confident to show outward signs of talent, brilliance and beauty, letting our own light shine, it will give others permission to do the same. We model, we copy, we repeat.

We must learn to become liberated from our fears by clearly understanding it is other people who have made us feel bad about ourselves. This is devastating for developing self-esteem, self-respect and self-image. When I walk down the street today, I hold my head high, push my shoulders back, smile my face off and know people are looking at me because I am a woman who knows what she wants, where she is going, and will let nothing get in her way. You probably walk down the street with your head down, not knowing what you want or where you are going, thinking everyone is staring at you because you are a failure and a mess. The main difference between you and I is confidence, the innate ability to not give a damn what anyone else is thinking. When people talk behind your back, it means you are in front. If you are feeling insecure, then so is the rest of the world.

When you are driven by low self-esteem, you are more likely to sabotage when something good happens. This is because you don't believe you deserve it. My advice is, never tolerate this kind of disrespect for yourself any longer. You are missing the point of your life. Never apologise for being you and remember confidence comes from not always being right but never fearing being wrong. I understand the life coaching clichés and common-sense mantras all sound great and possible in an ideal world, but you no longer live in this kind of world when you have let your beliefs, feelings and fears dominate your entire thinking strategy. I need you to see, the stuff I am preaching was not read in a book or learnt from a teacher. It came to me for real from the depths of despair, where you are now. If there was hope for me, then there's hope for you.

Everything that happens to us in our lives reflects what we believe about ourselves, so developing self-esteem really is the foundation for your success and happiness, outside the depression, misery and anxiety you constantly feel. To constantly spend your life wishing you were someone else is a waste of the person you really are. Other people's opinions of you truly don't matter and must never become your reality, no matter what has been battered into you. Only your opinion counts. Driving slowly through your life with low self-esteem as your companion, is like driving a car with the brake on; every time you try and move forward, your fear holds you back. You never move closer to your own hopes and dreams. Looking at your life through the opinions of other people, without ever having a say, makes you a back-seat driver in your own life, desperate to speak up but petrified you'll be criticised. Once you learn some balance and harmony through your meditation and you honestly check out your own behaviour, you will manage to remain centred and rational when you find yourself in the eye of the turbulent storm within yourself.

Fear and anxiety are the two main reasons for low self-esteem. Those who suffer these extreme conditions believe there is something innately wrong with them and often experience panic attacks when doing something they deem to be stupid. These panic attacks can also manifest when they think others have noticed their perceived stupid behaviour, confirming further a deep fear of inadequacy, incompetence and insecurity. This vicious cycle of fears and feelings may last for a few seconds, minutes, days or weeks depending on how seriously the person suffering sees the mistake. We all make mistakes. I have made the biggest ones you could imagine but that doesn't make me inadequate, it makes me human. Working on building a wall of confidence around yourself—the very first chapter in this book—because without it you will fail, will help you create the space between the mistake and the negative emotional reaction to the mistake. This wall you build around yourself will help you develop the principle of your energy balance, helping you to reconcile your inner and outer conflict, stopping the vicious cycle of feeding your low self-esteem. You are not a victim.

People with obsessive or compulsive addictive behaviours will spend their whole lives trying to feel better and often engage in relying on alcohol, drugs, overspending, illicit sex or practising perfectionism to try and feel better. I know what it feels like to find comfort in the moment by engaging and over-indulging in so-called pleasure zones, but I don't have an addictive personality, so for me, it only set me back short term. So why do some people use their addictions to feel better but end up feeling worse than before they began?

Some people have a serotonin deficiency, the chemical in our brain that produces balance in our emotions. This problem can be a common contributor to mood swings. It is the key to our feelings of happiness and helps defend against anxiety and depression. Others believe altering the state of their mind by constantly escaping reality, they can avoid having to take personal responsibility for their life, living in their imagination instead. It is hard for me to understand today why people want to escape life because I almost lost my own, but I guess the truth is, it's much easier to ignore pain than it is to face it. Getting to know the authentic you in my opinion is the first step to overcoming walking down the lazy route of your negative bias.

By making sense of your past and the feelings that go with this is the best way to form healthier attachments to the future, other people and potentially your own children. If when you were a child, you formed the wrong idea about who you are, it could potentially mean you will spend the rest of your life trying to prove or disprove this false identity. You never get the chance to be who you really are deep down. So much of what we perceive we are as we have established is projected onto us as children by our caregivers. If we are pushed down the wrong path to please others and never given the chance to express our own uniqueness, how we live our lives can end up with disastrous consequences.

I knew a girl in school like this. She was beautiful to look at—tall, slim, outwardly confident, always curious and always the centre of attention. She appeared healthy, balanced and was popular with the rest of the school. As we moved up the ladder around twelve years old, she suddenly dramatically changed both physically and mentally, becoming more of a loner and more uncomfortable in her skin. She gained weight, cut off her long hair, became introverted, sad, shy, unable to mix and sometimes crying at the tiniest thing. Her hopes and dreams appeared to be fading daily, replaced by uncertainty and unexplained insecurity. She dreamed one day of becoming an actress and a dancer. When I talked to her during this difficult insecure time, she told me her parents had decided they wanted her to live out their hopes and dreams by becoming a doctor or worst-case scenario, an accountant. Her father was an accountant and her mother a doctor. The idea of their only child becoming something creative, in their opinion a daydreaming fantasy, was never going to happen if they had anything to do with it. She told me one day she was in her bedroom freely dancing with the music turned up, having creative freedom and fun in her mind, when her father came in, switched off the music, beating her before locking the door behind him. I found out many years later at fifteen she hung herself. It turned out her parents were deeply religious, and she'd gotten herself pregnant after a drug-fuelled party, with a one-night stand, a random boy from the local council estate, their worst nightmare. I met with her best friend years later who told me in more detail about the severe control and inappropriate expectations from her own father before she hung herself. This kind of controlling behaviour created internal conflict in the mind and heart of the young optimistic dreamer and rather than living a life in long-term misery, becoming a doctor or accountant, it ended tragically in suicide.

Once we accept our earliest relationships and memories in childhood drive the way we feel about ourselves in adulthood, we can give ourselves permission to break down the barriers of the past and build a more realistic sense of self. All positive change, remember, begins with you. As you begin to hold more value for your own life, through developing more self-love, self-belief and self-respect, you will finally be empowered to begin the spiritual journey inward to finally find some peace. Depression and misery are not a way of life; they are a waste of life. When you start to share from your heart, magic happens. When you listen to your heart, you understand why this happens. Stop letting the thoughts in your mind and the belief in your fear become the glue keeping you stuck in the past. It's time to let your truth be the glue between the bricks holding you together instead.

The definition of insanity is to repeat the same behaviour and expect a different result. I use this persistently when working with people in talk therapy. As human beings, why do we keep doing the same thing over and over, never getting the result we desire, often leaving us more depressed, yet we keep doing it anyway regardless? The answer is simple. It's all we know. If you spend your life predicting the outcome of your future in a negative way, you believe nothing will ever go right, nothing can change, you are experiencing fear and anxiety. This is an emotional reaction to something deeper, not connected to the present. How can you predict today what will happen tomorrow? You can't. Remember once again, no one is born with depression or anxiety. Both are products of the mind. Start thinking about your limitations, asking yourself if they are real or planted there by others. Getting yourself prepared for change will be even harder if you believe you will not do well, so try to beat this feeling before it happens by preparing yourself when it's on its way. Keep reading your journal, focusing on what you have learnt about your negative self and what helps trigger your feelings of anxiety and stress. Set yourself small goals to begin with. You don't want to aim too high and end up back at square one defeated.

The more you achieve a small goal, the more successful you will become at achieving bigger goals and when you achieve a big goal, you create unbreakable confidence. If you are uninspired by all of this and cannot bring yourself to achieve even a small goal, you may want to face the fact you have become more comfortable with your misery than you think. If you are still using alcohol or food for comfort before you go to bed, you are waking up in the morning feeling like staying in bed, you are not being mindful or productive. I suggest you go back to the beginning of this book and start again.

Mindful thinking with mindful meditation is the only way you can change small negative daily habits through clearing out your unconscious past, planting new positive seeds in your subconscious. Once you have created a safe peaceful Garden of Eden in your unconscious mind, after you have weeded out all the repressed memories and pain, as the head gardener you can consciously plant your seeds of intention through visualisation in your subconscious. Stop relying on stress or addictions to make you think you feel better. Try and rely on something new, something healthy instead, and see how much better your life is at the end of the day.

Today I have a solid tree in the centre of my unconscious. It is strong and healthy, tall and beautiful, stretching from my mind in a straight line down to my toes. It represents me, is immoveable, consistent, powerful, rooted in integrity and humility. All around this tree I have planted various flowers that represent various personal attributes I want to develop in my heart where my soul lives. These attributes include joy, self-love, gratitude, grace, courage, forgiveness, faith and peace.

I have reprogrammed my subconscious with positive affirmations of emotional support and encouragement towards the development of my new core beliefs. They are always at the forefront of my mind, ready to pull out when I need them, like my pin number or my phone number. In my meditation, I visit this garden every night now, fully grown and in full bloom. I become the tree looking out over my personal core beliefs, the flowers, enjoying the way they make me feel, always checking myself to ensure I am being authentic in my daily life. When I wake up in the morning after a peaceful sleep, refreshed and raring to go, I am always ready to face the day with purpose and it's a marvellous way to start the day. I am not going through the motions anymore, dreading my life. I am not allowing my past mistakes to influence my future goals. I am gracefully, in humility and gratitude, working every day with joy to create my authentic self with only purpose and passion by my side.

Once you can let go of the past, your repressed memories and negative bias in your subconscious memory because it serves no purpose in your present life, replacing it all with your newly developed core values and beliefs, you will be on your way to create a positive healthier mindset. You may have gathered by now this book is repetitive and consistent in its simple message, connected to a complex subject matter. The complex problems arising from human conditioning, the way we develop mentally and how we learn to respond or react, create many different patterns in behaviour due to different experiences of learning. Our behaviour is learnt, our beliefs are copied, our insecurities are fear, our fear is not real, our dreams are suppressed and a life without purpose is set on autopilot. When you start to think about all of this, it is really depressing for those with deep-rooted childhood demons and memories. Their problems become more impossible to unscramble, face or forgive. None of us are born with a life manual, how to succeed or survive. This we must learn as we go on the journey of life, so at least let us make it exciting.

It is only when you come face to face with death for real, you realise just how much you want to live, just how much your life means to you. I know because I have been there, survived and changed dramatically for the better in gratitude. You may think the only way out of your internal pain and turmoil is to block it out with drink, drugs or end your life, but you would be wrong. There are options but they only come with more gratitude, compassion, humility and forgiveness. Your life is just like this book, each chapter building towards the end and that end depends on the writer, the story, the inspiration, the facts or the fiction. You are the writer now and you decide the way your own story ends.

Remember, when you feel compassion for another rather than pity for yourself, it helps you realise suffering is all part of being a human being, you are not alone, it's a shared experience. Learning to love yourself requires a balanced approach towards the negative emotions that overpower and consume you, when the dark mood takes over. You must make sure these feelings and emotions are neither suppressed deeper, nor exaggerated out of proportion, they get faced in the moment instead.

If you are still reading this book, chances are by now you'll be having a really bad time. Maybe you have lost your job, broken up with a partner, had a death in your family or maybe you just hate your whole life. It could be you have hurt someone, lost someone, need someone or maybe you think the world owes you something, whatever the reason, it's OK to feel angry, sad and desperate, but you must never let these feelings control you. You might feel every time you take a positive step, the big bad world throws something unexpected in your path, and you feel suffocated with stress, then buckle under the fear and pressure. Learn to be grateful. Uncontrollable things do happen in life. Be brave enough to not let them define who you are. You are bigger than the problems you face. What you believe is an obstacle, a problem, a negative force against you, can turn out to be something completely the opposite, so learn to take things as they happen with faith in yourself you can cope; there are many people out there worse off than you.

Working with addicts and the homeless has taught me empathy for my fellow human beings, which stops me being too focused on myself. Their suffering and pain truly fuel my empathy, I have been there myself. I was lucky enough to escape and for this I am grateful. I remember back in LA when it all came crashing in on me, going outside for a walk to escape my overwhelming thoughts of death, my lowest point, coming across a homeless man begging for food. Unfortunately, I was starving myself at this time, so I had nothing tangible to give him except eye contact and my time, two valuable assets when money is scarce. As we walked and quietly talked on the beach by the ocean, I explained I was pretty much homeless myself, dying, with a few weeks to live. His kindness in that moment was uplifting, as he produced from his dirty jacket pocket a small orange he had found earlier that day. He gave it to me without hesitation and told me to enjoy the fruit of God; it would nourish me and bring life back into my soul. In my old life, greedy, rich and consumed with only myself, I probably would have ignored a homeless person trying to talk to me out of fear or embarrassment. This I am still ashamed of today. I was blown away by an act of kindness from a total stranger worse off than me. I knew I was dying, so the misery for me would soon be over. He had no way out of his misery, just a small orange to share on that sunny day back in LA. I suggested we share the orange as well as our stories, our fears, our regrets, and it was not long before we both felt better and not so alone.

Instead of recognising the differences between people, try and see the things you have in common with people. At the end of the day, we are all human beings. We need food, water, shelter, crave love, recognition and above all deserve to find happiness, regardless of past mistakes and circumstances. The deeply interesting thing about the man I met on the beach that day, sharing the small orange, getting to share our pain, forced me to reflect on how much I wanted the world to stop suffering. It was in this very moment I began to think about my own true purpose in life.

I would highly recommend you take twenty minutes every night before you go to sleep to reflect on your day, even if it consisted of doing nothing because eventually you realise, unless you try, nothing will happen and nothing will change. Random acts of kindness, regardless of how small, will lessen stress level, improving self-esteem, something proven to reduce depression and anxiety. Practising kindness is good for your heart and soul, the place where the secret to your eternal happiness is stored. You will reach this inner happiness not by rearranging your circumstances but by rearranging your attitude towards yourself and those around you.

The eternal quest for happiness will never be found outside of yourself, this is a fact, so stop seeking what you cannot find in what you have. Having balance and harmony between your beliefs, thoughts, words and actions is now the key to your happiness. Everything painful in your life must become something you learn from. You must see it as an opportunity to grow and develop, shedding your layers of self-protection, without fear or regret, until one day you emerge as the solid tree, alone and unbreakable. Start to imagine the day when you can feel love, joy, excitement, passion and hope, things we all deserve to feel. Happiness is not an exclusive club for members only. It is a shared experience. Your life is a valuable important commodity when it is working to full capacity, so learn to be content in the moment and comfortable with yourself.

Underneath the layers of your conscious thoughts, you will find a powerful awareness, the subconscious memory bank I have talked about before. Remember, the subconscious mind obeys commands from the conscious mind. The seeds you plant in your subconscious must now become positive instructions, manifesting only positive beliefs going forward. I am going to say here again, this is not self-help or life coaching; if you decide to consciously plant a positive idea in your subconscious, like you are going to grow more self-confidence and you work on this consciously every day, eventually you will become self-confident. Remember also that the subconscious mind will make you feel uncomfortable or emotionally uneasy when you begin to try and change old habits and patterns. I want you to begin to stretch yourself more everyday out of your comfort zone, bit by bit. If you truly want to overcome misery, depression and a lack of interest in your life, you must train your subconscious mind to believe you can be a person who is organised through self-discipline. Don't let the old you destroy the emerging new you. Let it go and start again. I am convinced when we have nothing left to lose, we start to win.

Self-acceptance, learning to have love and compassion without regret, never judging your past mistakes, allows the space for new beginnings. Often it is our biggest regret not that we are useless and underachievers but that we are strong and powerful beyond our belief. How many times have you thought about saying to yourself you are brilliant, beautiful and brainy but are unable to do so because you think it sounds bigheaded? This is your subconscious mind dragging you back into your comfort zone, making you feel uncomfortable, uneasy, but if you do it in private in humility, you are doing it for real and this is OK.

You are a child of the universe, part of a greater energy. There is nothing now to stop you shining your bright light through the darkness. Come on, step out, be brave and let go of the past, stop being afraid of the light within, for this is your true self. When we shine, we allow others to do the same, which liberates us all and before long, this positive powerful collective energy creates miracles beyond our belief. Activate your inner spirit from within your heart—your infinite light, love and power—then authentically declare your intention to change, resolving your issues, freeing yourself, breaking the ties with your mental bondage. Reclaim the authentic you hidden in the dark behind the shadow, the fake persona created to disguise your pain, and you will start to reclaim your unique talents and gifts.

When you accept yourself and your own values, you start to create what is right for you. You begin to feel whole, valued and valuable. This change in how you perceive your reality will help you build self-confidence. You will be heading in the right direction for once, following your heart, your truth and not the pack or your mind. When you learn to follow the beat of your own drum, you behave in a much calmer, more compassionate, positive, healthy way. You get your clean energy back and wake up, as you start to really live the life you deserve. Once you can resolve your problems naturally, by finding the right solutions, you will start to see things more accurately as they are in the present, not what you want them to be or falsely believe them to be. If you hide or deny your problems from your existence, you cannot separate the problem from the solution. Once you begin to break away from your old patterns and habits of following the pack, driven by your unconscious ego, it will be difficult retaining your awareness, the reason you have to practise focusing on your consciousness through your meditation. Through your consciousness, you can start to create your new core values, then determine the point to your life. We cannot change our circumstances, but we can be more in control of how things turn out.

Most people today are battling something dark inside, an invisible silent enemy they are unable to identify. We have no idea what it's like to walk in the shoes of someone suffering unless we have suffered ourselves. Since I have been able to establish inner peace and more clarity in the point of my purpose, without the constant need for money or power, understanding the importance of my core moral values, I have finally arrived at a mature spiritually balanced place, with a real stability in my mind. For you to arrive at this place, once again you must first take personal responsibility for what you have allowed your mind and consciousness to express to the world in the past. By becoming free from your past, your unconscious ego, your demons, fears and insecurities, to travel to a higher level of thinking, applying your core values to all you do, you too will connect to a journey of inner expansion.

On this new journey to the new emerging you, the person you should have always been, recognise your character will be tested every step of the way. Mistakes are inevitable, we are human. Learning how to surrender to these mistakes will be much easier during your practice of meditation. Remember you are learning to be mindful, that what you are giving to the world mirrors your integrity. Stopping the cycle of self-sabotaging is a critical part of learning how to revalue you, others and the universe. Your meditation and breathing will help you delve deeper into the problems creating your emotional anxiety, shifting you away from attachment by becoming an observer, not a victim.

My goal as your therapist is to take what you have learnt about yourself in this book, your vulnerability and courage, to finally help you to feel safe and secure in being authentic, completely transforming the way you live your life going forward.

Lying: The Master Manipulator

The main reason most people struggle today to dare to be unique is because the natural blueprint we start out with is contaminated right from the start by our environment, our circumstances and the opinions and beliefs of others. There are not many geniuses in the world, those allowed to shine through, nurturing their inner talent for the rest of us to admire, learn from and be inspired by them. The painters, the writers, the dancers, the scientists, the doctors, the teachers, the philosophers, the musicians, all the people who share their talent for the greater good of humanity.

From a very young age, I always wanted to be a businesswoman in a pinstriped suit working in the City of London, yet I had never been exposed to or been anywhere near such a place in the past. I knew instinctively from an early age I wanted to be rich and successful. My creative side never had an opportunity to develop, coming from a poor background. Any advancement through private lessons or extra tuition was sadly non-existent. No one in my family had creative talent like playing a musical instrument, singing, painting or writing. It was all about working hard to bring in cash for survival of the family unit. I modelled on hard work right from the start, watching my father work his fingers to the bone. I developed my steadfast confidence following my own dream of climbing to the top in business. Today I am truly grateful I got to model on this serious work ethic because without it, I would never have been a success on paper. I am dyslexic, with no formal education. My whole school life was about survival. Reaching the City of London, becoming a top financial headhunter, making millions, was quite an achievement in the big scheme of things for the girl from the council estate in Leicester.

Although my start in life was not the best, by focusing on just one goal to escape poverty, I managed against all the odds to avoid being pulled and torn apart by emotional troubles and hurdles. I was able for some reason to keep my mind free and open, fearlessly travelling towards my goal. Working in the City of London—a fast-paced, frenetic, dog-eat-dog environment—where being the best was essential for beating the odds, I managed to make it big by manipulating my truth to fit in. Once you begin to believe you know your truth, you stop looking for it and this is what happened to me. I created my backstory based on lies, then over-identified with the lies in order to be successful. I was forced to become the master at fabricating my truth, exploiting my inner spirituality and core values in the process. I lost sight of who I really was authentically, constantly producing misleading information that didn't belong to me to get on in the world. My unconscious ego became the perfect screen to hide behind and the more I relied on it, the less I connected to the real me. Subconsciously creating this empty distance from my true self resulted in a permanent feeling of unease.

Your unconscious ego will always create a feeling of unease. Anxiety is an illness of our time and comes from our inability to live in the present. As you develop and grow from a child, you begin to form a mental image of who you are based on your circumstances and conditioning. Your unconscious ego starts to develop in the early stages of infancy. It is a concept of how you feel inside and will be influenced by what happens to you throughout your life. It is a totally unconscious process and constantly demands satisfaction. The unconscious ego, the false you, never focuses in the present. It keeps you fixated on the past or projects you into the fear of the future. You will always miss the moment if you only live in your mind.

As babies, we don't need an ego. We depend on others to think and do for us. We have no idea how to distinguish ourselves from others; we just need security and a sense of belonging. As we develop more and more our own sense of self away from our caretakers, we are forced to face reality and grow by interacting with the rest of the world. We evolve in stages the same way our unconscious ego develops in stages. When we reach around three years old, we start to develop our curiosity. We become impulsive in our behaviour, testing the boundaries, open to either punishment or reward from those controlling our personality development. Around the age of five, the super ego begins to develop, the moral side of us. The moral and ethical restraints placed on us by our caretakers will dictate our own belief of what is right or wrong. At this stage, there is rarely an opportunity for us to make our own decisions and choices about what is right or wrong for us as individuals. Understanding this is truly important when you start to understand why you keep doing the things you do, without thinking, that just don't make you happy.

Your unconscious ego is all about you, how you were brought up, how you learnt things, how you were taught to react and the process of all these things that develop in your mind. It is important to have an ego. It can help protect you. It is just a question of not letting it rule your life. Maybe what you learnt along the way is not right for the authentic you. Part of the unconscious ego in our early development remains focused only on our basic impulsive needs, our immediate gratification and because we are incapable of meeting our demanding needs, we end up immersed in ourselves.

As we develop more into middle childhood, the unconscious ego reaches the self-protection stage. This stage is more cognitively sophisticated than the earlier impulsive stage, and it's when we learn how to get the things we need from others. Many people remain in this self-protecting stage throughout the rest of their growth, right into adulthood. Those who remain in this stage through adolescence into adulthood become manipulative and opportunistic with the main aim of getting what they want from other people. They will immediately blame others when anything goes wrong in their lives, never maturing and often getting into trouble. This is where the lying starts. For those who don't remain in the self-protecting stage, they naturally move on to the conformist stage. This is where the super ego fully emerges. It is the time when we become focused on belonging and pleasing others through seeking approval and acceptance. Some people remain in this stage into adulthood. The final stage of ego growth, and sadly the part few ever reach, is the self-awareness stage when we develop into full maturity, thinking for ourselves beyond the impulsive, selfish self-gratification, approval seeking and pleasing others. It is at this stage we are supposed to develop our own unique feelings and independent thinking but unfortunately because we are guided, manipulated, moulded, and copy our caretakers, we have trouble finding growth potential and tend to remain impulsive or self-protective as adults.

The major problem with never being allowed to think for ourselves in our own unique way, through self-awareness, developing our own core moral values, we end up never exploring any self-reflection. We become the people we are expected to be and not who we really are inside. Without self-reflection, all we end up with is self-criticism, constantly feeling either guilt or shame because we find it difficult to live up to what is expected of us. When we are not free to explore or develop our own belief in the important stages of our growth, based upon our own unique needs and talents, we are forced to live by the existing beliefs of others. We end up doing what they want us to. We think what they want us think and we behave in the way they want us to behave to please them. Often these beliefs are based on lies or control.

Obviously when we are young, we have no understanding of the lies we are being told which then become our own beliefs and because we invest so much time and efforts in these beliefs, it becomes impossible to let them go. We grow up innocently believing everything we have been told is the gospel truth. We believe we know the way we see the world is right, even when we can see without doubt, the world is not always right. We grow up believing we know best in our comfortable bubble of a perfect world, designed and delivered by our parents, to give us peace of mind. The trouble is we have all ended up with little peace and a sore mind.

The majority of what we experience in our lives, these underlying beliefs, emotions, feelings and impulses are not always available on a conscious level. Most of what influences and drives us comes from what is buried in our unconscious mind. Basically, what you believe is consciously right, will often be unconsciously influenced and not be right for you at all.

As our conscious mind only makes up a small percentage of who we are, our personality, basically the rest of who we are is buried and we cannot access it easily. We have no idea it's even there, influencing everything we feel and our decision-making process. Whilst we are fully aware of what is going on in the small part of the conscious mind, the unconscious ego should serve as a good thing; it is meant to keep us safe, helps us understand other people's needs and stops us being impulsive or selfish like a child. The unconscious part of the mind is a different matter. It contains all sorts of difficult, disturbing stuff outside of our awareness. It is not rational to our conscious mind. When this disturbing stuff starts to manifest, we end up creating a bunch of self-defence mechanisms, such as repression, to bury the unwanted memories and thoughts, avoiding having to face what our true feelings really are. The mind in general is a survival machine, collating and analysing information. This is what it is good at but when it comes to anything creative or enlightening, we have to rise above our thoughts, listening into our hearts—the purpose for your meditation practice.

As we age, we have a much harder time holding onto ourselves, realising our self-worth, our purpose, our goodness. It all gets tied up with what we could have done once upon a time but cannot do now. Feeling rather than thinking, being rather than doing, shrinking from the world to just exist, rather than embracing who we really are inside, takes understanding that when we are not thinking, we are in fact creating.

The unconscious ego in my mind does not serve as a good thing. It allows us to escape our reality and confidently create imaginary fantasy ideas, thoughts, emotions, governing our behaviour in ways more than we understand. The truth is, if we do not mature, we remain impulsive, selfish children, unable to have empathy or self-respect, always miserable, always escaping, taking no personal responsibly for our actions. Maturing with grace, peace and wisdom can only come from detaching from the unconscious ego, connecting with the authentic self, letting go of the past, forgetting about the future and enjoying the present with no regrets.

Our fast-paced lifestyle today, our mental health combined with our physical workload, can cause our bodies to become ineffective at releasing built-up stress, which remains trapped inside, manifesting in fear and anxiety. This stress builds up, causing us to feel permanently uneasy or afraid; if not released, it remains stored in the body, resulting in health problems like depression, insomnia, anxiety, depleting the power of the immune system. Since stress accumulates on an unconscious level, healing the body must happen on a conscious level. Changing lifestyle habits through the daily practice of breathing, meditation and relaxation, bringing awareness back to how your mind is harming your nervous system, is the best basis for good health. Good health, regardless of what you think or how much you don't want to change, is the main key when it comes to feelings of self-power and inner happiness. Your mind will destroy your body and your body will destroy your life if you do not take care of it.

I discovered through working on myself with self-awareness, making my unconscious conscious, it was my unconscious ego that had become the barrier to me reaching my unique reality, my sense of identity. I am now aware the primitive urges in my unconscious did not protect me from my anxiety and mistakes. All my positive information processing came from developing my consciousness. The more I was able to let go of my unconscious ego, the self-protection stage, not acting on my impulsive reactions to my feelings but to my conscious thinking with integrity, the more I began to actualise my own potential.

The truth is, what we have been set up to believe right from the start, to give us peace of mind, has not turned out to be the truth in real life, leaving us disappointed and sad. Once we begin to feel this disappointment and we realise we don't want to face the reality, everything we have learnt is potentially a lie, we end up creating new lies to replace the old lies. We don't look inside ourselves to find the truth. We hate the unknown, it scares us.

When I reached the bottom, I abandoned all my lies. I was thrust headfirst into the unknown without a safety net in place, leaving behind the fairy-tale dream life and fake concepts to face the harsh reality of my truth.

The money had given me a false sense of security; it defined me and without it, I had nothing of any spiritual value to hang on to. Almost losing my life a few years later sent me tumbling into unbearable fear, recognising I had no idea who I was. Once I was able to break free from the chains of my false beliefs and leave them behind, with another chance to be the real me, I did not hesitate. The fake me and the lies suddenly had no place in my new world. When I stopped looking outwards for the answers to my problems, stepping in front of the shield of my unconscious ego, I found the gateway, the authentic path to the real me, finally finding peace in my mind. Very quickly I became less attached to material things, letting go of my bankrupt empty values, becoming more real, open and curious. This kind of transformation is nothing to do with religion. It is just about self-reflection, facing the made-up me, then leaving it behind, rising from the ashes like the phoenix brand new.

It is our fear of being out of control, the I–know-better mentality that keeps us lying to ourselves but try and imagine how this has put your life out of control and this should really be where your fear lives. We lie to ourselves basically because we cannot face the truth. The cruel inner critic, the voice inside our heads producing endless abuse, telling us we are stupid, awkward, incapable, is a trigger to keep you indulging in self-sabotage. The main reason this voice is hard to shake off is because it starts very early on in our development process. When the cruel inner critic voice is in the driving seat of your every move, it will be hard to remain positive and confident when trying to achieve personal success. We cannot shine and be brilliant when inside a voice is telling us we are stupid.

Start by thinking of your unconscious ego as your lying mind. A mind that has already decided who it thinks you are and because it is ruled by fear, it has set limits on what it believes you can accomplish. Once you begin to judge yourself, your unconscious ego starts to put labels on things, it categorises everything, but I have discovered the unconscious ego knows nothing. I can promise you what you think, what you do, truly matters in the bigger picture. You matter, your energy matters, and it has been proven by science that energy cannot be created or destroyed, only conserved or transferred.

The time has come for us all to make some valuable adjustments both physically and mentally, gaining a better understanding of the unconscious ego versus the soul. Thinking in a limited way stops us valuing our lives. To finally be yourself in a world always pushing you towards being something you are not, constantly struggling against the odds, like I have said a million times, will take enormous courage but in this struggle to achieve a stronger sense of self, we will learn to resist temptation.

Stepping into my own authentic life with wisdom and maturity, I discovered my innate desire to be part of something whole. I am sure you too want peace and harmony in the world, without war, poverty and conflict. I am sure deep down inside you want the planet to survive. Being truly open-minded means being receptive to new ideas, new thinking, being able to adapt to change, especially when it comes to the safety and survival of the planet. My goal is to get you to be more mentally open and flexible through feeling empathy, humility, compassion and gratitude. To not be scared or threatened but to look at real information that shares real knowledge for the collective good of humanity. Our whole existence is currently under threat whether we like it or not. This is a time in history when we cannot bury our head in the sand and pretend we are watching a Tom Cruise disaster movie any longer. Greed and overconsumption for real is contributing to irreversible climate change if we do not change. We are currently facing the biggest environmental challenge this generation has ever seen. By lying to ourselves and being lied to by the template, we have changed the balance of nature through greedily living beyond our means, burning too much oil and gas, breeding too many methane-producing livestock wastes, cutting down forests and not to mention the dirty business behind cheap fashion, costing us the earth. This unethical, selfish, greedy need for over-indulgence, our plastic fantastic convenience and self-gratification, is causing not only ill health in the western world but catastrophe and devastation in the third world for those already enduring extreme poverty. This unnecessary, impulsive, stupid behaviour is having a serious impact on the world's water system, and this is not a lie or propaganda, it's a very scary fact.

Fresh water environments around the globe are under excessive pressure from dredging and pollution, and climate change is making this problem much worse. Droughts and flooding causing displacement and conflict is becoming so common, it is almost becoming normal. As average temperatures rise in areas crucial for regulating the planets climate, there will be no ice cover left over the sea and this escalation of ice melting will have a devastating global impact as sea levels rise around the world. The sad thing for me, even with the best scientific environmental experts in the land banging the drum so loud it's impossible to ignore, screaming at us planet earth is at risk of extinction, the masses still yearn for the damaging convenience of a fast fashion fix with a Big Mac and fries.

Being mindful of your own personal behaviour helps you to improve your mental flexibility, connecting you to a higher intelligence beyond the ignorance of greed and money, and this will have a positive impact on your conscience and ethical footprint. Once we centre ourselves on a spiritual connection through peace and contemplation for the good of the universe and everything natural beyond materialism, money and greed, it helps us to have more compassion. Once you can reinforce gratitude for all the things you take for granted in your own life, your health, fresh drinking water, your freedom, the stars, the moon and the sky, you begin to nurture more goodness inside and behave in a more ethical, caring way.

Learning to think deeper and explore more through a wider knowledge, beyond the endless distractions and temptations of your impulsive consumption, always taking more than you give back, requires you to have a deeper knowledge of your consciousness. I know it is overwhelming when it comes to thinking about climate change, we tend to think on a small level with this subject matter, when in fact all we need to do is switch off lights and recycle more—the basics. We need to systematically organise our minds better, to think about how we deal with the biggest problem the world has seen, recognising collective action is the only answer. When you start to think beyond your own problems, by changing your own behaviours, you naturally develop a broader perspective around the idea the world is changing. When you really know the facts about climate change and you see the evidence, it can be emotionally distressing, so often people will avoid the emotional labour involved in changing and not get involved. It is the same principle of emotional avoidance in doing the hard work to overcome depression and personal misery, often we have no idea how to deal with emotional stress, so we give up.

As adults with our own mature mindset, we are capable of making informed ethical choices beyond the pack mentality, learning to have faith in our ability to problem solve will help us to build trust to surrender our unconscious ego, bringing us into the current state of what is happening right now. What use is huge profit to business if there is no planet? What use is another throwaway fashion garment if there are no discos to be seen in it? What use is money if there is nowhere to spend it? And what use is a balanced healthy person with a conscience if the rest of the world doesn't give a fig? Think deeply about these questions right now and see it makes no sense to keep buying, eating, drinking, consuming, lying and cheating at the cost of the very thing that keeps you alive. We need to stop and change before it is too late. Changing the behaviour of one person is hard enough, let alone the masses. Education is one thing but getting people to act can be challenging, even with concrete evidence. I guess the truth is, if people feel climate change is psychologically distant, it won't affect them, they don't worry so much about it in their daily lives, they feel it is less urgent.

Refocusing your mind through being mindful of your behaviour, learning to shift your impulsive, selfish needs, taking better care of yourself and the planet, restoring clean energy, will strengthen your spiritual growth and connect you back to your soul. Your soul is the connection to your divine authentic self, your gut feeling. The very thing you have unconsciously clogged up, believing your unconscious ego instead of listening to your open heart. Remember your unconscious ego is responsible for feeding you information that isn't true. This information has now become your existing belief system and negative thoughts. Most of it stems from fear and is designed to keep you trapped and unable to change. How many times have you examined your thinking objectively? Do you believe the planet you exist on is in trouble? Do you believe you can make changes to prevent a disaster happening? Do you care if the food you are eating is killing you? Do you believe you are invincible?

Sadly, we are living in a consumer driven world right now, believing from the beginning what we own makes us good people. Let me tell you right now, this is the biggest lie of them all. What you own, what you desire, where you live, what you drive, is just your unconscious ego looking to measure you against someone else, leaving you feeling superficially good about your choices and your life. Your unconscious ego is fickle. One day it can tell you how clever and amazing you are on the days you are lying to yourself. The next day it will remind you what a failure you are on the days you fall short to please it. On these bad days when you fall short to please, it becomes that cruel critic whispering in your ear, your internal dialogue, yet nothing has really changed from the good days. You are still doing what you do, trying your best, getting on with things. The only thing that changes between these up and down states is the story you are telling yourself in your mind.

Anyone under pressure or given enough incentive will lie. We are all in denial about something through self-deception. Lying to ourselves is simply motivated by a false belief. We all have secret desires to some degree. Think about a man who on the surface is happily married with kids, a loving wife, but deep down inside he knows he is gay, desperate to break free and engage in sexual activity with another man. It would be very hard to contain this kind of painful secret without feeling depressed, anxious and desperate, especially if he had been feeling like this from an early age without ever having been honest with himself. Is this a mental weakness or is it wrong? Should he be brave, open and honest, putting his authentic feeling before the feelings of his wife and children, so he doesn't go mad and kill himself? Should he confess, creating short-term pain for his wife and kids in exchange for his own long-term happiness and personal freedom? The truth is, if he stays in the marriage unhappy, he is lying to himself in denial, hurting himself with no choice but to consciously lie to his wife, preventing hurting others, forcing him to indulge in fantasy secrets and lies. It's a no-win for him.

When you start to look at situations like this without judging through compassion and empathy, you get to see how living life through a lie would create depression and deep emotional unresolved pain, manifesting into dirty energy. This scenario may seem miles away from the lies you tell yourself but in reality, any lie that causes you to not be your true self, is going to create a permanent feeling of unease in the end. We all have things we don't like about ourselves, we have all made mistakes, spending our lives pretending we are happy, when in truth we are not. We all have things we are desperate to change but we also know changing is difficult and tricky to do consciously. Even just a small lie can create uncomfortable feelings of unease and anxiety inside. Because subconsciously, we are just waiting to be found out, humiliated, embarrassed or judged by other people.

Think about how many people stand before a minister in a church, full of friends and family promising faithfully to be faithful but later have indiscretions and affairs with other people in secrets and lies. Think about how many times people tell lies to show off and pretend to be something they are not, especially on social media where lying, airbrushing, photoshopping and manipulating is normal and acceptable. We have all done it, told a lie to look bigger, better, fit in, stand out and then been forced into telling another lie to cover up the first lie and so the cycle begins, pushing our truth deeper and deeper inside, until we feel bad. We have all told lies to ourselves to convince ourselves what we are doing is right, we will never get found out, it won't do any harm, but this is false evidence. It is truly harmful to your soul in the long run. Once we sell out, giving in to the quick-fix mentality, the addictions, the turning a blind eye to situations, and we allow denial to cloud our judgement, hoping for a quick, fast route to relief from our problems, we just become spiritually weaker.

Developing spirituality is always centred on the deepest values and meaning by which we live. It helps embrace the idea of an ultimate selfless reality, discovering our inner path to the true essence of who we really are. We seem to have forgotten or maybe never even understood how important it is to consciously observe ourselves through examining and taking personal responsibility for the consequences of our actions. We don't know how to self-analyse or learn self-modification for personal adjustment, we are just constantly modelling on each other's mistakes and misery. We have dulled our senses to the point we have little realisation we have sold out, choosing money and materialism over personal ethics. We have sold our souls to the falsehood of our lies for short-term relief from our anxiety and fears over facing the truth head on.

All I am doing on this journey is trying to help you develop a better level of self-awareness, so you can begin to reconnect with your inner spiritual self, the authentic you, to help you overcome your pain, resistance and fears, currently limiting your ability to be an independent thinker. I am not here to force anything on you or make you feel bad. Self-will and freedom of choice is down to you. Self-honesty is the only true pathway to spiritual freedom. If we continue to constantly choose self-deception over the truth and we choose denial to deal with our internal pain fear and misery, it will stop us having access to developing our own unique character. As Jung said, learning only to people-please as a child prevents growth in our other characteristics. I am really sorry if I have burst your bubble or pushed you further into the comfort zone you are accustomed to hide yourself in. but if we are to eradicate mental health problems, develop healthy happy people and save the planet, we have to face what is really happening today and understand why the world has literally gone mad.

Woody Allen has been vocal about how much therapy he has had. His films often brilliantly prove this by his attention to detail in the subject matter. His ability to show us the human condition, the madness, the anxiety, the dysfunctional behaviour of his crafted characters and storytelling is brilliant. One film you could watch to use as a case study to explore and explain what I am talking about in this chapter, how lying and social anxiety can escalate to unimaginable levels with drastic consequences, is *Blue Jasmine*. This brilliant movie adapted from the Tennessee Williams' play *A Streetcar Named Desire*, another movie I recommend you watch, is so true to real life, it must have been written by someone who understands it. Both these films show beautifully how the choices we make, for all the wrong reasons, create the people we become and when life throws these choices a curve ball, we end up back at square one, starting again from scratch.

This is exactly what happened to me. Just like poor Jasmine, I lost all my status when I lost my wealth. I had become accustomed to a certain lifestyle and I was consumed more by what people thought of me than what I thought of myself. Once I lost everything materially, I felt the most incredible anxiety, paranoia and depression. Although I had no respect for my money, it did give me security and status with others. Once the truth is out for all to see and the person you've been pretending to be is all you know but you no longer like or trust, the only place you can go to is madness, self-harm, a nervous breakdown or death. I was lucky, unlike poor Jasmine. Although I did become anxious, depressed and isolated, attempting suicide as a last resort, thankfully it didn't work and I managed to recover from the loss of my money to start a new life in LA, without wealth or status.

For five years with my sister-in-law, divorced herself by now, we had an incredible, unbelievable journey doing everything we could to make money, make it work, but Hollywood is not a place for the faint-hearted. It is the most brutal place on the planet if you are poor, old or broken. All the bright lights turn off and the sharks swim around waiting to eat you alive, then spit you out, but Rome wasn't built in a day and all that, so we finally concocted a concrete plan to survive. If you cannot beat them, you join them. I had always set my sights high in the past, so getting to Harvey Weinstein, the most powerful man in Hollywood seemed the perfect plan, an ideal person to help us if we could track him down. During this difficult personal time, it became a natural progression to want to help others. It stops you having to think about your own problems, so we opened a small art gallery, Art Interiors, by the beach to make money and help geniuses the world had forgotten about. It was not long before we came across a penniless Russian artist on Venice Beach, starving and desperate to show his work to the world and the right investor. It turned out he was one of five fresco masters left in the world, the modern-day Michelangelo, capable of restoring the Sistine Chapel. It could only happen in Hollywood, right?

His work was magnificent, a real genius with qualities it turned out that matched our friend Harvey Weinstein and the idea was born. We would simply go to Harvey and ask him to help fund the work of the Russian genius, elevate his profile and showcase his work to the rest of Hollywood. Getting to Harvey Weinstein was set in motion, as we composed begging letters, endless invites to lunch, flattering flirty emails, orchids to charm him, stalking him from Cannes to Timbuktu, spending money we didn't have, to create the impossible dream, in order to survive. For five long years, we set about looking for Harvey Weinstein to help us save the modern-day Michelangelo.

Getting to Harvey turned into a silly story so unbelievable, so tragic, yet so funny during the dark nights of reality when the red wine had worn off and whilst the bullshit slept, I would sit at the computer getting it all down into a manuscript. If you want to know what happened, you can read *Looking for Harvey Weinstein*, a self-published book, documenting what I now believe to be my own nervous breakdown in Hollywood.

During this difficult time, I had been bleeding non-stop for over a year and without medical insurance, I was unable to take it seriously. I just got through it the best I could. In May 2005, I woke up one morning, collapsed from a cardiac arrest and died for a short time, before being resuscitated and given blood transfusions that saved my life. The rest you already know. We came back to England broke, broken with an eight-pound fibroid, some old designer clothes and a few copies of the self-published book *Looking for Harvey Weinstein*. I was alive, free and ready to start again without money, regret, lies or fear, just the raw authentic divine me with a true gratitude for everything. I was finally free from the past, not interested in the future, just curiously open to living in the moment.

The very first step to unconditional love and respect for yourself and others is to learn to have sensitivity to the spiritual side of yourself. Our soul is the deepest seat for our emotions and will benefit greatly from the gift of a more spiritually connected relationship with our mind. Spirituality feeds the soul, which ultimately heals the psychological wounds we collect through the battle of life. What we see with our own eyes is made up from memory and much of what we see is manufactured by our minds, so we can never be sure what is reality and what is an illusion. Basically, most of our thinking cannot be trusted.

I wanted to write this book for many reasons, but the main reason is because it is what I did for myself. I am hoping to help you do the same. I want to show you what your psychological survival mechanisms are, help you understand what your fears are, your strengths your weaknesses, your habits, your patterns and so much more, so you can go beyond your own limits and truly understand yourself for the first time. Most of the time our problems are created because our inner child is lost and buried, insecure, never feeling safe, fragmented and split, constantly looking for ways to cope. Once you can connect back to your inner spirituality, you will start to mature and then take the hand of the trembling infant, guiding it out of the darkness back into the light. As you develop into this greater spiritual maturity away from the fear and insecurity you have clung onto for dear life, the trauma, the conflict, the pain, you will stop resisting change and blossom like a flower in nature, becoming the beautiful perfect creature you are inside.

By working on yourself through meditation and mindful learning to pay attention to acknowledge your current experiences, accepting them without judgement, you will improve your moods, decrease anxiety and improve your physical body functioning. The next time your unconscious feelings begin to surface, try not to repress or deny them. Be committed to shift out your pain, recognising it is the only way to gain emotional freedom and acceptance, so you can finally move on with your real life.

The Power of Intention

Your conscious mind determines your actions. Your unconscious mind determines your reactions. Your subconscious mind is a huge memory bank, storing your beliefs, memories and life experiences through your feelings. Many of us have a subconscious idea of what we believe we are, but when life doesn't represent what we believe we deserve, we become frustrated and stressed, leading to self-sabotaging behaviours, played out in fear and self-doubt. By now hopefully you understand your subconscious mind runs the show. It has the power to create obstacles we often have no idea about, preventing us reaching our desired goals, our hopes and dreams.

Autosuggestion is the hypnotic or subconscious adoption of an idea originated by oneself. Whenever we are engaged in it without being completely sure of ourselves, we are basically sabotaging our ambitions. The subconscious communicates via our feelings, so our feelings need to be real when making autosuggestions. Increasing your level of self-awareness prevents you from communicating with your subconscious via negative autosuggestion. You automatically stop saying things like, I am not good enough. Once you can master mindfulness through being more self-aware, you will slowly begin to erase the negative programming inside your mind, creating space for more genuine truths to be phrased in a positive way, about how you really feel about yourself. This change will create a whole new perspective on how you feel about your life.

We need to learn to get to know ourselves authentically to able to see ourselves and communicate with our higher spiritual self. The steadfast part of us that is real, not the false side trapped and limited by fear. You cannot communicate with something you cannot see or acknowledge. Once you empty your mind, throwing out your false negative beliefs you have clung onto since childhood, making clear, definite, positive affirmations, repeating, repeating, repeating religiously the truth about what you desire, will literally change the way you think forever. Remember, your subconscious mind has created all your negative thoughts and actions. No matter what you say or do originates from here.

Our beliefs are the foundation of who we are. They are programmed and wired within us as a result of a lifetime of conditioning and represent a powerful influence on our behaviour. When you start to begin to really think deeply about this, you get to see clearly how your beliefs would influence your moods, your relationships, your self-esteem, your confidence, your career, your physical health. Our existing beliefs and values come only from our life experiences. They are stored in the subconscious memory bank, creating the way we perceive and respond to challenging situations. Our beliefs will establish the limits of what we can achieve in our lives. The biggest obstacles to changing our mindset are already programmed in our subconscious, and this will be limiting our success when we attempt to do something new, outside of our comfort zone. The constant conflict between your conscious mind and your subconscious comes from recognising what you say you are going to do one day can completely change the next. Your conscious choice cannot compete with your subconscious memory. What you say you are going to do consciously gets compromised and defeated by your limiting beliefs in your subconscious. This conflict then creates unconscious unease in your body, resulting in both physical and mental illnesses. This happens because your subconscious mind controls all motor functions, the movements in your body.

Think about it like this. If you were asked to make a speech at a wedding and you consciously agree, believing you will be fearless on the day, overcoming your dread of public speaking, then you get up to make your speech and freeze, your subconscious mind suddenly reminds you about your belief, you hate talking to crowds. You suddenly experience intense fear, dry mouth, racing heart, leaving you speechless. Your subconscious beliefs can literally sabotage your whole life. It is where all your emotions come from. If you consciously believe you are going to be good at something, when in fact your subconscious belief is you are a failure, you've always failed in the past, you will never be successful. Your body sensations will make you freeze, and you will fail every time you try.

Think about all the times you consciously decide to change your unhealthy eating habits by going on a diet. Deep down you consciously know it needs to happen because you are unhealthy but subconsciously you believe you cannot live without the comfort you get from the bad diet you crave. The delicious takeaway, the divine cream cake, will always override your conscious decision to eat healthy, low-fat, low-sugar foods, and this happens because your volatile roller coaster moods will ruin any highs, unless you are consciously mindful of how you are feeling moment to moment. It is true mindless eating comes from not thinking. Unconsciously, you automatically run to comfort without even realising you are doing it. Subconsciously, you are soothing an underlying, unresolved emotional issue holding you hostage, preventing you from taking back control of your life. Sticking to big life changes with determination such as dieting will take you reprogramming your subconscious first before you can stick to self-control in the discipline. You must retrain your subconscious mind into believing you are a success story and not a failure because you have failed in the past. Ninety percent of what you do is done subconsciously.

Once you can identify your subconscious existing beliefs, taking an honest look at your negative automatic patterns and habits, anything self-sabotaging, you will begin to see how they come to the surface, so you can consciously change them for the better. When you start the process of asking is what you believe true and real or fake and made up, you will begin to feel uncomfortable but don't worry, this is normal. You are not used to self-monitoring. Once again reinforcing your conscious mind that you are going on a diet is only a tiny part of your mind power. The main reason why when you decide to do something like make a change, you fail miserably and then believe you are a useless failure. Feeling like a failure leads you automatically to the old bad habit you consciously intended to change. Now if you really think more deeply about this, at least three quarters of your mind power and potential is never used. Delving into your subconscious means you can unlock, then access knowledge and wisdom never utilised before. The only way you can do this is through the religious practice of your meditation.

Meditation literally changes the pattern of your brain to reach a deeper level, exploring beneath the surface of your conscious thoughts, gaining full access to your subconscious. The deeper you delve to get beneath the surface of your thoughts and beliefs, the more you gain the ability to connect with your deeper consciousness, solving your problems in a more relaxed open manner, unlocking your inner power and strength. I can tell you from experience without doubt, if you can nourish your mind with the right things, eat healthier foods, remain optimistic, exercise your body daily, you will unlock the magic power within you and true progress on a deep level will be made.

If everything we do subconsciously has been programmed through our experiences, the common-sense advice would be to get out of the negative mindset and have more interesting positive experiences. If we remain in the same mindset or environment for too long, the subconscious mind begins to form a belief system based upon what it sees and feels. Think about how you feel when you are around positive exciting people or you watch your favourite actor in a film, you end up wanting to be like them because it makes you feel good in the moment. Now think about being around pessimistic depressed people for too long, you end up feeling low, miserable and cannot wait to escape to lift your mood. They bring you down, not lift you up. We model, we copy, we repeat.

Our own beliefs are formed on thinking repetitively in a certain way and because we are quite lazy in our thinking patterns, we are more likely to rely on what we have learnt in the past over trying out something new. If your parents and caretakers have been negative thinkers in the same job, in the same town all their lives, chances are you will start your adult life in the same job, in the same town, with the same mindset. What we think and believe dictates how we feel and translate into how we behave. Positive thoughts generate positive actions and positive actions improve confidence.

Your mind controls your actions and because we are lazy thinkers at the end of the day, automatically reverting to what we know, the comfort zone thinking, our subtle thoughts and deep-rooted habits in our subconscious leave us victim to our negative bad thinking habits. By consciously repeating positive thoughts with commitment, belief, courage and intent through self-honesty when you go to sleep and when you wake in the morning, visualising what you want to manifest, your subconscious will begin to act, then deliver. Remember here, your subconscious does not differentiate between your imagination and your reality—

what is good or bad—it just obeys what you consciously tell it, so command wisely.

Every time you act on something, start to stand back and decide if the action was driven by your self-deception of it, you did it intentionally for the right reasons for you. Is what you are intending in your best interest. If you start to do this regularly, you will eventually protect yourself from constantly feeling bad or guilty and that is a good thing. Constantly having a distorted view of your own self-concept, the perception of how you see yourself and your abilities, allows your subconscious mind to make this your truth. If you believe you are a fat, undesirable person who will never get a good job because of it, your subconscious mind will not motivate you to do anything to lose weight and potentially become more desirable to a prospective employer. A distorted self-concept will prevent you from making better choices, like going on a diet, so you can buy more attractive clothes, making you feel more confident and likely to help you get the job you truly desire. Once you begin to change and develop a more realistic self-concept, you start to believe in yourself more. You have more confidence in your ability, then your subconscious mind will do everything accordingly to help you fulfil this new belief in yourself. When it comes to being over-weight—and in this current environment, this is most people—it's important to distinguish the difference between health awareness and cruelty. I never criticise or judge people for being overweight, I just try and point out, obesity is the second leading cause for lifestyle-related cancers, a fact many people are just not aware of. Mental health and self-esteem play a huge role in our ability to control our weight; anyone suggesting a size twenty is just as healthy as a size twelve is not a positive body image message, it's an irresponsible form of self-denial.

Have you ever thought about why sometimes something that makes you have a disgust response, say like eating brown sauce, makes other people lick their lips? This is because the difference between your hate and their love is down to the influence of the subconscious mind. We have all felt emotional reactions, things like disgust, fear, trust, and this is because we have constantly reinforced existing beliefs into the subconscious of what we are afraid of, who we trust and what we like etc. We communicate these beliefs, feelings, likes and dislikes— we hate brown sauce—into our subconscious and by doing this habitually, we end up never challenging things. It is because our mind doesn't understand language; it only understands images, emotions and feelings. This is the reason why learning to meditate is the key to changing how you think. When we are fully relaxed with an empty mind, the conscious mind does not have to respond to external stimuli. It allows the subconscious to take over, then we can influence it by visualising success. The exercise I gave you earlier, breathing on your bed in a cotton wool cloud, is the perfect way to relax and begin to visualise what it is you wish to change, like how you love brown sauce, reinforcing in your subconscious, most of your brainpower, you are no longer disgusted by brown sauce. It is not a quick process to change old negative existing beliefs, especially if you are driven by your unconscious ego, keeping you believing you should think in a one-dimensional way. If you are prepared to be dedicated, your new choices will eventually become as automatic as your old ones and you will be eating brown sauce with everything and loving it.

Relaxation and a clear empty mind are all it takes to change your old habits. When your mind is always active, wandering and constantly taking in what you perceive as reality, it's impossible to remain focused on visualising what you need to change. Basically, once you code into your subconscious mind the things you want to change, solving your problems will become much easier, as you make conscious decisions about what you want to change.

Your intuition, the thing you currently have no idea about, you are automatically doing things without thinking, is the ability to gain insight before you make your choices. You just know instinctively without doubt what to do and why you are doing it. A positive intention helps you to build resilience through repetition and practice, setting realistic expectations helps you to begin to shape a better reality in your truth. Have you ever consciously thought deeply about your existing beliefs and how they have become part of your story? Have you ever questioned if what you believe is really what you believe? Have you ever changed what you believe to impress another person, look good or fit in?

Knowing yourself, the real you, is all about understanding the way you think, through self-honesty, self-awareness and integrity, never just bumbling along, changing like the weather to please others, otherwise you end up an empty, fake, depressed people-pleaser. Following any repetitive behaviour that reinforces a distorted self-concept, the way you see yourself, will always prevent you from achieving your goals. Remember how you feel about yourself right now, your self-concept was formed from your existing beliefs, developed in your subconscious mind in childhood. You were not born with all your negative feelings, fears and insecurities, so you must start facing why you are now over loaded with all the wrong information about yourself. A simple thing like lying can literally make you physically ill. Every time you tell a lie, deep down subconsciously you know you are doing it. It plays on your mind and makes you feel bad. Every time you lie to yourself to get what you believe you want, you never get what you need or deserve, only what you want in the moment.

My own self-concept, the way I saw myself before losing all my money, was quite good. I believed in myself. My intention was always followed by an action. I was action-driven right from the start and everything I wanted to achieve happened effortlessly. My overconfident, optimistic outgoing personality did affect my behaviour. It allowed me to manipulate and compromise my core values, my morals, to get what I wanted, to be rich and successful. Once I reached the top, my out-of-control behaviour began to affect my moods. My self-confident optimistic bullshit took a bit of a blow as self-doubt, guilt, remorse, regret and humiliation took over. Therefore, I understand how these negative feelings can pull you into the depths of despair and destroy any self-esteem you have. For quite a while, my own self-concept changed. You cannot be a big shot calling the shots, when you've lost everything without thinking, gambling on the stock market, regardless of how big your ego is. In the past before my catastrophe happened, my inner dialogue was driven only by my unconscious ego. I was invincible, permanently convincing myself my conscience was clear, I was doing all the right things, I deserved to be fabulous because subconsciously I had worked hard for it.

When my material world collapsed before my eyes, the virtual money disappeared, my unconscious ego took a knock and my internal dialogue changed. I suddenly had no confidence to hide behind, no hope to look forward to, no fake bullshit to spout. I became isolated and alone, self-sabotaging, feeling like a failure. Basically, I was nothing without the money. Overnight I went from believing I could rule the world to believing I was not good enough for the world. I now know this is what happens when you are empty spiritually. You realise just how shallow you have become. I was not used to blaming circumstances, conditions or others for my own failings. To be honest, I'd never actually failed at anything. I was always self-assured. Suddenly finding myself broke, broken and humiliated sent me to the darkest place you can imagine. This is what I now know to be depression.

Life doesn't always go the way you would imagine it would go and difficult times produce difficult circumstances, some so unimaginable they go beyond your own capability and strength. Deep down I knew I wasn't a victim, depressed, weak or unconfident, I was just stupid. I wanted to stop the internal battering I was giving myself so badly. It was such unfamiliar territory for me, so getting drunk and taking the pills was a godsend. By getting drunk, thankfully I didn't swallow enough pills to finish me off and I survived myself. As you can imagine, I have learnt a lot of things about myself from this unexpected event back in LA. The main thing I have discovered is that negative thinking is like a mental chisel used by the mind to shape the wrong beliefs, changing your moods and outlook, leaving you incapable of thinking straight. Once my unbearable, unpredictable period of negative thinking was over, I accepted the money was gone and was grateful to be alive, the horrific self-defeating attitude lifted. I let it all go, faced the pain of feeling ashamed for even contemplating suicide, then set about some serious self-reflection with unbreakable faith and an optimistic approach to survival, without the false security of money. I have learnt if you never face yourself, your denial, when you constantly suppress painful feelings of shame, guilt, humiliation, you end up creating a permanent feeling of unease inside, and this will manifest in almost everything you do think and say. You will not only be hurting your physical health you will also be creating a mental health problem as well.

When we can assume a positive intent, we seek to do good for ourselves and others around us. We don't have random emotional reactions of anger because we don't get defensive. If you hear yourself say in your head I am a failure, I just got the sack, reply with something like, it doesn't matter I got the sack because now I have an opportunity to find out what I am really good at, a chance to do what I have always wanted to do. This is how subconscious brain training works. When you begin to reframe what you are telling yourself in your mind and you keep doing it repetitively, you will begin to believe it. It is all down to how you talk to yourself in your internal dialogue with yourself remember.

It has been established through research only forty percent of lifestyle intentions are successfully realised. The likelihood of performing any change in behaviour is all down to function of the person's self-regulatory capacity. So why are we so irresponsible towards ourselves and our intentions? Monitoring bad habits is the key. We must make any action to change consciously part of our routine and recognise, change is not something we can just say we will do, we need to act by rewiring our brain circuits, ignoring our built-in survival triggers as much as we can. If we have a better understanding of the cause of our own behaviour, we can work better to keep the behaviour in line with our plans and goals. The nature of the goal, the basis of the intention, the properties of the intention, each influence the quality of the repetitive intention and its likelihood of enactment.

Many times, we set goals that are over optimistic, which reduces the likelihood they are achieved. In my own experience of working with people to help them change their behaviour and negative patterns, the biggest obstacle that gets in the way is they have more reasons to continue the habit, always overriding the one conscious intention to change. Think about a bad habit like smoking. The doctor would have one single purpose in advising you to quit. Simply it is proven to be unhealthy; it can kill you, so his intent is to get you to give up, saving your life. That's his/her job. The smoker has no intention of quitting with many different positive reasons for continuing the habit, outnumbering the doctor's one overwhelming reason to quit, which are enough to convince the smoker to keep on smoking. The smoker would say they need to smoke in the morning to wake them up and get them going. They would need a cigarette to help them concentrate. They would need a cigarette to stop them snacking. They would need a cigarette to reduce stress. They would need a cigarette with their glass of wine to relax and because it gives them pleasure. If we are honest, smoking is often used to cover up stress from our negative emotions. The smoking habit gives us comfort, not pleasure even though we have convinced ourselves it's about pleasure. To change a bad habit we feel is positive and gives us pleasure, it is vital to establish a viable alternative which in some way will satisfy the purpose of the old habit. Unless we can do this, other problems will arise just from quitting alone. Once you begin to nurture gratitude as a core belief, you obviously begin to nurture appreciation for your lungs. For the smoker, the positive purpose of keeping the lungs healthy would establish a viable alternative to the smoking habit. Obviously, withdrawal is not easy. We have unconsciously become reliant on smoking to handle our emotional stress, but it is a fact craving only last for a few moments at a time, so learn some diversion techniques like cleaning your teeth or chewing gum instead. Bad habits or cravings are triggered by certain situations, places and emotions you have learnt to associate with your bad habit, so make a conscious effort to mix things up and start to work on alternative coping strategies. Like with anything we are trying to change, don't be so harsh on yourself. If you fail the first time around, talk to yourself compassionately, be kind to yourself. learn to get back on board with your self-discipline and try again by visualising yourself as a non-smoker, until resisting temptation subconsciously and automatically becomes a piece of cake and you begin to resist automatically.

Encouraging positive self-talk to work for you instead of going against you is the key to changing how you feel about yourself but remember positive affirmations live at the surface level of your conscious thinking, limited beliefs live in your subconscious. If you are telling yourself constantly you are thin, you are going to be healthy, you love yourself, but deep down your core belief is different, you are a miserable, sad, fat failure, not good enough, your mind will be permanently at war, in conflict. If you are telling yourself you have nothing to feel guilty about but struggle to stop using your imagination to fantasise about things that are not real, your subconscious will keep reminding you all the times you are disappointed, when your expectations are not met. You tell yourself you are not to feel guilty anymore yet subconsciously you still feel guilty, even though you've told yourself something different. When you begin to see this, you begin to realise just how much you are being controlled by your negative subconscious thinking.

For people who are depressed and full of anxiety, optimistic thinking can trigger self-defeating thoughts, especially for those with little self-regard and self-confidence. This is where having forgiveness as a core belief, alongside gratitude, can truly stop you beating yourself up. Once you have forgiveness in your heart you can redirect your energy to more manageable thinking, so what you think about yourself becomes less painful. The simple act of self-forgiveness will allow a true appreciation of your feelings and you can begin to build real self-esteem again. Once again, the way in which you speak to yourself through your inner dialogue, the cruel critic who throws untrue accusations at you, is truly the only way you can change how you feel about yourself. Self-investigation helps you to connect to the side of your brain that deals with problem solving, something you didn't learn to do as a child. How we communicate with ourselves consciously, subconsciously, cognitively and emotionally must come from a deep place of self-belief. Every day from now on, try and be conscious and aware of how you are communicating with yourself and remember you are a work in progress, not perfect but always grateful for your life. If your intentions are based on your core personal values and not social pressure, you are more likely to experience a greater moral obligation, and this will encourage real honest change in your behaviour.

Sorry to keep repeating but what we are told and what we learn as young children has a massive impact on what we believe, how we think, feel and behave as we evolve into adulthood. I want to prove this in the next case study to show you just how powerful intention in children can be, so you can understand more about maybe what you have been told yourself in the past, could be the reason you are making poor choices today.

Recently I read a story from a psychological case study of a six-year-old girl who consciously walked straight in front of a fast-moving train, purposely killing herself on the surface for no logical reason. It turned out the little girl in question had just lost her mother tragically in a car accident. On her own with a confident intention, she decided herself to go to heaven to be with her mother after being told by her father that's where she was with the angels and God in the sky. This powerful story shows us just how strong the power of intention is when you believe something is real and worth sacrificing everything for. It shows what you believe, you want, can outweigh what you need in the moment. It also proves what we learn as children, the fantasies, the lies, the fairy tales can play out in real life. If the little girl had not been introduced to the idea heaven was a real place, she would have reconsidered her action when facing the painful loss of her mother. Some people who are steadfast believers in God and this magical place called heaven might believe the little girl had justification in killing herself to be with her mother. Others might argue it is a real sin to take your own life. But sensible, realistic, mature people like me would argue she was ill-informed without all the facts. Would you rather have facts so you can make an informed decision, or would you rather hang on to a fantasy and make your decisions based on sentiment?

We are in a constant battle between logic and our emotions every day. We all know deep down inside we should stop smoking, give up on a toxic relationship, cut down eating high fat foods, yet we are driven to go against what we know to be true, in order to satisfy our perceived belief in comfort. Then we feel guilty as a reaction, never before the event, always after the event. Why is this? We all have strong impulses, intentions, based on what we are told, what we see, what we believe often without any factual or logical information. We believe we know better, often better than the experts. Why is this? Once again like climate change, we believe in a psychological distance from the harm we are doing to ourselves, believing nothing bad will happen to us.

As we have already established, your unconscious ego, the image you have of yourself, the social mask you put out to the world is something you have learnt to live with, but you don't have to believe what it has to say about who you are. It's not the real you. Your soul is the authentic you buried beneath the mask you wear, the roles you play, it never changes. It gives you your gut feelings, your intuition, your inner voice of reason that never lets you down. It helps you discover your true purpose and what you are meant to be doing with your life. You can learn to listen to your soul as it speaks to you in the silence of your meditation and through being open-hearted, connected back to nature and free from the constraints of your unconscious ego. This is where you will find a connection with your truth and all the unconditional love you need, without having to sell yourself short anymore.

The more I connected to my soul, my clean energy, away from my stupid unconscious ego, the more I got closer to understanding the incredible world of nature and the universe. I got close to understanding better about all creatures great and small, that plants have life as well as animals and yet this is not perceived by humans as conscious life. Both plants and animals get nourishment from the earth, just like human beings. It is true what is from the earth is the greatest of worth and with this deeper thought process, beyond my mind, my one-dimensional thinking, my feelings about eating meat changed. I simply did not want to eat flesh anymore, so I naturally became a vegetarian. I didn't have the intention of giving up meat, I didn't plan to do it, it just happened with certainty. People always want to have certainty before they are prepared to act on something, but we must always remember, it is the action that creates the certainty. Knowledge can never be found in doubt. If you believe in something strongly enough, it takes you beyond resistance; you will discover courage as a personal power, expanding your consciousness and developing insight and wisdom overnight.

If you listen to the brave inspirational stories of people devoted to a certain sport or been very fit and suddenly have an accident, they lose a limb, they will say the experience made them stronger to go on and participate at a very competitive level. This is what we call the power of intention, placing all attention in the direction of a particular objective, then directing all our energy towards it, to cause what we are focusing on to manifest because of that very focus. The athlete with the limb missing wants to run and be a winner so much, they fight through the pain to make it happen, then focus until they are as good as they were when they had two limbs.

The power of intention is about you intending to practise every day to become focused on what truly matters in your life. You need to keep evolving, moving just like the planet revolving around the cycle of time, always precise, always reliable and always in control. We all have an ability to harness personal power within, but it is up to you and you alone to put in the work, the practice to make changes to make something bigger happen. If you can start to accept maybe the choices you have made have potentially left you depressed, keeping you stuck in the negative bias is not your fault, you can then start to think about the athlete who loses a limb but fights back. The man who keeps on smoking when he has lung cancer will die if he doesn't listen to his doctor's advice. The man who has his limb removed after an accident goes on to live and he wins. He has the will survive. The difference between the two men is simple. One has an ego believing he can defy death and the other has faced death and wants to embrace life.

The power of intention for me when I had to face a massive mountain to climb back from homelessness, penniless and dying on the dole in Leicester has driven me to where I am today, not fully there yet but on my way to saving the world one by one. With good intention, I have managed to create a new business from a personal need, making sure this business reflects my ethical and passionate beliefs. If it has been possible for me to do all of this with nothing but the power of intention and gratitude for my life, health and wellbeing, then I believe anything is possible for you.

There is big difference between your mind and intelligence. Your mind prefers to do things it enjoys, regardless of whether it is right or wrong, intelligence, on the other hand, relies only on facts. Learning how to control your mind takes understanding intelligence, so try and begin to make your choices based on knowledge and facts, never on desire or fantasy. We can start to begin the intention to create something different for ourselves and whilst there are outside factors that may affect the outcome, in the end, we must trust in ourselves, to confidently jump each hurdle as it happens, until we get there. Our intention is the most powerful of indicators, but we must truly desire a new reality more than anything else and see it through to the end, the difficult bit. Curiosity is the motive to help you reduce a negative mindset. It is crucial for you to create curiosity now. It is a way to explore and discover new things like reading this book to find out why you feel the way you do. By being curious, you get to understand more and when you understand more you change for the better.

I remember reading Carl Jung *Modern Man in Search of a Soul* and because I was curious enough to take my time and break it down, it's not the easiest book to read, I discovered how much of what he was teaching me had happened to me for real. I can tell you now from a clean fully functioning healthy place myself, when you are in tip-top shape because you have put the correct fuel into your body, positive energy inside will radiate and shine, attracting back everything you desire. Improved self-esteem is a key psychological benefit of regular physical activity. When you exercise did you know, your body makes its own pain relief triggering feel good vibes? The natural way to get a positive energising outlook on life. Surely, this is a better option than using medication or fake highs to feel better?

Psychological illnesses of the mind are all down to a lack of spiritual maturity. Acting and thinking like a child, never feeling happiness, never feeling satisfied, always searching, making mistakes is fine when you have the excuse of youth on your side but as an adult, you will remain depressed without spiritual growth beyond your perception and existing beliefs. We must grow up, by this I mean like the tree, grow towards the sky reaching a higher level of maturity, expanding our energy back out into the world. It is time to stand tall, healthy, curious, vital, optimistic and stop slowly and painfully killing ourselves through stress, addiction, misery, ignorance and denial. It has become too easy to remain in denial, be out of control, easily led by marketing and other people's opinions. This, like I have said, is because money and big business have taken over from nurturing ethics and morality for the good of humanity.

There is a whole new world waiting for you behind your unconscious ego beliefs. A world where how much money you have doesn't matter, how ugly you feel, how insecure you are and how afraid you are, all disappear. A world where you will learn to face adversity with courage, always aware to never project your problems onto others. The most important thing is to allow yourself to feel unbearably uncomfortable, in order to develop deeper clarity, allowing you clearer transparency to the things influencing you externally. There will be no spiritual growth without facing personal discomfort. Spiritual maturity is all about the process of expanding your consciousness. Remember patience is the key to developing and gaining strong moral core values, nurturing a deeper strength inside of you. If you continue to remain unaware of your subconscious reactions and negative thinking, you will continue to project your unconscious poor qualities onto others through blaming and denial, weakening your intention to cultivate a spiritual awakening inside.

Hypnotise, Tranquilise and Analyse

Poor self-esteem due to a lack of trust in our ability to problem solve is probably the biggest block to overcoming our mental health issues, shutting us down and stopping us learning how to think positively. By learning to explore the mind beyond stress and anxiety, we begin to be more open and curious, creating a space for reflection through deeper knowledge about our true abilities.

A pessimistic mindset will take its toll on your health in more ways than you could imagine. It is a fact negative thinking is the biggest cause of mental health, relationship and lifestyle problems. They don't call it unease for nothing. The main symptoms of depression and stress come from blaming ourselves. Although it is important to take personal responsibility for the past, if we don't have forgiveness in place as a core belief, we end up believing we have ruined everything as a failure. It is impossible to step back and look at something positively, take a balanced realistic outlook, when everything seems dark and pointless. When we have negative slumps, constantly predicting doom and gloom, it makes it impossible to manage the mind, preventing further negative thoughts, forcing us deeper into the depths of despair. The reason I am talking about this now is to remind you once again, just how dangerous and powerful your subconscious thinking is—it is so powerful it can push some people too far.

The biggest tragedy today is we have little time to concentrate. Life is so chaotic and busy it becomes impossible to focus our minds on what we want to achieve, by giving it our undivided attention. Imagine if your mind was emptied of all your subconscious memories and negative self-talk and you could just listen to one conscious positive voice, telling you to trust in yourself, believe in yourself. In meditation you are going to learn to do exactly this. You are going to quieten down your conscious mind, so you can become more aware of what is going on in your subconscious, enabling you to evolve beyond relying on unconscious ego drives, comfort and addictions, currently controlling how you think. You will learn to identify the difference between the weak moral values of the false imposter self and the strong moral characteristics of the authentic truthful self. Unless we become grounded with core moral values and deep ethical beliefs, we will end up relying on negative untrustworthy behaviours, which continue to influence low moral conduct, including self-betrayal, causing deep depression and low self-esteem.

Most of us have no understanding how deeply critical and negative the process of self-identification really is, the degree to which we define ourselves through the cruel lens of the inner critic, the negative voice, constantly undermining our true potential. You must start to see now it is this inner cruel critic slowly but surely diminishing your ability to be the courageous best version of yourself. By you reinforcing these destructive thoughts and memories from the past, you end up pushing your self-doubt into feelings of self-hatred, this then becomes your depression.

The key to success when it comes to managing depression and preventing it becoming all-consuming is to first nurture forgiveness for yourself and then for those who have created the cruel inner critic inside your mind. It doesn't matter what other route you try, whether it be drowning your sorrows, looking for a diversion in your imagination, until you nurture more forgiveness, you will always relapse, then feel bad. Once negative untruths and dark thoughts get logged in the mind, we are unable to act naturally or be ourselves in truth. If we define ourselves as stupid, we are going to have a difficult time ever believing we are cleaver, not because we have something wrong with our intelligence but because we are telling ourselves we are stupid. Sometimes we are so wrapped up in the negativity of the cruel inner critic, we have a tough time understanding what is really going on in our lives. We end up reacting to everything in the wrong way through distorted beliefs, based on language imposed on us by someone else.

Many people who suffer depression have no idea why it happens. The conscious mind informs the subconscious mind, the main reason talk therapy is so effective to help alleviate episodes. We all carry heavy baggage from life and past experiences around with us, but some people let it drag them down to the depths of despair without a way back. If we never offload this baggage, heal it or talk about it, we end up over stressed with pressure building inside, causing severe mental and physical problems, until on an unconscious level we truly believe there is no hope left. All this negative baggage build-up is your dirty energy and is carried around in the subconscious mind, slowly nagging away, constantly reminding us we are worthless, tired, unhappy and we give ourselves more grief by consciously reaffirming it all as our truth.

I am always trying to encourage people I work with to be mindful to not let this mayhem build up inside, by making sure their conscious mind is not letting negative false beliefs and thoughts get through in the first place. We can avoid depression by consciously putting healthy thoughts and core beliefs like gratitude, humility, forgiveness and compassion in place, until they become part of our subconscious. This is how I managed to do it for myself. Any negative thoughts I had, had to go through a conscious filter of my new core beliefs and values first. If I found myself automatically thinking negatively about someone, I would consciously put the trigger of compassion in place and the wrong feeling soon got replaced automatically with sympathy, immediately wiping out my frustration. If I found myself beating myself up for making a mistake, I would consciously put the trigger of forgiveness in place and the wrong feelings got replaced by tolerance and understanding, immediately wiping out my anger. Obviously, this kind of work cannot be done consciously until your mind is free and quiet, away from the overload of your internal madness, through the practice of meditation and breathing. Unless you do this in meditation, your anxiety will undermine your ability to hear your truth. I want you now to really think about what I have just said because if there is way you can replace the wrong feelings you are having, through nurturing forgiveness and compassion, there is no excuse left to let depression define you anymore. You can make yourself feel better.

There are many external ways to numb the pain, diluting the internal battle you have with yourself short term. The fixes, the addiction, the comfort but, trust me, this will only make things worse long term. They never deal with the problem for real. Constantly struggling with yourself through anger, arguing and fighting has not got you anywhere except imprisoned in your own mind. Once you start to recognise this, you can begin to change things by allowing some room for error or weakness, not totally beating yourself into submission. A person who is forgiving will allow themselves to make mistakes, allow for weakness. Giving up the right to hurt yourself by learning how to respond properly to feelings of being misunderstood, offended, lied to or rejected, is one of the basic ways you can nurture a happier more fulfilled life.

When we forgive ourselves in humility not ego, we get to wipe the slate clean like I did when I foolishly lost all my money. I cancelled the debt out, forgave myself with grace, then moved on confidently from the self-persecution of regret, bitterness and self-harming to be free from my feelings of failure. It is important to be able to understand forgiveness can never be granted because we deserve to be forgiven. Instead it is an act of self-love, mercy and grace, the things we nurture and grow, not just expect to arrive without doing the work. By forgiving ourselves we free ourselves up spiritually and emotionally. It is an act of our own will to bring emotional healing, regardless of our programmed negative subconscious thinking. We become lighter, less burdened and more open to facing ourselves without shame or guilt. Taking the time to gently forgive yourself and those around you, allows progress through the steps of forgiveness, beginning the journey of releasing the pain holding you back, once and for all.

As human beings we are part of nature and must be grateful we are the only ones lucky enough to be in control of our lives. This is a true gift when you start to look at every other living creature. We can make our own choices. We create our own destiny. We decide who we are, what we are and what we want to be. This unique gift of free will must not result in someone choosing to just laze around waiting for the meaning of life or their purpose to turn up. Our true calling comes from action and exploring the many wonderful possibilities outside the comfort zone bubble, the ego life template, designed through greed to keep us stuck, almost disabled.

Today in this current culture of narcissistic, phone obsessed, selfie-driven, shallow-minded social media madness, being consumed in a bubble of likes and admiration neurosis: the only way people know how to value themselves has become limited through little global exposure to anything else. If the conscious mind is focused on watching a starving woman in Malawi, feeding her three children with one corn on the cob because she cannot afford to farm the land to grow food for herself, the obsession to be liked by strangers diminishes. It puts things into perspective, and we see the bigger picture. She has little choice but to keep going for her survival. She doesn't have the luxury to laze around and wait for the phone to ring, a big red sale sign to go up or a slap-up meal to look forward to. She has no time to be depressed. She's too busy surviving day to day. When you put this into perspective—and I am not belittling your depression—then question your own ability to survive day to day, you might just find hope in your circumstances compared to hers. Focusing on the real difficulties people in a situation like this face every day and it is happening all over the planet right now, outside the confines of the bubble mentality, redirects any thinking from the opinions of the mind to the strings of the heart. Without feeling, compassion and sympathy for those worse off than you, it would be hard to ever nurture self-compassion.

No matter how much you believe your life is pointless, how much you have failed or whatever mess you think is not possible to change, there is always someone else, somewhere else worse off than you who needs your time, kindness and compassion. Learning how to explore your own thinking patterns by giving yourself time and space, outside the madness of your mind, during your meditation, you will start to notice how detached you have become from the real world. Within the silence of your meditation, you will start to learn something new about you. You will start to find answers to your problems in the most unexpected places, as you delve deeper into your consciousness, becoming less afraid to face the world. You will start to put faith back in your trust, in your own abilities, knowing whole-heartedly you can now depend on your own mind, feelings, emotions and abilities. You will begin to build even more trust to develop a better relationship with yourself through your strong core beliefs, so when things get rocky you have a higher knowledge to step in and help sort it out.

A closed ridged mind will always result in a hardened heart. The more flexibility you have in your mental mindset, the softer your heart becomes. Love and compassion always beat pain and bitterness. This is how you start to develop warmer, kinder feelings inside of yourself. Think about all the times you feel down. Then you go and see a film that inspires you, makes you cry and changes your life. Or you read a book that makes you laugh or feel something. Connecting to external things through feelings from your heart, not your mind, can completely change your mood. Obviously, these feelings are sometimes short-lived once the laugh is over, you forget about the film and you remember you are down again. Nurturing and connecting internally with your authentic self through your heart, is a direct experience, not short-lived and will change your brain structure. Understanding your brain can strengthen and change in response to how you perceive things, how you think about things, how you react or respond to experiences, helps you to recognise the structure of your brain changes by what you choose to think about and not what you feel. Losing control internally over your feelings, through either internal suffering or external distractions is extremely stressful and happening because you are only connecting with and listening to your mind. This is creating your anxiety.

Your goal throughout this book is to learn to focus on what is going on beyond your mind to stop you running around in negative cycles, draining your precious clean energy on fruitless false deceptions and a distorted perception of your reality. You are not condemned to be a slave to your mind any longer. There is always hope outside the mind. The key is to understand how to connect back to your heart by developing new core beliefs, so you feel positive and authentic. Most of us in this cruel selfish ugly world have had our happiness hijacked, being exploited disillusioned and imprisoned by self-gratification. We have been forced through greed to focus more on developing the negative unconscious ego, over building a higher consciousness, through better morals and ethics. No matter what is happening in the world, your life, we have to now try and learn how to remain centred, calm and still, moving away from toxic unhealthy thinking and behaviours, gathering strength, no longer tolerating self-abuse, all the things you do when you have given up on yourself.

With age should come experience wisdom and good judgement, the amazing useful qualities that make us wise and sensible. Wisdom is the ability to think and act using knowledge to make good decisions. When old age and wisdom have become invisible to young people, they think they know better, in my opinion, the world really has gone mad. Unless we grow and evolve to a higher level of thinking and mature with forgiveness, grace and gratitude, we will never learn from our mistakes and these mistakes will just get passed down from generation to generation. For all those young people out there consumed in the bubble who think they know better, suffering unbearable levels of anxiety, depression and social anxiety, the many faces of mental health will never be cured without more exposure to the real world.

We have to face the reason young people cannot look to older people for the answer is simply because most haven't found the answer themselves, so youth is not attracted to anything they have to say. The mass midlife malaise currently happening across the western world is not appealing or beneficial to anyone young. I have heard many young people say in therapy, their own parents are stupid, out of touch and don't understand the way things are today and because beauty, the way we look is the perceived key to success, old and wrinkly in their words becomes invisible and rejected, as out of date. From what I can see young people today truly believe money buys beauty, beauty attracts money, money buys holidays, holidays are great for a picture-perfect life, showing off on social media, creating likes and envy, all the wrong things for personal growth and maturity. A Chanel handbag does not make you successful if it has been purchased with money borrowed on a credit card and you have nowhere to go to use it. It has no purpose except creating nice pictures on social media that ultimately puts you in debt.

I have a social media profile because I have a business, I am a life coach and my purpose is to inspire others with consistent truthful messages, not showing off a fake illusion of who I am, to look better than I am. I never gift my fashion garments to bloggers or pay them to write reviews. It would not be the truth and I would be conning my customers. They must find out for themselves. This is how you build a new kind of brand based on what your customers think about your ethics, your passion, your products, your consistent message that never changes and is never manipulated for profit. This is the definition of authenticity and integrity in my mind. I would never consider paying for likes on my posts to improve how popular I look. To do this I have to con myself and others and look where that got me in the past, in the gutter, homeless, penniless and dying. The only true way to be popular and shine bright like a diamond is to not see yourself as a celebrity or fabulous lifestyle guru because unless you have done all the hard work to justify this position, you are not worthy, you are a fake.

Learn to switch off the fake relationship you have built with your phone and forget about all those endless numbers of likes you rely on to define who you are. Start to develop a real relationship with yourself, the real you inside without doubt to help you feel better about yourself, stabilising your moods. Interacting with real people and real life, bursting the bubble you have created, stopping you living a healthy happy life will be achieved when you accept the information you have been exposed to is all wrong. The reason you have lost all connection with your authentic self.

We have all been lied to in every possible way by the media, TV, big business, the government and like I have already said many times, we need to learn to stay neutral and focused on our own unique needs and opinions, to be able to realise our own mental freedom. The more you manage to get away from the insular, fake world you have created on your phone and travel, meet new people, see new things, the quicker your mental health issues will diminish, your consciousness will expand, and your real life will start to take off.

Social media and the way it can influence how we think today, is basically a dark mirror reflecting the level to which we have become self-obsessed, small-minded, driven by aspiration not purpose. This reality sadly, has created mass depression especially in the young. If we are never exposed to the bigger picture, a life outside the constant need to be liked and accepted by others, we end up disconnected from each other. If you believe getting plastic surgery, bigger lips, a bigger bum will get more likes or change your life, perhaps it would be wise to go and visit a burns unit in a children's hospital and face the real reason people must be reconstructed. Then you might think twice about what you are doing to yourself. I am not judging here because everyone to their own. What I am trying to do is get you to think more rationally and feel less insecure.

Risking surgery or putting poisons like Botox in your face to freeze muscles, iron out expression lines in my opinion is unlikely to make you more desirable or popular, especially if you are a teenager with the gift of a perfect face already. The lines on your face draw a picture of your life. The happiness lines around your eyes come from all the smiling you have done and that's a good thing. The lines across your forehead come from all your frowning and the lines round your mouth come from potentially smoking. So maybe you should think about changing your lifestyle, so your beauty outside radiates from within. For me personally at sixty-two, I cannot understand why anybody would not want to radiate the natural beauty internal happiness and a healthy lifestyle creates. There is nothing more attractive than a smiling face and twinkling eyes at any age.

An expressionless society of avatars with frozen faces, fake breasts, flash phones, fish face pouts, obsessed with money, designer lifestyles and little common sense is the perfect environment to create disappointment. Once again it is not about judging, it's about recognising we have been fed all the wrong information by big brand marketing, lying to us for money and personal gain, over providing responsible, informed information, to encourage us to make better choices for our wellbeing. When you can step away from the pack, pay attention to your own gut feeling, your heartfelt intuition, what you really feel about yourself deep down will become stronger and you will rely on courage with steadfast integrity. Having the courage from nurturing more integrity, questioning your values, reflecting self-worth, self-respect and self-belief without the constant burden of worry and stress, you will find freedom in your mind. Drifting through your life automatically without intention, allowing your current circumstances to define who you are in my mind, is to be avoided at all costs now, if you truly want to evolve and make the most of your time here on earth. Plastic surgery is not a beauty treatment, it is either a necessity because of injury or deformity or it is another addiction in this crazy world of self-obsession.

Depression and internal misery like I said is the backbone of mental health issues, a kind of cancer of the mind. It's all about numbness inside, a feeling of being completely disconnected and absent from your true feelings. This sense of isolation and emotional disconnection from the rest of humanity, is a deadness and emptiness that permeates your whole being, stripping away any joy and this is happening because we are not being real. Any emotional numbing, blocking out your feelings, is not done on a conscious level. You may not even be aware your negative behaviour is happening. To you it has become a normal way of behaving through your socially acceptable persona. The truth is, you have locked yourself away from listening to your heart and have become imprisoned through listening only to your mind, driven to madness by focusing on the past. The only true way you can begin to defrost your emotions and engage in feeling safe again is to learn to self-regulate. We all need protection, a shield to defend us against painful feelings but allowing this shield to define who we are, means we never move forward or get past the pain.

Being vulnerable and confident enough to stand alone, like the solid tree in the wind without protection, as we have already established is not going to be easy, especially if anxiety is crippling you. Anxiety, the symptom of your fears, is casting a dark shadow over your whole existence and attacking anything positive and good about what you have to offer the world. The truth is anxiety has become the most common emotional distress experienced by human beings right now, so there is little need to be ashamed or embarrassed when the whole world pretty much, is suffering in silence.

Building integrity allowed me to transition to adulthood after my own life-changing experience. I did experience anxiety for a short while when everything collapsed in on me, so I do understand how paralysing it can be. Once I stopped looking back at my mistakes, dwelling on the past in despair, letting it all go because I had no choice, I truly became excited about the future, even though at the time there appeared to be no future for me. It was just a feeling of almost relief. This feeling didn't come from imagining something was going to happen or from hope. It didn't come from money, it didn't come from another person, it truly came from finally understanding gratitude. I no longer have an ideal picture in my mind of who I am. This would allow me to fall short of expectations. I know who I am, I also know we all make mistakes. I no longer make decisions to give me temporary satisfaction in the moment. I make better choices based on my gut feeling or intuition, not my need for glory or validation. When we start to think about a person's character, we are referring to their moral qualities balanced against their imperfections. This doesn't mean we need to be perfect it just means whatever we do, say or think can be trusted. The idea of self-perfection should not be about how you look on the outside but about the solid person you have nurtured on the inside, your trustworthy qualities like integrity, compassion, humility and empathy.

A strong moral character might sound old fashioned on Instagram, but it is the foundation required for being a good person, a happy person, a rich person in spirit. These qualities we seem to have passed over today are more valuable and attractive than money and obsessed empty vanity. I am hoping to encourage you to start developing a strong moral character yourself, so you are guided with passion by your ethical principles, not your self-gratification. That hasn't really got you anywhere, has it? When you care with a passion about what you are buying into or supporting, doing what is ethically right over personal gain or for vanity, treating the planet with respect, you begin to feel good inside. Once again, this feeling is not manufactured or created, it comes again from truly understanding gratitude. We all know if we cheat, deceive, steal, are dishonest, turn a blind eye, bully, be unkind, we end up feeling bad inside, even if we believe we don't, we do. It is these unconscious bad feelings inside creating your accumulated dirty energy, the reason you always feel guilty, shameful or have regrets. Your dirty energy is a build-up of your morally non-existent characteristics, it creates an energetic weakness that has translated into depression and ultimately become your anxiety.

Many psychological theories today suggest factors such as biological, religious, environmental and cultural will influence the development of moral characteristics in children and the importance of our moral values, rely on parental bonding. Without secure, healthy parental bonding in early development, children will often make a connection with other things. This can become unhealthy obsessions with body image, fixating on food diets and personal scrutiny, creating a lack of self-worth and self-esteem. Understanding this, you get to recognise how potentially devastating this can be to the personal development of our character and learning habits. In my opinion, the sooner you give a young child the chance to make their own choices, the sooner they learn to feel more relaxed and independent about their mistakes. They get to rely on their own natural instincts through problem solving.

The many faces of mental health today range from eating disorders to addiction, thoughts of suicide, depression, anxiety, misery, self-doubt, irrational fears, lack of confidence, OCD and many more new ones like status anxiety, social anxiety and post traumatic panic disorder. Emotional wellbeing is the key to a healthy happy mind. I cannot use a magic wand to give you a dose of mental wellbeing. It is up to you to do the work required through desire and courage, facing yourself head on, looking beyond your bad habits and pattern behaviours. Once you can learn to go beyond the fear and anxiety of the things worrying you, like you are alone in the world or the only person on the planet with problems, you begin to open your eyes wide and see we are all the same. We all have challenges. We all need the love and respect of each other. Once you can look in the mirror and no longer see yourself but see others, you stop focusing on the past and do what is right in the moment.

Learning something new encourages brain cells to develop. Focusing your attention on a new skill or project will give you the feeling of a sense of achievement, so try and sign up for a course or a class or take on a new challenge every day. By revising your own inner core values, letting go of the ones you have inherited through the trials and tribulation of your past, you can begin to take a positive approach to nurturing your own unique talent inside. Once you start to feel authentic feelings in your space of calm and serenity, you can begin to work harder visualising your strengths, over your weaknesses. Start to face your lost potential through strengthening your coping skills. You might not feel safe to begin with, but this will pass, as you develop more courage inside.

Once you consciously make choices and decide what your personal priorities are, what is important to you through the creation of your own core values, you can concentrate on these qualities, so they align perfectly with your choices going forward. With more clarity in your own personal core values, without worrying about what other people think, you will start to make better more informed choices and be grateful for what you have that is real not imagined. Deep feelings of gratitude will always override the cruel critic inside your mind, once you are able to find the courage to stand up to it. Forgiveness will always override the cruel critic in your mind when, showing bravely through humility, weakness is not about being a failure, it is how we learn and grow. Compassion will always shut the cruel critic up, when you have sympathy for the times you intentionally hurt yourself. Unless you become aware of how you are treating yourself then allow yourself to grow, you will always struggle to follow your own internal moral compass; how you navigate your emotions and feelings. How can you ever be sure of the direction you are heading, if your mind is permanently fixated in the past or you are afraid to look deeper into the future?

Failure is the highway to success, so we must never be discouraged by it. It leads us closer to recognise we are not perfect and never will be, no matter what you have been told by the media. Failure always encourages us try harder, trying hard means we are progressing, learning and ultimately stops us being stuck in mental torture.

Mental illness is not choosy. It does not discriminate. It does not warn you. It is a bit like the wind. It doesn't smell or taste of anything but that doesn't mean it's not there. It just gets you, takes you down then ruins your life. I am here to remind you all, you are not an accumulation of all your mistakes. You are a free individual with your own mind. It's time to wake up. Your soul, your spirit, your guiding light is the missing concrete between the bricks in the corridors of your mind and without your soul holding you together, things can never change. Recognise the bricks are falling, the walls are collapsing, and it all needs gently but firmly putting back together, rebuilding the authentic you. I can tell you from my own experience of putting myself back together, gratitude is the start of healing mental health and this is backed up by conclusive evidence gathered through research. It increases happiness, decreases depression, enhances empathy whilst reducing aggression, counteracting toxic emotions such as guilt, greed, envy and victimisation. If you can learn to be grateful to be alive, it will push you away from giving up or thinking of suicide. By acknowledging all you are grateful for, all you have been given for free by nature, you start to move away from negative thinking then the inner cruel critic loses its strength over you. Gratitude interrupts the destructive ways depression makes you feel and behave. I know without doubt from personal experience, nurturing gratitude is strongly associated with the emotions that help us to enjoy greater health and wellbeing. I promise you by understanding the benefits of being grateful, over the dangers of being miserable, you will begin to know the quality of being thankful, desiring only kindness and appreciation in your life.

Choices

Why is it everyone wants to change the world, but no one ever thinks of changing themselves? We can only change the world if we are prepared to change ourselves.

I spent the first half of my life succumbing to the needs of my unconscious ego, ignorant of my own spiritual power inside. I was in denial about my own happiness and security. I created a life based only on my driven quest for money, success and power. I rarely sat back in reflection to look at my behaviour, my thoughts, my feelings, open and willing to take personal responsibility. Being brave enough to own your emotional conflict without blame or projection on to others, is the unique attribution of personal responsibility. Making the choice to accept self-responsibility was the very first productive step I took towards clearing my unconscious ego. Today, after making the best choice of my life, reinventing my own story, letting go of the old me, I am finally authentic, having taken ownership of my mistakes, forgiven myself and realised how much I value my life and how grateful I am to be here. I am no longer climbing the mountain to success. I am heading to the ultimate summit of enlightenment.

I have reprogrammed and taken ownership of all my subconscious fears, offloaded all the dirty energy inside my body, the blame shifting, projecting blame on others, my defence mechanisms and I no longer allow my shadow side, my unconscious ego to make me feel threatened by lies. I have faith in me, the authentic me. By doing this hard work I have changed my negative false perspective of what is important in being a human being, allowing me to be amazing, successful and accomplished without being shallow, guilty or depressed. I am finally free to be me. For the first time I know what it feels like to be truly alive.

As you develop the ability to accept self-love with dignity and you start to appreciate the finely tuned workings of your mind body and soul, stepping away from the idea you are invincible, you too will begin to see how lucky you are and how perfectly you function on your own. For you, once you have accepted self-love, you can begin to evolve to the next stage of your spiritual development, going beyond your closed off mind to authenticity without the crutch of other people's opinions dictating who or what you should be. Evolving beyond your need for money or power, understanding materialism lies in your darkest fear for survival, your unique life purpose will start to be revealed. Remember as adults, no longer children, only we can make the choice about who we want to be. Only we challenge the negative definition of ourselves by identifying it as a false belief. And once we begin to embrace this reality, we can separate out the true self and differentiate it from the past.

Talk therapy and self-reflection helps us to grow by looking at what is going on behind the depression to give the person suffering tools to change their thoughts and moods. We cannot always identify what the event was that created the mood change because there is a lot going on in the mind at any one time and things do get easily cluttered and clouded. Never being able to resolve your problems or satisfy your needs, basically, is the main cause of why you feel depressed, frustrated and stressed out. If this is experienced continually over a long period of time, it's obvious we would end up believing everything is hopeless. Learning how to expand your ability to feel comfortable with yourself by interacting with others is not easy when you feel hopeless and a failure. I know this because even though I was the most confident, outgoing person in the world, when I found myself isolated, hopeless and defeated, my own confidence went out the window.

Today I am determined and happy regardless of what situation I find myself in. I learnt from experience the best part of my happiness or misery comes from the inherent quality of my heart, my character, not my circumstances. I have learnt life is about the process of finding solutions, problem solving. So please try and understand there are significant and substantial grounds for you believing there is more to you than your mind and your body. You just haven't found it yet. Your inner destructive negative voice controlling your thoughts and provoking your feelings is currently programmed to instruct your body and mind to fail. It has been set on this negative, destructive course for a long time, since you were a small child. Now you understand what is causing your misery, you must acknowledge it, reframe it and then reprogram it in your favour. You are going to achieve this shift by creating a safe space in your meditation, standing back as an observer from your mind and confidently questioning your existing beliefs, eliminating what does not mirror image your authentic truth. You are going to make the choice to no longer give your power to your material attachments, your past perceptions or your irrational fears, anything that goes against your new relationship with your spiritual emerging self. All your power, your energy from now on is required to reach your higher self, your inner being, your truthful beautiful emerging soul.

The soul, your inner being, like everything else unexplainable, is open to personal interpretation. In my opinion, because I have experienced connecting to my own soul, it is the real you, the thing that does your thinking, your feeling and your seeing. It is not part of your mind or your body, it is something separate and something you may never have thought about deeply. I am of the opinion today, finding myself a more open and enlightened individual with a unique purpose, no longer driven by greed or false aspiration, my soul is my choice. I have learnt to make choices now aligned with my inner soul needs and desires, not those of my unconscious ego from the learnt beliefs of others. When I am at peace in the stillness and I let go of everything else, my soul becomes present within me and I feel grounded. In this place as the observer outside of my mind

I always ask the same question. Are the choices I am making today good for my higher soul self tomorrow? Once I surrendered and was openly willing to listen unconditionally to my inner soul self, the real me, I was able to act on my feelings and no longer react to them.

The simplest way for you to think about all of this is to remember, if your unconscious ego oversees your choices, based on your existing beliefs and they do not align with your authentic core beliefs, you create an emotional reaction when things don't work out in your favour. If your soul self oversees your choices and they align perfectly with your authentic core moral, beliefs and values, you will act intentionally, overcoming your self-imposed limitations, reaching your true potential. Choice is the essence that goes beyond personality, character, the mind, the body and the teachings from our parents. It is something that goes beyond our social programming, encouraging us to be more honest with ourselves.

In my old life, I will openly admit I was soulless. I believed I had no choice but to make more money, behave in an unethical capitalistic way to reach the top of the money mountain, always selling myself short in the pursuit of world domination. To be honest, it never occurred to me I had a choice to be ethical with integrity, a choice to be a vegetarian, a choice to be celibate, a choice to be compassionate towards others. I was just driven, selling my soul, compromising myself to get what I wanted, at any cost. Today after discovering my soul self, this will be my legacy based on the choices I make about my behaviour, my actions and my purpose. This life-changing experience, discovering my soul, my choice, has helped me to evolve greater maturity and the direct knowledge of self-realisation. I no longer spend my life walking on eggshells afraid to be me for fear of upsetting others. I have finally mastered me and my emotions. I am no longer dragged into the drama or bondage of my mind. I have realised how short life is, so I am living it for real in every way.

You can make the choice to remain plagued by your circumstances, ruled by your existing beliefs, hurt by your experiences, shallow in your thinking, lost in your depression, walking on eggshells yourself or you can wipe the slate clean and start again. Unlike me, you can make the choice to wake up from your coma, open your eyes and expand your horizons beyond what you have been fed by others and begin to question why you have been sleepwalking through your life for so long. Listening to your soul, the choices you make from your heart not your unconscious ego, the cruel critic in your mind, your subconscious lies, trust me, is the only process to developing self-awareness and your unique creative talents, beyond the pain and limitations you have chosen to put on yourself by not believing in yourself. By remaining true to your intention to follow your soul self-choices, you will finally release your old patterns and negative habits of resistance, awakening your internal power going forward. You need to start to trust in yourself that whatever happens will be right for you. Remember, it is you who oversees your choices, so it is up to you to decide which side is in charge, the strong good you or the weak, negative afraid you, the unconscious ego self-versus the soul self.

I have tried my best to explain a very complex mind mapping process based around your current belief system, your assumptions, your perspectives. How you negative your internal dialogue needs to be observed outside your comfort zone, in silence and meditation, so you can begin to consider a new way to think for yourself. I want you to now grow some new wings, then give yourself permission to spread these wings and fly. Don't do what is expected of you anymore. This will only keep you disappointed and frustrated. You need to finally break free from the heavy chains of your internal misery and become a beautiful butterfly in nature. Start to celebrate a sense of freedom from your mind by listening only to your heart, then marching to this beat.

Once you begin to realise every single moment of your life counts, every choice you make matters, you will start to develop a deeper connection with the rest of the world. Always remember what you are feeling is what you spend most of your life thinking about and focusing on. What you see and what you experience is based on your perception of your reality and you change this through expanding your self-awareness and your focus. The downside comes from the existing programming in your subconscious mind, so don't expect anything to happen overnight. You must put in the hard work to see results.

As you know I battled myself with my subconscious even with all the confidence in the world, so I totally understand the yo-yoing back and forth, the bingeing and purging when dealing with your mindset. Any change is difficult and daunting, especially on the days you feel bad but blocking it out is no longer an option, if you want to evolve. If you are waking up wishing you were still asleep, if you sleep instead of thinking because it's easier, if you drink, over-eat or take happy pills for comfort, this is stopping you sticking to the plans you make in your mind on the days you feel positive. Life is not meant to be a battle ground where you find yourself constantly under attack from your negative emotions and mood swings, it's supposed to be a walk in the park and maybe this is what you need to start doing outside, instead of beating yourself up inside. I would always force myself outside of myself when the inside of me felt bad because outside is where the real world exists not in my mind, the place I created all the stuff not useful to my emotional wellbeing.

Once you begin to realise everything bad is happening because of you and the stories you tell yourself, there will be no need to feel shame or guilt anymore, you can start to cast it all aside, striding back into your real life with only gratitude and humility. Acceptance of what you see, do, believe and feel is your truth, and this creates your reality. The more you look outside of yourself for the answers, the longer it will take for you to find your truth. I can give you a million different ways right now to change your mindset, empower you, change the way you think. I am also convinced if I got you alone on a slow boat to China, one to one talk therapy would have you thinking straight but this is not possible. All we have is our time in this book together. As you experience a direct communication with who you really are behind the mask, you will begin to see you always have a choice within you and this choice, if it's the right one for you, will always lead you back to your truth.

The truth is, if you are feeling miserable, unfulfilled, lonely, sad, defeated, and depressed it is because you have a massive hole in your soul, an empty void you find yourself constantly trying to fill. It is the place that forces you to constantly search for comfort and the perfect place for your anxiety to thrive. If your anxiety is filling up this empty hole, the place reserved for your soul, you will never feel comfortable satisfied or centred, you will always feel empty. There is no single problem in the world that cannot be solved if you put your mind to it. Anyone who tells you that life is fair is lying and has not lived a day in the real world with their eyes open. Life is unfair. You only need to look at how many people are suffering globally due to poverty, famine and war. So much of what we believe today is down to brainwashing, marketing and fake news. Our emotions and actions reflect our environment. We prefer to complain over adjusting or changing things. It is easier to remain in denial with the pack mentality, rather than stand alone in truth and fight for what is right.

Nurturing humility truly will allow you to mature and recognise there is little point in accepting negative emotions. I advise you now, learn to accept failure with calmness, never conflict or anger. Maturing is never about getting emotional unnecessarily, that is for children. Growing spiritually to become more mature through humility, confidently walking away from conflict and situations that threaten your peace of mind, your inner values, your self-worth and your safety is the key to understanding courage. Maturity is about letting go, listening before jumping to conclusions, learning to accept and see things for what they really are, instead of pretending, showing off or lying your way out. Self-respect is about growing up, leaving behind the damaged immature cruelty of your past experiences. Once we lose self-respect it's hard to get it back. People will always remember and use negative things against us, it's human nature, so we must be aware we are not selling ourselves short.

You start to realise as you grow up, many things about beauty and the power of maturity. Speaking ill of others in their absence is not only unkind but tells a lot about who you are, so I now try to avoid doing it. You realise when someone is hurting you, you learn to understand their situation instead of hurting them back. You realise you must accept your mistakes and do your best to never repeat them. Maturity for me today is all about being centred in myself not being self-centred. Maturity does not come with age, it comes from learning from our experiences and more than anything, it comes from accepting our personal circumstances can change.

A common trait in leaders is being highly aware of who they are and where they are heading. Your destiny is constantly being shaped and mapped out by your thoughts, emotions, beliefs and behaviours. If you are not focused positively on your thoughts, goals and choices, your mind will be wandering all over the place influenced by your unconscious ego decisions.

When you learn to ask yourself questions and begin to self-analyses through reflection and not denial, you get to understand yourself better on a deeper level. The choice to develop more self-awareness, allows more self-control. A growth mindset is a sign of maturity. Don't waste anymore of your time going through the motions of your life waiting for a miracle or something amazing to come along to wake you up. It's never going to happen.

The resilience of the human spirit is something I have experienced myself. It always amazes me how people can withstand multiple crisis or even severe illness, then get back up with a fighting spirit, so there are no excuses for you. When you start to think about the idea you are not a human being having a spiritual experience but a spiritual being having a human experience, it changes everything. Your soul is the part of you that makes you who you are. It is the moral side of you, the nonphysical side of you, and the part of you that never fades. It quietly observes everything you think, do, believe and feel. It existed before human life began and will exist when human life ends. It is the essence of the real person you are, the authentic you, the bigger picture. Where the soul goes after we die is of course a big question with many answers depending on religious teachings, belief or personal interpretation. I am of the opinion today if we are made up of energy that can never be destroyed, this must be our soul and it lives on forever in the universe after we die moving, changing and evolving. As I have said many times, the importance of understanding and having a connection with your soul is vital in the pursuit of happiness and fulfilment. Your well-being comes not just from your physical health but from your mental health as well.

The practice of meditation, yoga, walking in nature, helping others will all have a profound impact on your happiness and wellbeing, leading you to a better connection between your mind body and soul, beyond the need for self-gratification. If you are clogged up, tired, run down consumed with lies, judging, complaining, blame shifting and constantly at the doctor, you will unlikely be able to change and make better choices. Unless you are prepared to believe wholeheartedly you need take care of yourself and recognise your soul exists as a human essence, guiding and driving you towards change, personal growth and wholeness, the spark of light in your depression, you will have little hope of ever beating your demons.

I found the best way to connect with my soul was to listen to my instincts and intuition, understanding they are never wrong. Once I was able to face my problems with a non-judgemental awareness, I discovered an incredible ability to grow through the experience of the most challenging of times. Being non-judgemental means, we can be open-minded, expanding because of our experiences, gaining a much clearer perspective over the whole situation. I realised I was not the only one on the planet going through troubling times. This allowed me to be more sensitive to the needs of others. It is called empathy, something I had not been aware of in the past. This idea of shared collective empathy for others, facing challenging issues without being superficial, allowed me to step into the shoes of someone else who might be in trouble. And this was real progress for me. Think about the homeless man with the orange.

The time has come now for you to work yourself out, so you can leave the blues, the booze and the black dog behind, getting outside with mindfulness, using your energy to heal yourself through the power of self-awareness, revisiting the past, then closing the door through forgiveness and humility.

Practice makes perfect, so if at the end of this journey together you still feel like nothing makes sense, go back to the start and read it again. No matter what excuses you have, you must at least try and change. The choice is yours now and you will only reach your limit when you can go no further. There are no rules set in stone when it comes to life. We all have our own crosses to bear and ways we get through it but there are common sense rules that teach us not to take things too seriously. This is not a dress rehearsal, it's your life. A basic human trait is we love to have more than one choice. Intuitively, we believe the more choices we have, the better chance we have of finding the right choice that satisfies our needs. The truth is, this intuitive assumption is in fact an illusion. The more choices we have, the less likely we are to decide. The reason, having an overload of choices paralyses the decision-making process, leading to avoidance behaviour. We get to the place where we cannot see the wood for the trees, the whole picture. When we are faced with too many choices, we then face the fear of making the wrong decision. Having two choices is fine; we have a fifty percent chance of getting it right. When it comes to planning your life, your wellbeing, your mental health, there is only one choice and although this choice results in you having to face your fears, it is the only route to taking back control of your mind.

This important choice and remember, it is your soul talking, is all about you changing, talking less and listening more, not to other people's opinions but to what is going on inside of you. You are no longer a people pleaser constantly trying to live up to everyone's expectations, petrified to make a mistake, always looking to find validation outside of yourself. You are now working on finding your own self-worth instead.

Self-worth is based on the opinions you have about yourself, the values you place on yourself. This is how you optimise your happiness levels through identifying with your own core beliefs and values, not those of other people. It is important to be able to view yourself now without feeling anxious about how you see yourself. If you can make the choice to be more accepting of yourself, you are less likely to be anxious about your failings and be more realistic about whom you are inside. We all have failings but the difference between a happy positive person who accepts this and a depressed, anxious, unhappy person who believes their failings and flaws are fatal, is self-confidence and self-belief. Hopefully by now, you are learning to go beyond who you think you are and venture more into looking at your real identity, coming out of your comfort zone, your shell, letting go of your imagined self.

Jung and individualism are what this is about, uniting personal and collective unconscious into conscious. The journey of personal development is the evolving process of self over a lifetime. It is a constant work in progress. Who you really are inside, the authentic you, your real identity will come from nurturing self-awareness. By letting go of all your conditioned thoughts and beliefs, your choices will start to align with your authentic self. If you continue to violate and ignore your true values and beliefs, you will only weaken your sense of self and this is the reason you are depressed, unable to be happy. It's crucial for those living with depression and anxiety and it's pretty much all of us to some degree or another to know, our thinking and our choices create our misery. For each possible scenario we must know whether the best possible outcome is worth risking the worst possible outcome. If you cannot live with your choices, then don't pursue the option.

Personal growth should focus over a lifetime but as we age our growth fades in favour of family and careers, which can leave us putting our spiritual development on hold. If we reach midlife without establishing personal growth and creative thinking, in other words we have not worked on ourselves; chances are we will feel unfulfilled and disillusioned by earlier choices we are stuck with today. This is often what people mean when they talk about a midlife crisis. When we begin to accept to be individual, we must create our own experiences and be totally responsible for our actions, we can stop looking to others to blame for the problems we have created for ourselves. We can only expect perfection from life, when we are committed to be perfect ourselves.

My intrinsic value goal of nurturing self-acceptance and my contribution back to society through self-actualisation has helped satisfy all my insecurities, psychological problems and needs. Once I was forced, I had no choice to give up looking outward for approval, I started to place value on my life, my health and my emotional wellbeing over everything else. The search for happiness is never ending. There is nothing material or tangible on this planet that comes close to the importance and value of your health and wellbeing. Without it you have nothing. I can tell you without doubt any search for happiness through materialism and status is short-lived. The more you raise your standards, buying bigger or better to impress others, the people you are trying to impress will outdo you. I understood through my own personal experience of gaining great wealth in the world of capitalism and greed, most fortunes are made largely on deceit on who you know or luck.

With only a greed and status mindset you get materialism but are vulnerable to emotional bankruptcy when it all fades away. Gordon Gekko, the stock market investor on Wall Street once said, "Greed is good, greed works," making it acceptable and encouraged in our current climate of materialism. Personal experience has taught me greed is never good, since we can never attain everything we desire, we will always end up with some level of dissatisfaction. I have learnt the secret to getting what you want is, still wanting it after you've got it.

Today I practise generosity over the desire for wealth and possessions. I don't covet another person's life or money. I value my own life above the idea of a fancy unrealistic fake existence. When you make the choice to connect with your soul and you are guided by it, the yearning for materialism stops. Once you become more practised at making soul-based choices, you start thinking with your heart. This will be the total opposite to how you have lived your life in the past, so it does take a bit of getting used to. We all need money, but it must never define who we are.

Personal Responsibility

When we look at our lives, we have two ways to see it. The outside, what goes on externally around us, what we see, smell, touch and hear and what goes on internally through our thoughts, feelings and emotions. These two should work in harmony if we are doing everything possible to take care of ourselves both physically and mentally. Like all creatures great and small in nature, we also work perfectly.

Think now about how amazing your body functions are. How your lungs help you to breathe, your eyes help you to see, your voice allows you to talk, life miracles we all automatically take for granted, without thinking or being grateful. The mind should work perfectly in the same way if your body is giving it the right messages, you are happy, healthy, centred, fulfilled, purposely working every day at what you truly love. Obviously, life for us all is not that simple. Our minds can become easily influenced by what we think, what we see, what we feel and what we perceive or imagine depending on our environment and circumstance at the start of our development process. We have been on a long journey together through this book to try and help you understand why you have found yourself either depressed, miserable, crippled by anxiety, ruled by negative bad habits and patterns, unable to work yourself out to be happy and fulfilled in your life. We have established the mind is the main problem, the barrier preventing you overcoming your fears and fantasies. We have also established your unconscious ego is not helping you survive yourself either. It is keeping you stuck; believing you know better, when if you did, you would not be needing talk therapy. I hope also by now you have established you have to somehow learn to think before you feel because feeling before you think is why you cannot get anywhere. Your emotions take over your rational thoughts and before you know it, you are sinking, not thinking straight.

We have looked at how the past influences the future and how all your fear is potentially irrational, based on insecurity and immaturity. So that's why you need to grow up now. The lost wounded child inside has become unable to evolve, grow up, and this stagnation has blocked the pathway to your deeper spiritual needs developing. I have hopefully inspired you to recognise, a more self-aware you could contemplate the profound idea of having a relationship with the authentic you, to expand your consciousness through connecting deeply with your inner soul. By this process of awakening, moving into deeper self-realisation, you will start to be more aware of a true state of being conscious, adapting your brain power to develop changes in your expanding reality. By rewiring and remapping your brain, you will start to see a radical shift in your consciousness, your emotions, your behaviours and your thoughts. This shift will play a huge role in your ability to activate higher thinking levels, leading you to positive change and a spiritual awakening.

Hopefully, we have established mindful meditation is the tool to help you create more self-awareness through improved brain function, strengthening your nervous system and reconnecting your disconnected soul connection. Basically, by meditating you are nurturing higher emotional behaviours through empathy, humility, compassion, gratitude, forgiveness and peace. When you learn to relax in the inner peace of stillness in your mind, the place that exists without thoughts, once you feel safe with honesty, it will open the pathway to empathy for yourself. Empathy is the main function of your soul. I am hoping you have also started to realise compassion and empathy are the cornerstones of love, the thing that interconnects us all to other living things in the world. With this in place we can reflect on our own sense of identity through simply understanding, what we really feel inside. At a time of self-realisation when we can deeply feel empathy, we have no choice but to experience how others are feeling. The sense of isolation and separation from the world begins to fade, as we begin to feel connected to something greater.

The more we travel through life with our new set of core values, new pathways are created in the brain by the soul. The more we practise empathy, compassion, forgiveness and integrity, the more we understand self-reflection. As we shift out our negative dirty energy, we stop creating internal conflict. Once we become more self-aware, we begin to evolve beyond the ego levels of a cognitive lack of harmony. We make better choices based on deeper feelings. Our lighter sensory side from the heart, our spiritual intelligence can then guide us beyond the conflicts of the mind.

I have been talking to you throughout this book about how much your personal progress is important. Without making life changes because we change as our circumstances change, we will stand still in an immature mindset unable to resolve our issues. Most of the time an immature mentality belongs to the lost inner child trapped inside. It is this child creating our irrational feelings of insecurity. This is the reason as adults we don't feel safe, so we create defence mechanisms to help us cope and feel more secure. When we feel insecure, we feel unsafe. We are disconnected from our core spiritual foundation, the solid tree. We have buried all our trauma and lies within the unconscious level of the brain and this has become the protection from the pain, basically what a defence mechanism is.

Your job now is to start to connect back to your solid, spiritual core foundation through meditation, releasing your unconscious trauma and lies, developing spiritual maturity, no longer being held hostage by your self-deception. We have not been taught as children how to think, problem solve or use the power of our brain, so we have ended up misunderstanding the meaning of life. We have ended up sabotaging our happiness, over enjoying it.

Inner reflection through your meditation will allow you to get to know the real you. No matter what is happening in the external world, when you don't know yourself, what makes you feel fulfilled, happy, peaceful, your personal success, will always be measured in the material world. Once you clear a space for healing, remain present in the moment of awareness, feeling safe as the compassionate witness and observer of your mind, without judgement, you will start to gain access to your consciousness, your spiritual power within. As you become more conscious and aware through developing spiritual intelligence, what has been hidden and niggling at you in the dark shadows of your psyche, will slowly begin to surface. You will learn to be free from your mind, from your fear and experience the real spiritual protection of what inner peace and safety is meant to be.

Understanding your mind truly is the key to getting better. Once you have mastered some discipline over your unconscious impulses, the work of your unconscious ego, you will automatically stop being controlled by your fear-based thoughts. This process will lead you to listen to your heart and gently force you to face your moral, ethical and spiritual beliefs head on. Once you can break down and release your unconscious ego personality, the false you, and walk away from the control it has had over you, you will be free to discover then develop your spiritual nature. When this connection happens for real, you will realise just how lost in the past you have been. It is not going to be easy, like I said, to face your truth, who you are and what you have become, so you will need to be strong spiritually to see the dark shadow side of self.

There has been a long debate about the mind being a mental process, thought, consciousness and the body being the physical aspects of brain neurons, basically how it is structured. The big problem is understanding how all of this can work together in harmony. Is the mind part of the body or is body part of the mind? Which one is in charge? Are they separate or the same thing? We have freedom of choice, which is a mental process, yet it can cause physical behaviour to occur as a response or reaction to a thought. Many biologists believe the mind can be found in the brain and they are the same thing. Cognitive psychology has recently placed a new debate in the argument based on the computer analogy of artificial intelligence. The brain being like the hardware on your PC wired and connected to the human body, the mind being the software that allows the different reactions people have to the same stimulus. The more work I do on myself, the more I understand and recognise this as a reality. If we have an active body, we have an active healthy mind, common sense. A healthy lifestyle is the key to having a healthy mind.

Learning to understand how the brain reacts to certain stimulus or how brain structure can affect our health, personality or cognitive behaviour helps us to see a better picture of how we work as human beings. We are not useless bits of flesh ruled by fate. Despite all our amazing capabilities, our finite knowledge and power, there are many things we have no idea about in the universe, but this is never an excuse to stop learning, evolving or asking questions.

We seem to have lost our dignity when it comes to creating the upmost respect for the real things that matter in our lives, like our physical and mental health, believing we are forever eternal, instead of being eternally grateful. This further influences and shapes what our collective unconscious creates as the main value in society. Money and materialism are highly valued by the masses. I have already talked a lot about how we have become obsessed with money and I conclude, we have simply forgotten about a sense of self, our self-respect and our self-empathy.

The higher your mental agility and stability and this means going beyond materialism and greed, the more likely you are to develop and maintain a healthy body and mindset. A healthy well-balanced routine, eating a good diet, daily meditation, regular fresh air, exercise, even just a walk in the park will not only change your body, it will change your mind, your mood and your overall attitude to life. I am finding myself since giving up alcohol, meat, caffeine, becoming a vegan, I not only look and feel healthy, I am reversing the aging process, something I am quite excited about. It has already been proven exercise improves insomnia, reduces stress anxiety and poor mental wellbeing but you will never get to this place if you believe you know better, hate the idea of healthy living and have given up on believing in yourself because you prefer a comfort zone instead. If you really want to start the process of lifting your depression, reducing your anxiety so you feel better and less miserable, it only takes exercising twenty minutes a day to boost your information processing memory function. Common sense, if you look after your body, your mind will function better. Remember your mind is shaped by your experiences and thoughts. You are what you think. You can decide what you feed your mind just like you decide what you feed your body. It's about taking personal responsibility for taking care of your machine.

In the early stages of your awakening, the first goal is to help you clear your fear established over years, your body pain. We do this by refocusing your destructive habits, shifting your negative perspective and observing it from a healthier more optimistic place. Goodness, a healthy lifestyle, regular exercise with devotion and dedication to good virtues may sound old fashioned, not very trendy but having a moral compass is the only way to point you towards a life that will allow you to flourish. Think about this deeply. How is it possible that goodness, good health and morality have become old fashioned? At the end of the day being a good person and living a healthy lifestyle is all about creating a balance between your emotions and your needs. You might think you need money for the reason you believe it will make you happy, but money is no use if you are damaging your health and cannot enjoy the freedom it brings. If you had to choose between winning the lottery or being super fit and healthy, which would you choose?

Our greatest life struggles, problems and challenges occur when we are not in alignment with our own internal needs, our natural rhythm, which is defined once we have an alignment with our soul. Accepting you have let yourself go, you are not treating your body with respect. Or facing the fact you are addicted, relying on comfort, is not easy. But if you want to change things and start to value your life, rather than destroying it, you have got to be honest with yourself. Learning to be mindful, basically thinking before you feel, like I have said throughout this journey is the most important thing you need to change, especially if you want to stop feeling guilty and miserable. Ask yourself why you don't find getting on top of yourself an exciting challenge. Have you given up on yourself because you don't like yourself?

This build-up of stress, guilt, judging, condemning our existence as worthless, useless, incapable of being happy, is all coming from the negative dialogue you have with the cruel critic in your mind. Only mindfulness can halt the escalation of these thoughts defining you. The more attached you are to the material world, the more you will be out of control and the more you will suffer when you embark on the spiritual path of unconscious ego break down. Developing a growth mindset spiritually, going beyond your limited existing beliefs, recognising you are in control of your own choices, gives you the underlying truth, it is only you who can oversee your destiny. When you can no longer hear your truth, you are lost in your pain and your negative perspective about yourself. This is what has made you unhappy.

To end this book, we are going to look more at why it is vital for us to grow up, mature and take personal ownership of our mind body and soul. We are going to move away from a fixed mindset, the only reason you get discouraged by setbacks and see these setbacks as an opportunity to try harder, by learning something new. When we begin to understand virtues and good morals are the qualities of goodness and it is goodness that defines the quality of our character, we start to make sense. The quality of our thinking shapes our belief system and attitude; it is our mind that distorts our perception of our reality. Once we can identify triggers, that lead us to a distortion of our thinking through an awareness of anxiety or tension, we can learn to shift our feelings through meditation, releasing stress and relaxing more into real life. Let's remember again, denial of your truth is the root of all unconscious ego defence mechanisms. We can never be defined by what we own, how can we. It makes a mockery of all the amazing natural life gifts we have been given for free by Mother Nature, things we can never buy in shop or replace when they break down.

To change your thinking, your negative perspective takes finding the silence between the external and inner mind noise, then be brave enough to listen to what comes up. When you are going through something no one else understands, when your heart is hurting, you are crippled with anxiety and nothing makes sense, you must find something within you, stronger than this perception. You will only do this when you start to believe in yourself. Many times, the answer to a question lies within the question itself, so your understanding of what you really fear or what is making you hurt will only change, when you can identify the basis of your fear. Then you can mitigate it.

In this life regardless of what you think, right now you have accomplished a lot, way more than you realise. If your whole life is spent focusing on only the negative, you forget to remember the positives and there will be some somewhere. I am sure of this. It is just a matter of changing things around. The time has come to stop telling yourself you are not good enough, not strong enough and not worthy enough to be fit healthy and fabulous. Your self-care must now become a necessity, not just an idea in your mind you don't believe you deserve because you do, we all do. You need to start caring about yourself in a mature way, no longer acting like a robot trapped in fear waiting around for someone else to sort out your mess. At the end of the day, you have two choices. You can either sink or swim. If you believe you cannot swim, you've tried, and it's not worked out in the past, remember learning any new skill takes reprogramming your short-term memory. Ask yourself now, how hard have you really tried to change in truth?

When we feel scared or threatened, living our lives in survival mode, abusing our consciousness we find it impossible to assert healthy boundaries. We become a victim. This then destroys our self-awareness and we allow life and other people to walk all over us. You must no longer deny the person you really are inside. Remember you are the only one who sets your rules and boundaries, it is your life.

It was only when I was forced to reflect on the meaning of my own life, during my close shave with death, I realised how much of it I had wasted maintaining the illusion of my vain pursuits. All I can tell you from my own experience, never lie to yourself. You will end up being unable to distinguish the truth within. You may not fully understand what I mean when I talk about self-deception, we all like to think we are good people and the life we have chosen is an honest, upstanding, noble one. We all have a basic need to think positively about who we are, even with our many defects and flaws. It's truly hard to overcome the desire to resist any change. Our natural tendency is to self-sabotage, particularly in the environment we live in today. It is tough to practise the art of acceptance. Although our resistance to change serves as a self-protection function, we can no longer be forced to be held captive by our childhood or circumstances.

Think back about the married man who at an unconscious level wants to sleep with another man but at a conscious level finds this behaviour unacceptable because he has a wife. To diffuse his anxiety from his internal conflict, he is likely to deploy a defence mechanism like anger or denial, which will ultimately become repression or projection. His resistance to change is massive. Not only is he participating in self-deception, he is living a lie to protect the illusion of his whole existence. Many times, we choose repression to either forget or distort our own truth which then becomes unconscious. A wife who has been beaten up by her husband may choose to not remember the attack, instead seeing the husband as a loving caring man who cannot help his behaviour. We all have secrets. We are all cracked in some way and often need putting back together. At an unconscious level, you may have been lying to yourself for years about how you feel inside, pretending on the outside to be happy, balanced and fulfilled. It is this repression that eventually creates your dirty energy.

The lies we tell ourselves and others will only perpetuate our addictive behaviour, our addictive thinking. Think about how many times you lie about how much you have had to eat. How much you have had to drink, how much you weigh, how old you are, everything from small insignificant lies to massive life-changing untruths. At a core level, we deceive ourselves all the time because psychologically we don't have the courage to deal with the consequences of what may follow from telling the truth. Carl Jung put it beautifully and plainly when he discussed taking the easy road instead of changing. "We may think there is a safe road but that would be the road to death. Anyone who takes the safe road, is as good as dead." Do you think by ignoring your deep inner needs you are taking the safe road? If the answer to this question is yes, think about being as good as dead right now.

Showing yourself, the real you without holding back for fear of rejection or judgement, will involve feeling everything, the good, the bad and the ugly. My truth came through by gaining more wisdom and self-discipline towards things essential to developing more meaning. The idea of self-analysis and talk therapy is to understand, suppressing your hidden fear, pain and emotions behind a mask or false identity means you will never be able to tell the difference between what is true and what is false. This is what we call self-delusion. Once we begin to understand this, we start to look deeper to reach the core self, to create emotional and spiritual healing. We start to search out the root cause of our problems and where the pain came from in the first place. The idea in this book of you becoming an expert in self-mastery, means you will finally be able to take back control of your own life, confronting your limitations to reach reward and satisfaction. This satisfaction is not only rewarding but way more lasting than the quick fix feeling of instant gratification.

Human beings are programmed to fear the unknown. It's a primal instinct. I understand from my own personal experience just how hard it will be to let go but, please remember, if you resist the process of the change required to face your pain, you will remain forever mentally and physically crippled by it. Taking personal responsibility by accepting the consequences of your actions, without expecting anyone else, particularly parents to protect you, is essential for making mature independent decisions going forward. You must learn to walk to the beat of your own drum now. The journey to discovering your unique identity, finding out who you really are, how strong you are and how you fit into your world is a deeply individual experience. This journey begins by accepting discomfort as a normal state, a vital part of the process to uncovering self-sabotaging patterns. By being willing, curious and open to finally delve headfirst into the unknown world of your internal pain with integrity, takes you closer to maturing with intention, instead of constantly running away masking it all with comfort and addictions. Like I keep repeating, it won't be easy to take an honest look in the mirror and accept personal responsibility for your mess. You have become used to projecting the blame onto others. Understanding this projection becomes clearer, when in your meditation as an observer you start looking deeper at your behaviour. You cannot do it when you are in it. The way you learn anything in this life is through patience and practice, setting your intention to have a truthful conversation with the vulnerable, emotional and sacred you. Part of becoming emotionally mature is about understanding what vulnerability is. Nurturing humility allows you to share deep hidden feelings you might at first feel ashamed of, afraid of or humiliated by. Trusting yourself to share these feelings openly, without hiding away from them anymore, will create a space for compassionate, freedom from your inner critic. You will start to notice you are bringing the past into the present by repeating the story in your mind and at some point, for your own peace and sanity, you will confidently let it all go. You will start to bring all your actions and thoughts into alignment with what it is you really want in your life. As you move past your pain with grace and compassion, refocusing your mind on being more productive, you will start to be of service to the world and no longer fight against it.

Our goal during this journey is to help you understand you must heal your pain, then stop the emotional triggers, which will bring a feeling of safety back as you surface and resolve your issues. Once you set a practice in motion and you religiously follow the same path in your daily meditation, with time your negative automatic way of thinking will start to change, and your subconscious will follow suit. Basically, you will begin to feel healthier mentally and be emotionally stronger. Once the door is open, your mind is open, you will be curious, no longer closed off. You will learn to hold your hands up when you make a mistake without feeling like a loser. You will learn to hold your head up in humility when you are proud of something new you have managed to achieve. You will learn to laugh at your pain, once you recognise it never belonged to you in the first place.

Thinking in a new, healthier optimistic way without judgement or fear is how you build self-confidence, especially once you have let the power of your unconscious ego go. You can now start to think for yourself without worrying what others think about you. Learning to think outside of ourselves, focusing less on our own needs, wants and desires, becoming more sensitive to others, allows us to understand we are part of something bigger, something more collective. If you are honest with yourself, you will start to be honest with others, then you establish integrity both internally and externally, removing the heavy chip on your shoulder once and for all. Once you become a spiritual thinker not a negative robot, you will travel through life without doubt, arriving at a place of peace.

Training your mind to go beyond your perceived negative thoughts expands your clean energy and your consciousness, opening your heart feeling centre to more easily process your reality with clarity through intuition. Once you notice in your meditation associations and judgements against yourself, through searching your heart, not listening to the cruel critic in your mind, you will stop your tendency to create false identities. Through more self-awareness, only communicating with your conscious mind, you will begin the process of refusing to form any attachment with your false unconscious ego identity and negative bias. Suffering in the mind can only happen if we harbour judgements and lies.

The most important thing you must do to change depression is to silence the inner critic, developing only pure thoughts in your meditation. This will lead you to a much deeper self-awareness and then a state of higher consciousness. Your meditation will activate a more realistic assessment of your reality. By paying more attention with patience and empathy to yourself in your mind, you will begin to see just how mean and cruel the voice in your head has become. With confidence and clearer insight as the compassionate observer, you can begin to question your negative thoughts, instead of automatically believing what is not productive, healthy or real. If every time you say think or do something that starts as a reaction, not a response, this will become a trigger to let you know you have not been present in your mind, you have automatically jumped in without being mindful of the bigger picture. By identifying your negative belief system drives, your reactions, creating your emotional and mental conflict, causing your anxiety, you start to see how it all results in your physical and mental structure shutting down in fear. Through learning to observe your automatic mind behaviour, remaining present with your physical body sensations in pain or fear, not running away, masking them or letting them translate into anxiety, just staying present until they pass, you get to see them for what they are. You are not physically in pain or in any real danger. The whole episode of anxiety is being driven by your unconscious ego. Your mind is dictating the fear and pain based on your hijacked self-belief, not your reality.

Allowing you to be open and emotionally vulnerable is not a weakness, it's a strength. How can you ever build courage and integrity, if you are always escaping your feelings and truth? Learning to remain present in your fear and pain is the key to getting through it. Whatever you are afraid of or avoiding because it means having to face yourself, your truth, will never go away until you feel it, deal with it and let it go through unconditional love, self-compassion and courage. It is better to be a lion for a day than a sheep for the rest of your life. If you believe letting go of your fear and pain means you will lose your sense of security, your personality, the essence of the person you believe you are, remember what you are losing is made up in your mind, in your imagination and nothing to do with the real person you are under the mask.

The truth is, you have no idea about the real you, the authentic you or how strong and courageous you are deep down inside beyond the false protection of your unconscious ego. This protection is a defence strategy designed to stop you facing your demons, your truth your choices, your pain, your misery and it will fight you to the death to protect its survival. It prefers you to be depressed, suffering self-deception and anxiety, lying to yourself instead. It has no interest in allowing you a free passage to your authentic core beliefs, your inner beautiful unique nature, the side of you never free to be alive and vital. This got kicked out of you years ago. The more you understand your unconscious ego and practise your meditation, you will start to take control of your negative dialogue, irrational fear, gaining more self-control, developing a stronger spiritual connection to your soul self. Once again to remind you, your subconscious patterns will try and surface. Don't deny them or repress them anymore. This will only prolong your suffering. Work with all the things I have told you through being a spiritual observer committed to discovering your emotional freedom.

Aligning your old self with your true self through nurturing love, peace, joy and compassion, your heartfelt feelings, not your emotions or beliefs in your mind, the real aspects of the divine you, your truth will be triggered, not by what is outside of you but from somewhere deep within you. Unconditional love and compassion will develop more within you as you gain more strength. Your clean energy will come from a spiritually untapped universal source, available to all of us when we become a good, ethical, well-balanced, honest, trustworthy, reliable, caring, courageous and open person. If you can begin to focus your attention on building this foundation of core beliefs inside of yourself, you will wipe out the fake trembling mess behind all that is ugly and false. The past will no longer be the driving force behind your emotions, thinking and behaviour. You will start to emerge as a brave human being with a spiritual connection to only the truth, goodness and self-honesty. All you have been missing will be restored in complete awareness and my friends, this is real progress.

Remember your beliefs are just a state of mind. You can think something is the case without there ever been any evidence to prove it is the case. Without factual certainty, our personal attitudes, associated with either true or false ideas and concepts, get confused then misinterpreted. Basically, our brain becomes emotionally attached and becomes entangled with ideas and concepts we come to believe are true, paying more attention to our existing beliefs over changing them. If we had modelled, learnt and copied as children good moral values and core beliefs, based on understanding compassion, gratitude, forgiveness, humility and integrity, our thoughts about how we feel about ourselves inside would be solid and unbreakable right from the start. Your parents would not be handing over to you the curse of their neurosis and existing beliefs, passed onto them by their parents, instead they would have given you the gift of how to operate, problem solve and be centred with a mind of your own.

Now imagine if we all had a mind of our own, thinking believing and acting out everything we did in life, based on simple universal core beliefs. We would not be looking outward for approval from others, we would be able to rely on ourselves for how we think, feel and act independently. If you had started out centred, happy, bursting with compassion, gratitude and joy, valuing every second of your life because you are grateful for it, you would never have been tempted to abuse it. You would appreciate you needed it to survive. If you had started out positive, honest, full of humility and forgiveness because you care about your purpose more than materialism, you would have become rich both financially and spiritually. This is what real success looks like.

To fully heal we must discover our authentic nature, taking purposeful steps towards aligning our lifestyle to our circumstances. This is where we find and feel connection, acceptance and our unique purpose. I never imagined a life without my mask, my false identity. Dropping my unconscious ego, building more self-awareness by developing gratitude and humility in my life truly connected me back to the spiritual source of my soul self. It was this experience that led me to ultimate freedom from my internal suffering. The stress of losing all my money was my unconscious ego making me upset about the situation. It did not lead me compassionately away from the pain, it didn't allow me to surrender in humility, it didn't protect me from the discomfort and shame of being greedy and stupid, instead it tricked me into thinking I was better off dead. My mind played the worst tricks possible when I was at my most vulnerable. It took me down, it stripped me of my confidence, it made me believe I was worthless useless and worst of all it made me question my own survival tactics.

When I was truly at the bottom five years later and my life was potentially over for real, the process of dropping my unconscious ego happened through resilience and dedication to listening only to my heart. I had a spiritual awakening during a midlife crisis. It was a truly freeing experience to let go of all the pain, the regret, the lying, the past, the fake façade, the discomfort. I was not afraid to embrace death in the moment and this is the reason I know it is possible to escape depression, suicide and anxiety. Although I only experienced the madness of being out of control for a short period, it was enough to let me know and advise you, reaching the bottom and killing yourself is never the answer. All I can tell you through adversity, I discovered how strong and powerful I was inside without my mind pulling me under. Difficult experiences have helped me create a much healthier way to live my life today. I had to look at how ignorant I had become, how much suffering I was enduring. I realised how I knew very little in the bigger scheme of things. I got to see how fast things can change. How easily my life could be taken from me and it was all this that led me to be grateful in humility. Once my hard work was finished internally and it was really hard work trust me, I woke up from my comma and saw the authentic me with crystal clear clarity through open observation, allowing me to see my reality, understand it, then fully accept it.

I gained great wisdom through the wise action of letting all that mess go. The past served me no purpose in the future. The inner peace I have today is incredible, steadfast and never changes. My passion and purpose have emerged, through continued committed work on myself. I never regret what happened because what happened naturally for me through suffering is what changed me. I am not a hurt, silly, little lost girl anymore trapped inside a massive ego, pretending to be a clever adult without anything to back it up. I am grown up, mature, centred, spiritually driven woman, trying hard to save a big bad world.

It is hard to explain this incredible shift or make it sound aspirational for you. You have not been forced to change. You have a choice to make. The external world you believe in right now is random. Your internal space is deliberate and planned. So, which do you prefer? Ultimately for you to become mature and develop into a positive, independent functioning human being, you must throw away the crutches and support you have become dependent on, creating a false sense of security, recognising the price you will pay for this dependency is your spiritual freedom. Mature thinking is only developed through more exposure to emotional fear. You learn to challenge your own beliefs and re-evaluate them, either improving them or getting rid of them. Once we are willing to let go of them, we recover our own core beliefs. We regain control over how we feel about ourselves with a clear intention of where we are heading in the future. Nothing depletes self-worth faster than feelings of anger, fear, guilt and regret.

Digging deep for your own personal strength once again will come by understanding, all positive change begins with you. Arriving at spiritual maturity; the level to which you accept personal responsibility for what you have allowed your body and consciousness to endure, you will have undergone many conflicts between strength and weakness. As you become less attached to things and become more willing to let go of your spiritually bankrupt values, in order to survive the inner transformation required to stand alone in truth, you will start to evolve in alignment with all that is imperfect but real. Strength and weakness are equally powerful.

Everything I have told you will help you shift from living in the wake of your past, catapulting you into the stratosphere of your future. The highest level of peace, joy and happiness but it can only happen if you take personal responsibility for yourself and commit to the work needed to get in touch with your authentic self, behind your fear, your mask, your denial. Unfortunately, this will mean you facing the prospect your whole existence to date is potentially a big, fat lie. The person you think you are is in fact an imposter, a fake persona created to mask your insecurity and self-doubt, to fit in and be accepted by others. Once you begin to honour and respect yourself, listening closely to what you are really feeling in your body, paying full attention to the internal warning of your emotional limits when in challenging situations, you will stop losing control over your emotions and behaviours. You owe it to yourself to be true to you by making the effort to respect the contents of your heart, generating love and kindness for yourself, through higher spiritual growth. Once you begin to heal your mental and emotional pain and you build self-respect by taking care of your health, through consistent meditation and avoiding exposure to self-harming behaviours, you will start to establish your inner safety.

I could just be another happy-clappy life coach full of good intention, spouting self-help mantras and mission statements learnt from a book but I am not. You know my story. Once you are forced to downsize your mind, clean out the cobwebs, then polish the empty space in healing until the negative voice, the cruel critic is finally gone, you will begin to see near death and losing everything for me was a blessing in disguise. I may not have all the money anymore, but I will have it again. I am even more driven today than I ever was before, not by greed, power and success but by passion and purpose. It's too easy to revel and wallow in a miserable life of self-pity, missing all the opportunities we have for personal growth and wisdom, the two essential ingredients required to face adversity. All life struggles go towards building unbreakable character and are often the times in our lives we can be most proud of. When you overcome great adversity, it pushes you to your limits and you accomplish something worthwhile. This is what I found to be true on my own journey. The experience of adversity pushed me to my limit then beyond, forcing out of me inner strength and power I had no idea existed.

By facing your own life challenges, you will see yourself in a good light and a bad light—at your best and at your worst. The easy route is to temporarily escape yourself through addictions and comforts, but the greatest challenge is when you suffer to find assurance and security within. You can continue to ignore the evidence in order to preserve your unconscious ego, avoiding your inner conflict but sooner or later it will manifest into a physical illness, causing you further misery until you die.

Apparently, it takes ten years and ten thousand hours to be an expert, so I can say I am one today, having spent more time than this working on myself and with others. It might take you a lifetime to know yourself well enough to become an expert. We are all a work in progress. You have potentially given up on trying to sort yourself out, find a way beyond the misery, the depression. You have also potentially accepted anxiety, the symptom, as something you will endure to keep your unconscious ego happy. It is one thing to say you are motivated to change but an entirely different thing to find the motivation to translate your talk into action. If you think about it, you have become an expert at destroying all that is good about you, so it cannot be that hard to become an expert at nurturing all that is good within you. It just needs a shift in your existing beliefs.

I have always been a master of my own destiny. I have always charted the path to where I needed to be to reach any goal, I set myself. I have always known deep down inside I am only borrowing this body. My drive and spirit will always be free. It doesn't belong to me. It belongs to the universe. I am connected to something greater, something more substantial. I do what my heart tells me to do and it works for me. Learning to think for myself came from listening to my heart not my mind. Start to think of your heart like the engine in your car or the control panel in an aircraft. Recognise everything needs to be in perfect working order to keep the engines running, pushing it forward to reach the end destination. The wrong fuel, no movement and the whole thing breaks down. Every time you drink too much, eat too much sugar, salt, every time you hurt yourself emotionally, your poor heart must work like crazy to keep everything moving to keep you alive. Did you know your heart generates the strongest electromagnetic field of any other organ in your body? It can be measured up to a few feet away from your physical body and can change in relation to your emotions. Think about it now, if you are permanently depressed, full of dirty energy, this is what you will radiate around you, attracting the same back. Your heart generates the strongest electromagnetic field and the information stored in it affects every other organ in your body. The reason why the heart is the very first organ to form and function in a foetus. It has an intelligence of its own. It is known better as the fifth brain or the heart brain. Your heart is not just something you take for granted, pumping blood through your body. It has its own intelligence and plays a massive role in your life. It is the main conductor for connecting us all together in the universe. Sadly, the brain and the heart often work in opposition. Think about how many times you have been torn between your thoughts and feelings. A rational person would say the mind is the key to keeping us out of trouble, we think about the pros and the cons, the risks and the safety of our choices. The heart on the other hand helps us feel the best outcome of our choices. It connects to our intuition, what is right or wrong instinctively. Depending on your perceived ideas, the mind can make you think you are afraid to seek happiness outside of what you already know, your comfort zone. Your heart on the other hand often makes you more impulsive, urging you to try the unknown by doing something new. Think about it now, is it right to get drunk and damage your heart further, when you have a medical diagnosis already from your doctor it is broken? Is it wrong to stay in a marriage when your heart is breaking, when deep down inside you are gay and lying to everyone else?

These days I have learnt to follow my heart, always keeping my mind open. I have found this gives me the clarity and balance to always do the right thing, when doing the wrong thing would be way more fun. I am sure you will all understand this kind of thinking. I value my heart more than my mind these days. I need my mind, so I keep it in check, always remembering it tells me lies, it makes me do stuff that is not real and can be easily influenced by others, if I allow it. My heart never lies. It tells me the truth if I am open to listen. I listen to the opinions of others. I am open to change if something makes sense to me and I am not just doing it to impress. I no longer fear death. Death is part of living and when it comes, I want to be able to say I did what I needed to do to survive. I am not embarrassed or afraid to talk of my mistakes or my mental health issues. We all have problems. None of us are free from the madness of the mind. I am a creature in nature with the gift of self-will, not a programmed robot going through the motions. I am in control of what I think and do. I don't worry about superficial things anymore. Money is only useful if it is valued and well spent. I never repress my emotions. If something goes wrong in my mind, it wasn't meant to be in the first place, so I let it go. This means I carry no unnecessary baggage around anymore.

The secret and most crucial element to any success story in life is courage. You cannot live this life to the full, if you are unprepared to take risks. Change is the biggest risk of them all. Any change even a positive change is hard to embrace or sustain because it shifts us away from what we are used to doing, thinking or believing. Changing comes with adapting. A slow exposure to everything you fear gradually allows you to be more confident, formulating an action plan, then taking the plunge. Once you adapt to the coldness of the water, you can build courage through endurance, without running away or blaming others. The meaning of life is to achieve belonging and significance via cooperation and contribution in the interest of human mankind. Courage is a universal core value. Perfection is fiction and happiness, is the end goal for you.

I am slowly getting ready to say goodbye, but I will be with you all the way to the end. Remember you can always go back and start again if you fail. No one is monitoring your progress on this journey, except you. Don't have unrealistic expectations or be discouraged if you don't get it right. It took me half my life to get it right. Life is a journey never a destination. Too much time in one place is a waste of time so travel, be free, explore and endure. Only you have the key to unlock the treasure behind the locked door. Many things will change and become available to you, once you learn to detach from your unconscious ego, so never become dependent on experience or fantasy for pleasure, pretending you are happy, when inside you are really in pain.

As I come to the end of this book, I am very aware of not sounding like the type of person I once found it impossible to listen to. I don't have all the answers, but I have had a huge life-changing experience which led me down a path I know now has helped me evolve my spirituality, allowing me to finally heal myself and be myself. I am fully engaged now and aware, every choice I make has consequences, this is enough to make me stop and reconsider. One difficult day or bad choice does not send me to the depths of despair. I can always bounce back like a rubber ball.

It has been wonderful spending time inside your head provoking and poking. I hope you have at least gained some inspiration, motivation or encouragement to take some action-based steps yourself, to finally understand the beauty and pleasure in living the life you deserve. I am always here in this book, so if you need more support, don't understand something or find yourself going backwards, read it again and again until you are sick of me and change anyway. When you start to engage your mind in all the things presented in this book and you regularly practise the breathing and meditation, the mindful thinking, the truth, you will start to retrain your automatic existing beliefs, regaining control over your thinking, your life and your happiness. Alone you have been unable to problem solve your way out of misery. This is potentially because you have spent your life blaming others for why you are stuck today.

Back in my own childhood days, I managed to maintain consistent experiences and patterns to help me survive alone to get my needs met. I could self-regulate, and problem solve. This idea once looked grim to me before I matured. I always imagined my childhood lonely without my mother. Actually, it forced me to grow up quickly and survive. How could I blame my mother when she gave me freedom, confidence, self-worth and the best of herself before she left, leaving her empty, drinking herself to death? How could I blame my father who worked his fingers to the bone giving me steadfast work ethic and moral guidance through his goodness? How could I blame my financially poor circumstances at the start of my life, when everything I needed was provided? The big problem for me, I forgot about my truth as I climbed the ladder to the top of the world. I dismissed what was good about my past to create a better backstory to fit in with my imagined future. The thing you are forced to do when you sell your soul for money and success.

Understanding the importance of your own life, your purpose, your meaning comes from accepting you are free to create meaning yourself and not just expecting to find it in the universe. I can promise you for sure, you will flourish and grow with purpose and suffer severely without it. Suffering, sadly, is an unavoidable part of life, something we must come to terms with. How we choose to respond to and deal with this suffering forces us to find more meaning we would otherwise fail to see. The truth is, there is no universal meaning to our lives, other than to save humanity. There is a specific meaning to an individual's life, and this will be different for each one of us. Your inner world is never random unlike your external world. The modern world devalues your inner world and over values your external world, so you need to make a choice. Whatever you believe or whatever you decide about the meaning of your own life remember, you have very little time here, so do something constructive. Find your unique gift then give it away to the world to enjoy and learn from.

By shifting your perspectives, looking at your circumstances, you will learn, grow and strengthen beyond your personal belief system, then expand your personal consciousness. Basically, you are rebuilding a new foundation for yourself and when all the dust settles, after all your hard work, you can start to take the next step of living your real life, no longer being stuck in the past. Once you start to see your existence as a higher thinking self and this becomes your perception, all your own issues will dissipate, and you will no longer be self-absorbed in the madness of your negative emotions and suffering.

For me the suffering experience allowed me to be spiritually productive. I was willing to face the nature of the pain I was experiencing in order to get rid of it.

Accepting responsibility, owning your emotional conflict without blame guilt or projection on others, helps you to see we don't know everything about the people we are blaming and judging. The next time you feel upset, in pain or persecuted, accept it is your responsibility to restore the balance in your mind and feelings through listening to your heart. Only you can solve your problems. Once you start to recognise this and are willing and open to learn what your real issues are, by going deeper within, reflecting on forgiveness, you start to acknowledge real life. This is the first major step to diluting your unconscious ego. We all know people will only take responsibility for themselves when they are ready to do so, and this is usually through an attitude adjustment. No one can force us to change. We must be willing independently to face the truth of the matter ourselves.

Anyone who is faced with misery will automatically ignore any evidence contrary to their own belief in order to preserve their mental madness because it has become an important part of their social personality. In order to resolve mental madness, stress and anxiety, to resolve inner conflict resulting from inconsistent thinking, we must recognise only we have the power to make different choices, through thinking consistently. In taking responsibility for the choices we make, we learn to change the way we think, changing our behaviour to restore more consistency. Sanity is defined as remaining mentally open and mentally flexible. Insanity is defined as a shutting down spiritually. It closes us off, keeping us mentally ridged and this rigidity then leads to a mental breakdown of our nervous system, manifesting into a variety of different symptoms. By resolving or moving away from mental rigidity, we start to become more coherent and consistent in our thoughts, allowing us to make better choices. Trust me, if you remain inconsistent in your thinking and don't take responsibility for your choices, to resolve your inner conflict, you will remain depressed. Your thoughts shape your beliefs. When you escape from your reality, refuse to face and resolve your conflict, you are self-harming and undermining your self-discipline, the very thing that gives you the ability to overcome weakness. The most important relationship you have is with your higher self, through the inner relationship you have with yourself. I have found through my own experience, it is always better to recognise and face what is happening, than to allow pent up frustration and anger be expressed in uncontrollable outbursts, ending up in depression and anxiety. The more you start to really focus and understand why you feel the way you do, through personal observation, your negative feelings will begin to disappear through greater acceptance and awareness.

When we begin to develop and improve our emotional awareness in our meditation through self-observation, we become capable of making the changes required to take back control of our mental state and unconscious mind. Making these changes impacts our behaviour and physical actions. I am trying to help you become willing to see what is going on around you, through being interested in a higher learning, expanding your mind and your consciousness. Remember you are not one dimensional. You are multi-dimensional.

The only way I know as an expert to help you sort out your problems is through meditation. It is the only way to connect you to your higher intelligence. It will have a positive impact on calming your mind, so you can clear out your negative emotions. Once you are free of your negative emotions, meditation will then allow you to focus on positive emotions like gratitude, compassion and forgiveness, all of which allow goodness back in. Meditation has been proven to reduce stress, anxiety and depression, so start to be mindful to improve your mental flexibility, keeping you balanced spiritually, focused only on thoughts of self. Through practising love and kindness towards yourself, you will start to activate the parts of your brain responsible for empathy and increased emotional intelligence. This practice is all about overcoming your feelings of self-doubt and negativity. It takes personal dedication and honesty to face yourself in order to evolve past your chaotic inconsistent thinking and travel towards the higher clarity of your truth. Surrendering, truly allows you to resolve your life problems. It is never the job of your unconscious ego to solve the problems of the world. They can only be resolved when we give up fighting against them. All I can say is stop fighting with you and learn to act going forward, from a place of surrender.

This spiritual journey of gaining self-knowledge will help you to understand when you are feeling fearful and insecure with low self-esteem. You will also learn the reason you feel bad, miserable, depressed or unfulfilled is because you have disconnected from your inner spirit, shutting down your heart, leaving you a prisoner to your mind. It is a choice to travel beyond your fear to finally directly experience your true self beyond the world you have come to see as your reality. Once your core values, your solid tree is rooted, strong, stable and secure you will flourish with a heart-based devotion to goodness and integrity, beyond the selfish ignorance of your unconscious ego, developing good ethics and higher morals along the way.

Through a standard template belief system as a young child installed in you by your caretakers, you have grown up feeling unsafe inside, insecure and vulnerable. These unconscious feelings have disconnected you from a solid bonding of love, safety, acceptance and security, creating your lack of self-esteem. Your lack of self-esteem fuels your fear-based insecurities, and this then reinforces destructive patterns and negative self-talk. Basically, the same feelings and sensations you had as a child get repeated in adulthood and this has resulted in your unhappiness and emptiness today. This destructive cycle will keep repeating from generation to generation, until we accept many of us are learning a very painful lesson in a very painful way through negative replay.

Once you drop your unconscious ego and accept this cycle is causing you to become a victim of fear, you can stop giving it power, understanding what you own, money and materialism does not give you your sense of security. Your sense of security comes from reconnecting back to your soul. The greatest thing that happened to me, I transformed into a spiritual adult, so I could parent my lost inner child and finally escape the past in my mind. If you never adapt, grow or evolve as a mature, spiritual adult, you will spend the rest of your life suffering in unconscious pain, based on your inner child's ignorance. And this is not progress. The only real thing any of us can do is change ourselves through listening to the heart and not the mind. All change starts from within. When you have a true connection to life, you have compassion for others through mental openness and this openness allows for a higher sensory perception. You must decide now if you are willing to be aligned with your purpose of spiritual growth, accepting your mind's challenges through self-honesty, shattering all your illusions and delusions, to finally wake up, even if what you see is painful.

As you become spiritually strong enough to consciously remain open and vulnerable, releasing your dirty negative energy from past wounds and trauma, you will no longer be limited by the automatic unhealthy bad habits put in place, not by you, by your unconscious ego mind to falsely protect you. Going forward, your responsibility is to practise only unconditional love and peace with the rest of the world. All the madness, the pain, the trauma, the fear, the anxiety, the depression now needs to be shifted out, so your heart can be reopened, and you take back charge of everything you do. You are going to become enlightened, free, liberated from your past pain, even if you have no idea what you have suffered. You are going to be courageous and mature enough to change, dropping the façade, connecting back to your heart, so you can finally start to live the life you deserve, the life that was always meant to be. Life is not to be rushed, not to be taken for granted or be wasted believing what you are stuck with can never change; it can. I want you to always remember, what you see, think and imagine is all made up in your mind and your mind is a liar. I want to leave you with this greatest knowledge, you have access to extraordinary magic found only in your intuitive and spiritual nature. Your brain is full of neuro-networks, just like roots in the earth that all communicate beneath the surface. Your unconscious works in a similar way, especially when you are stressed, depressed, anxious or when your unconscious ego becomes filled with fear. This book is the path to the process of reconnecting back with the roots of your soul, understanding clearly and openly, you are NOT your thoughts. Discovering your soul is about discovering your authentic inner being and through this process you find your true purpose, your passion and that which makes you whole and real.